THE BEACHBOYS

AMERICA'S BAND

STERLING
New York

An Imprint of Sterling Publishing
1166 Avenue of the Americas
New York, NY 10036

STERLING and the distinctive Sterling logo are registered trademarks of Sterling Publishing Co., Inc.

© 2015 Essential Works Limited

ISBN 978-1-4549-1709-0

Distributed in Canada by Sterling Publishing
c/o Canadian Manda Group, 664 Annette Street
Toronto, Ontario, Canada M6S 2C8
Distributed in the United Kingdom by GMC Distribution Services
Castle Place, 166 High Street, Lewes, East Sussex, England BN7 1XU
Distributed in Australia by Capricorn Link (Australia) Pty. Ltd.
P.O. Box 704, Windsor, NSW 2756, Australia

For information about custom editions, special sales, and premium and corporate purchases,
please contact Sterling Special Sales at 800-805-5489 or specialsales@sterlingpublishing.com.

Design and Production by Essential Works

Manufactured in China

2 4 6 8 10 9 7 5 3 1

www.sterlingpublishing.com

THE BEACHBOYS

AMERICA'S BAND

JOHNNY MORGAN

STERLING
New York

Contents

Introduction

When exactly the Beach Boys became "America's Band" is uncertain, although if their co-founder and latter-day defender of the Beach Boys' reputation Mike Love had succeeded in his application to trademark the phrase "America's band," it could have officially been appended to their name soon after December 15, 1997. In the mid-sixties the Boys were always tagged as being American by teen mags, to differentiate them from the British Beatles. A decade later, a press campaign to publicize the release of *The Beach Boys Love You* album referred to them as "America's best loved band." In a 2012 *New York Times* opinion piece about the politics of the Beach Boys, Daniel Nester identified 1983 as the date and Ronald Reagan as the one to give them the title.

Whenever the tag was first publicly applied to the Beach Boys it has, nonethless, become a kind of unspoken rule that the term be applied whenever anything is written about them. Still, the examiners at the Patent and Trademark Office rejected Love's application on the grounds that "we conclude that AMERICA'S BAND is a merely descriptive phrase that is not an inherently distinctive trademark for a musical group."

THE BEACH BOYS

If there's one thing that has remained true about the storied, varied, convoluted, and at times confusing career of the Beach Boys, though, it is that they've always been distinctive. Like only Frankie Valli and the Four Seasons, the Beach Boys existed and succeeded before and after the Beatles-led British Invasion of America in 1964. Although the Jersey Boys gave up on making records in the mid-1990s, and turned Bob Gaudio's songs and the story of the band into a smash stage show and box office hit, Mike Love continued touring the world with the Beach Boys, who could boast one founding member (himself) and a long-standing (since 1965) member in Bruce Johnston. When the Beach Boys' twenty-ninth studio album *That's Why God Made the Radio* debuted at #3 on the U.S. album charts, it did so 50 years after their debut, *Surfin' Safari*, had barely scraped the top 30.

The Beach Boys have played more gigs even than the Rolling Stones, and possibly Bob Dylan, too. The longevity of the band's career alone has earned them much respect and admiration.

The tragic elements of their story and the often-painful honesty with which different members' lives were laid bare in the media has sustained a fascination, too. Everyone is aware of Brian Wilson's bouts with mental illness, his deafness in one ear, and the physical abuse suffered by him and his now-departed brothers at the hands of their father. For a while it was believed that Brian's eccentric behavior and withdrawal from public

Left: A rare publicity photo of the Boys wearing Beatles-style suits rather than striped shirts, printed in *16 Magazine Spectacular,* **summer 1965.**

life in 1967, was due to a bad LSD trip. Later, he was considered an unfortunate victim of a scheming and exploitative doctor, Gene Landy, and wrongly diagnosed as being schizophrenic. Since the turn of the millennium, however, Brian and the rest of the Beach Boys have been highly visible and increasingly beloved by a public who proclaim them as more than just survivors, but as victors of a sort.

The Beach Boys have grown old with their original fans while gathering successive generations of new ones along the way. They have always reflected what their admittedly mostly conservative and middle-American fans have lived through. After the teenage fun of surfing and drag racing, Beach Boys songs turned briefly psychedelic, and then anti-establishment (kind of, on *Surf's Up*), albeit five years after the hippies had first bloomed.

Following a decade of backward-looking reevaluation and smash hit "best of" compilation success, the Boys spent the 1980s as big fans—mutually so—of Ronald Reagan,, and enjoyed their biggest hit in twenty years with "Kokomo." The 1990s were spent in litigation and the courts, while the early 2000s saw them coming to terms with how the world was changing. All the time

"We all lived this wonderful life with The Beach Boys."

MIKE *Love*

there was always a Beach Boys gig happening some-where in America at which those great old songs could be danced to and sung along with. Even Brian came out of retirement to peform his old stuff live, to great acclaim.

Nostalgia has always been the Beach Boys' found-ation stone and secret weapon. As a teenager, Brian Wilson wanted desperately to be a member of the Four Freshmen, and all of his musical creations took the middle-aged, middle-American, conservative, cocktail jazz stylings (so loved by his father) as a starting and sometimes endpoint. The Beach Boys' vocal harmonies were not new or unusual in 1961, and neither was surf music, but Brian and Mike's talent in combining the two made them unique in pop music.

The Beach Boys songs written and recorded between 1961 and 1964 proclaimed the sunny California dream as a way of life, setting it to tunes that were nostalgic for the baby-boom era of the 1950s. Brian and Mike (plus Gary Usher and Roger Christian) wrote songs that reminded the listener of the era that they'd grown up in. The mid-to-late 1950s reveled in teenage trends turned into popular songs—think Chuck Berry's cars, Jerry Lee Lewis's high school rebellions, and numerous others' dance steps. So it was natural that the Boys would look

for their own musical hook on which to hang their career. When Brian's brother Dennis suggested surfing, the rest was pop music history.

Surfing, like pro football, hot-rod racing, NASCAR, and baseball are purely American pastimes, and any musical act championing them will be welcomed into the hearts and record collections of fans of each sport. Although surfing was only a fad as far as Brian was con-cerned, Mike recognized that it wasn't *just* a sport, but it was an essentially American sport, which made it hugely important. Anyone who believes that Brian was the only Beach Boy responsible for their career should consider that without Mike's driving ambition and innate under-standing of what their fans wanted to hear, as well as his songwriting contribution and commercial savvy, the Beach Boys would have ceased to exist in 1967.

While the rest of the Beach Boys toured the world singing their biggest pre-1966 hits, Brian stayed in California, constantly trying to recreate a 1963 single by the Ronettes. "Be My Baby" had a stunning effect on 21-year-old Brian. As well as the melody, chorus, and almost undefinable sense of yearning, lust, and regret in the voice, there was an incredible backing that illumin-ated Veronica (Ronnie) Bennett's lead vocal.

Producer Phil Spector had created an immense sound using instruments and arrangements that Brian Wilson could only wonder at and try to copy. He used Spector's musicians and even his studio in creating Beach Boys music, as he attempted to move the songs away from what Mike thought their audience wanted to hear.

"I was really taking Phil Spector's type of records and making them Beach Boys records," Wilson told Paul Williams in 1995. In truth he never stopped trying to make music as perfect, thrilling, imposing, and unsettling as "Be My Baby." Oddly though, he's only ever produced one version of the song—for Mike Love's solo LP.

Fifty years after they wished that everybody had an ocean across the USA, the idea of the Beach Boys remains as potent as all the other iconic totems of what "America" represents. Like their fans who have come through decades of political, social, and personal turmoil, the Beach Boys are still having fun, fun, fun.

What follows is one version of how the Beach Boys came to be known as America's Band. There are others.

Left: Brian Wilson in his living room at home in Bel Air, 1966.
Below: The Beach Boys 50th Anniversary Tour announcement, 2012. L-R: Brian Wilson, David Marks, Bruce Johnston, Al Jardine, Mike Love.

1

SURF (DON'T SURF)

1942·1961

California in the aftermath of World War II was a strange and wonderful place. In Los Angeles the Hollywood movie industry thrived and the city expanded at a rapid rate. New roads fed into swathes of modern tract housing that expanded the outer limits of the city, taking an ever-growing middle class into a new golden dream of suburban satiety. The Wilson family, who bought 3701 West 119th Street in Hawthorne, were just like every other aspiring first-generation Californians. The families of both mother Audree and father Murry had emigrated to the Golden State from the Midwest during the booming 1920s, when the biggest problem facing adults in America was how to legally get an alcoholic drink. Murry Wilson's father, Bud, always found ways of getting drunk, though, usually on dubiously fermented moonshine that never failed to turn him into a roaring, fist-throwing drunk. Back in Kansas, Bud had cursed and fought his way out of favor with all and sundry, and earned a reputation as being unreliable and therefore unemployable. As so many others at the time (1921) Bud shrugged off Hutchison, Kansas, as a dead-end town and moved west, a good decade before fellow Midwesterners were blown that way by the dustbowl and Depression, in order to find his fortune in the sunshine, hoping to play professional baseball. After stints in states that lay between him and the sun and surf, Bud took up plumbing, made it to Escondido and called for his wife, Edith, and brood of children to join him. Murry (b. July 2, 1917) was the third of eight children. By all accounts he was a chip off the old man's block, which resulted, as it so often does, in both males hating each other because of the faults they could see reflected in each. Bud took out his frustrations and rages on the family, beating them all regularly until there were enough kids of a big enough size to haul off back at him and join together in the fight. Eventually, by the time he was 16, Murry and siblings watched Bud walk away and he disappeared from their lives. If nothing else, Bud instilled in Murry a strong sense of independence and a will to make a life on his own.

Thankfully for successive generations of future Beach Boys fans, though, Bud and Edith also instilled in Murry a love of music. It's likely that the only occasions of familial togetherness during the late 1920s and early '30s in the Wilsons' Escondido household came when they arranged themselves into a rough kind of choir and sang along to Edith's clanking piano, Bud's lead

"My dad was always overbearing. And it just got to the point where I couldn't handle it any more."

BRIAN *Wilson*

age. Evenings and weekends for the first four years of
their marriage were spent singing and—for Murry at
least—writing music. By day he worked first as a clerk at
the Southern California Gas Company for a couple of
years, and then, following the birth of his first son, Brian
(b. June 20, 1942) at the Goodyear Tire and Rubber
Company, on the shop floor.

Before Brian was a year old Murry suffered the loss of
an eye in an industrial accident. After months of rehabilit-
ation and wearing an eyepatch, he returned to Goodyear
and the position of foreman. Talking to *Rolling Stone*
magazine almost three decades later, Murry recalled:
"When I was twenty-five I thought the world owed me
a living. When I lost my eye I tried harder, drove harder
and did the work of two men in the company and got
more raises." The raises, combined with the arrival of
a second son, Dennis (b. December 4, 1944), helped to
effect a move for Murry, Audree, and sons to that house
in Hawthorne, where today only a stone monument and
plaque remain to mark the beginning of the Beach Boys.

The loss of his eye and growing family (a third son,
Carl, was born on December 21, 1946) combined to
drive Murry from Goodyear in search of higher wages.
He went first to Garrett Air Research and then, after
a time working with his brothers learning about the
business of aircraft machinery importation, he risked a
mortgage on the Wilson family home in order to start
his own company, A.B.L.E. Machinery (Always Better
Lasting Equipment).

During those years of job hopping and company
building, Murry continued to write music, sending

voice, and—by his early teens—Murry's self-taught guitar
playing. In a home filled with anger and violence, any
kind of peaceful joint activity soon achieves golden status,
becoming a treat that makes a sense of life, if only for a
while. For Murry, making music together became the key
to creating a happy family atmosphere. It was something
that he'd pass on to his own children. Sadly, he'd also
pass on to them some of his father's less nurturing
parenting methods.

In 1938, Murry Wilson married Audree Korthof
(b. September 28, 1917), the daughter of a straight-
laced baker father. They shared a love of making music,
and Audree's piano playing and sweet singing voice
pleased Murry in the way that it can when a man meets
the kind of woman his mother might have been at that

out manuscripts of his songs to music publishers in the greater Los Angeles area, desperate for someone to record them and make him a fast and vast fortune. Having grown up during the first truly successful era of American music, Murry saw how sheet music sales earned authors of the Great American Songbook, such as George M. Cohan, Walter Donaldson, Gus Kahn, Irving Berlin, and—a great favorite of both Murry and Audree—George Gershwin, huge amounts of money. In the 1930s big bands had spread the work of songwriters across the country as they toured and broadcast over the ever-expanding local radio network. By the end of the 1940s record sales had outstripped those of sheet music, and people bought record players to sit alongside their radios and learned to sing and play numbers by ear.

When, in his thirties, Murry became management rather than foreman, he attempted to embrace a kind of sophistication that was expected of men of his ilk. Advertising had begun to talk directly to the hard-working, ambitious middle class, via sponsorship of radio shows, billboards, magazines, and even television (the first TV ads appeared in 1941; the first mass-produced TV set came to market in 1946). Men of Murry's kind wore suits and hats to work, drove brand-new American-made cars, drank cocktails before dinner, and took their wives to clubs for dinner and dancing. There, they'd foxtrot to smooth, lightly swinging jazz of the kind that Lawrence Welk's orchestra played.

When the 1950s began, Murry Wilson, songwriter, entered his most successful period of work. Aware that dance crazes and novelty songs were popular, he'd written a polka or two and a Western swing–style dance number that he was sure would be his own "Tennessee Waltz" or "Beer Barrel Polka." When Lawrence Welk's accordion

Right: Band leader, accordionist, and radio show host Lawrence Welk (in car) with his orchestra in 1954. The venue was the site for the first ever Welk TV show broadcast. Murry listened regularly along with his family, always hoping that Welk would play another of his tunes. He didn't.

wheezed out Murry's "Two Step, Side Step" in his inimitable "Champagne Music" style on his radio show in 1952, the songwriter was sure that he was destined for a major career in music. Murry became a devoted Welk fan for life after that, and passed on something of his love for the German-speaking North Dakotan to his eldest son. Brian's first musical instrument of choice was an accordion.

Welk's promotion of the song led to a couple of Midwestern swing artists covering it, but only with minor local success and not as the main side. In 1953 Bonnie Lou's version on King (rereleased in 2013 by Rockabilly Records) and the recording by Johnny Lee Wills, a former member of Bob Wills's Texas Playboys, were B-sides. In 1954 Suzi Miller (a wannabe Anne Shelton) and the Johnston Brothers (a kind of trad jazz-style Four Freshmen) released their interpretation on the B-side of "I'll Hang My Heart on a Christmas Tree" for Decca. They may only have been B-sides, but they showed Murry's name on the label. Each new disc's arrival at the Wilson home in Hawthorne meant a few days of calm and peaceful living with a smiling Murry—as long as none of the boys did anything to upset him.

Pleasing Murry was a constant struggle for all the Wilson boys, but they soon learned that showing any interest in music, particularly the kind of music that he liked, would make their lives easier. Murry's music was

Left: The Four Freshmen in action in 1956. L-R: Ken Albers, Ross Barbour, Don Barbour, and Bob Flanigan. Right: Brian Wilson (second from left) with (L-R) Bruce Griffin, Keith Lent, and Robin Hood at a Hawthorne High School assembly, performing a version of "Hully Gully" as a campaign song for fellow student Carol Hess's run for commissioner of the student government.

Brian's music in the 1950s, which is where the son got his love of the Four Freshmen. Speaking to the *Los Angeles Times* in 2011 after the death of a Freshmen founding member, Brian said, "Bob Flanigan and the Four Freshmen were my harmonic education. I saw them at the Cocoanut Grove in Hollywood in 1958. My dad and I went backstage and met the Freshmen. I was nervous because they were my idols. They were so nice to me. I was just 15 years old."

The Freshmen comprised two brothers, a cousin, and close friend, all in their thirties by the time Brian saw them. They played the kind of smooth jazz that Murry thought sophisticated and had the kind of sound that he could write. The Freshmen scored their first hit in 1952 with "It's A Blue World," all swooping four-part harmony, languor, and longing, set to a shuffling brush beat, plodding acoustic bass, and light guitar coloring. If you didn't know better you might mistake it for a Beach Boys imitation piece. It was a thousand miles west of "Two Step, Side Step," but Murry really dug that warm swing, and so did Brian.

Apparently, following Brian's quasi-religious evening at the Cocoanut Grove, he took to arranging every piece of music he could find at home to fit four voices: his, Murry's, Audree's, and Dennis's. Although Dennis was reluctant to sit around the family piano mimicking old-time jazz songs, so often Carl would sub in while Dennis wandered the streets getting into trouble or sat in a tree with the BB gun that Murry had given to him for his ninth

birthday. Years later Dennis would tell an interviewer that the gun had changed his life because, "With that gun I had something I could take my anger out on." Dennis would sit in his tree fort, shooting at animals, houses, trees …"anything. I was in a completely different world out there: my own. I was like that in school, too: in my own world. And I always made trouble, or it made me." As he went on to explain, any broken windows or minor vandalism within a 20-mile radius of the Wilson home in Hawthorne would have people proclaiming Dennis as the culprit. "And lots of times I did," he admitted. Although according to Audree, Dennis was "just like" Murry, the second son was the only one to challenge and openly antagonize his father. The gun allowed Dennis to act out physically against a world in which Murry was the ultimate, brutal power. Both Dennis and Brian called him a tyrant, and the second son often told interviewers that Murry had physically beaten the boys.

Dennis was always active, always moving, running and dodging. Carl once said that Dennis could never sit still, couldn't concentrate on just one thing for too long,

Left: Brian Wilson at 19, the college freshman who preferred writing songs about surfing to composing sonatas.

which sounds a lot like a condition that in more modern times would be termed attention deficit disorder. But it was more likely to get Dennis referred to as a "problem child" back in the 1950s. Both he and Carl failed to graduate high school, but while Carl left because of the success of the Beach Boys ,before his graduation year, Dennis left after striking a teacher with only weeks to go until his final prom night.

Until the age of 16, Brian was something of a jock at school—he played baseball (but couldn't hit a curveball) and was a quarterback on his high school team, as was Al Jardine, at one point competition for Brian's position. But after discovering the power of music to soothe his father's savage beast, Brian immersed himself deeper into making music as he grew up. A tall teenager, and with some physical presence, Brian may have been able to physically defend himself against his father's assaults, but years of abuse, punishment, and being made to cower before Murry's rages (and being forced to stare into his vacant eye socket) had made the boy too subservient

to confront his old man. But he learned that he could avert the attacks and rages by making music, especially the kind that Murry loved so much. "My dad was an asshole," Brian would later state. "He treated us like shit and his punishments were sick. But you played a tune for him and he was a marshmallow."

Brian's suffering at Murry's hand—which included being beaten about the head with a piece of wood and having a boat dropped off bricks onto his hands—could be assuaged by singing or playing a tune on the piano, accordion, or guitar, all of which he learned quickly and with only one good ear. Brian's defective hearing loss has been variously ascribed (by him and his mother) to an accident at birth or being hit on the ear by an unnamed kid from the neighborhood. According to others (who weren't there), it was caused by Murry whacking him with that plank. The charge was denied by Murry, though, in an interview with *Rolling Stone* magazine in 1971: "Oh I spanked his bottom, you know, like any father would do to a kid, just whap him a little bit. No, I never hit my kid on the ear. No, no."

As is all too often the case, parental acts of violence against children cause discord among siblings. There's audio proof (as reported by author Peter Ames Carlin

"Brian thinks in six-part harmony, instead of two- or three-part."

MURRY *Wilson*

in *Catch a Wave: The Rise, Fall, and Redemption of the Beach Boys' Brian Wilson*) that Brian argued with his younger brothers, although there's no evidence of his beating on them. For his sixteenth birthday Brian had been given a Wollensak tape recorder by his parents, on which he recorded family singing sessions. He also took to recording attempts to get his brothers into some form of singing harmony in their shared bedroom, and on one occasion he taped the then 14-year-old Dennis asking to record something but being denied by Brian, who talks directly to the tape and includes Carl in the argument. In other personal recordings, writes Carlin, you can hear Brian's anger snapping and his good humor failing.

Following a performance at a Hawthorne High School assembly with three fellow pupils singing an adaptation of "Hully Gully" (for a student government campaign) in 1958, Brian seems to have decided to make music with more serious intention than he was willing to give to organized sports. He quit the football team in his senior year and began to make music with a cousin, Mike Love, who had been a part of the extended Wilson singing network that would congregate at each others' houses on public holidays.

A year older than Brian, Mike (b. March 15, 1941) graduated high school in 1959 and worked for his father at the family sheet metal business by day, adding to his earnings by pumping gas at night. He wasn't qualified for anything other than manual labor and didn't seem to have much ambition to learn about anything else. Not that he could have made it to college anyway, because by the end of 1960 Mike Love was a father-to-be and had been kicked out of the family home by his mother, who threw all his belongings out of his bedroom window on hearing about Mike's girlfriend's pregnancy and their plan to get an abortion in Mexico. Mike was persuaded to marry Francie in January 1961 by both sets of parents, and their daughter, Melinda, was born in July of that year. By that time Mike had been fired by his father, and pumping gas was his only real source of income.

Mike may have recognized in Brian an ambition and the talent to make a career of sorts from music. He was aware that his uncle Murry would support most anything that his cousin wanted to do musically, and so he pushed Brian to work on songs with him, dreaming of becoming a rock-and-roll star. Simultaneously, that other Hawthorne High quarterback, Al Jardine, was learning to play the guitar and forming a folk act with a school buddy.

In 1958, the two younger Wilsons made the acquaintance of a new kid to the neighborhood named David Marks. Although four years younger than Dennis and two younger than Carl, David Marks (b. August 22, 1948) became a close pal to them and got into trouble with Dennis whenever possible. By the middle of 1959 both Carl and David had taken guitar lessons with a local musician named John Maus (later to find fame as a Walker Brother), who was three years older than Carl and happened to be a surfer and regular performer at bars and clubs in the area. Carl progressed well enough that Maus allowed the youngest Wilson to sit in and play at local bar gigs with his band and go surfing with them, too. Marks was too young for that, but not, as he'd later explain to a journalist, too young to jam with Carl. "He and I started doing Ventures tunes, sitting around the living room, learning them off the records for our own amusement."

As well as having a voice that Brian felt fit with his and cousin Mike's, Carl was a good enough guitarist by 1960 for his big brother to ask if he'd perform with them at some high school gigs. He went as far as to name the band Carl and the Passions in order to persuade his little brother to perform. Carl said yes.

Al Jardine saw the gig and was impressed enough to ask if he could sing with them in the music room.

The surf scene in California was first established in the 1920s at San Onofre beach, near San Diego. The beach was used by U.S. military for Camp Pendleton, a training center for the Marine Corps in 1942, but surfers still rode waves there—all of them marines. After World War II, tired and disillusioned with life, a few GIs returned to the then-abandoned Camp Pendleton to live and surf. Or to live for surf.

The GIs slept in old trucks and cars or pitched former army-issue tents and survived as best they could, taking part-time jobs in the surrounding area to buy food and beer. A handful became full-time lifeguards at tourist beaches along the coast. They'd take their boards with them for use when on down time—making sure that it always coincided with the best surf time, of course.

Because San "O" beach lay just off the Pacific Coast Highway, it was an easy find for non-military surfers too, and it soon became one of the coolest places to hang and surf from—not that amateurs were encouraged or appreciated by regulars and inhabitants of San O. The sense of exclusivity and outsider vibe that the surfers exuded was attractive to those young men for whom simply driving up and down the same old strip in a Nash Rambler was never going to be enough to satisfy their sense of adventure. Surfers were outsiders, rebels whose cause was catching the biggest waves.

By the end of the 1950s, sitting in a Rambler in Hawthorne, singing along to the radio as it spilled doo-wop and Chuck Berry and Elvis Presley songs into the air, was pretty much the best night out that Brian, Mike, and Al could imagine. For Dennis that wasn't

Top: Brian Wilson in his senior year at Hawthorne High School, 1959.
Bottom: Dennis Wilson in his Hawthorne High School yearbook, 1961.

enough, though. After getting a taste of the surf, neither was it enough for Carl. As much as he might seek the attention and approval of his big brother, he was not inclined to just sit around listening to the radio.

Dennis had noticed that girls liked surfers, and there was little he liked better than girls. Although cars came close, as he'd later reveal, "I was into carburettors, cars, peeling out, cruising, A&W root beers. I was also into tits, nipples, dirty pictures—I loved dirty pictures, magazines, Tijuana, surfboards on top of the car. Even if I wasn't going surfing that day I'd put them up there anyway. Anything to do with that—with having fun." He was not a good or even average surfer, as Australian surf music expert Stephen J. McParland wrote in "Understanding the Beach Boys," published in *Beach Boys Australia* magazine in 1992. "Dennis was no surfer. He simply indulged in the sport more as a fad than a lifestyle." To a lesser extent, Carl also adopted surfing as a fad and took to hanging out with surfers when allowed.

In Brian's senior year and Mike's first post-graduation year, they were listening to mainstream radio and hearing lots of pale Elvis imitators, such as Fabian ("Turn Me Loose," "Tiger"), Frankie Avalon ("Venus," "Why"), and Ricky Nelson ("It's Late," "Never Be Anyone Else for Me"). Their releases, along with those by Elvis, who had recently returned from service in the army overseas, set the midpaced, inoffensive tone of the pop music of America at the time. While it was all pleasant enough, most of the biggest hits in 1959 and 1960 lacked the musical complexity of *The Four Freshmen and Five Trombones* album that had so inspired Brian in 1955. Five years later he was still listening to the Freshmen and working out ever more complex harmonies for himself and anyone who'd sing them.

Al Jardine began performing in a folk group in 1960, and soon after Brian and Mike began trying out Kingston Trio songs; at least the Bay Area folk group

Full-time surfer and part-time actor Bob Gravage (aka Hammerhead) sits on his home (a van) with dog Cork McNork and surfing buddies at San Onofre beach, 1950. A tough ex-GI, Gravage became the surf idol of kids like Dennis Wilson.

had recorded an interesting version of "Sloop John B," and folk music was newer than rock and roll. The Trio's version of "Tom Dooley" had been the biggest record of 1959, and there was a buzz about folk singers and folk clubs springing up everywhere. Murry would have been happy to write a number like "Tom Dooley," but he hadn't, so Brian wasn't stepping directly on his old man's toes. If Brian tried to form a doo-wop group like Dion and the Belmonts, whose "Teenager in Love" and "Where or When" had instigated a revival in 1959, Murry would laugh and drop the needle on the Hollywood Flames singing his "Tabarin" (Fidelity, 1951) or the Jets' recording of his song "I'll Hide My Tears" (Aladdin, 1954).

No, Murry had done doo-wop, so Brian wouldn't, not directly, anyway—it'd be too much of a challenge to the old man and too dispiriting if Brian's group didn't get anywhere or were laughed at like his high school outfit had been when they'd attempted the Freshmen's "It's a Blue World," the previous year. If he was going to try anything it'd have to be a musical style that Murry Wilson hadn't got around to himself.

Dennis was 15 years old during the summer of 1960, and just as his big brother was preparing to go to college, he was getting a very different kind of education. While Brian and Mike were dabbling in folk music, Dennis was hopping beaches with the surf crowd, learning how to roll joints, get high, and speak the surfer langauge. His summer nights were spent at impromptu beach parties where older guys with acoustic guitars strummed Hawaiian tunes they'd learned while surfing waves at

Top: Carl in his Pendleton shirt, 1961.
Below: Mike Love in 1959.

Kahalu'u or Holualoa Bay, the bonfires burned, girls passed joints and bottles along quickly, and everyone sang when they knew the words.

Surf culture was a truly alternative scene in California, and it needed a soundtrack. Drawing inspiration from music that wasn't sung by Frankies and Bobbys, musicians who lived by the beach began making mostly instrumental numbers that mixed Hawaiian slack key and steel guitar sounds with rock and roll's reverb, 4/4 beat, and energy. The electric guitar in surf music hoped to replicate the sound and power of the waves. Unlike Duane Eddy's twang or Hank Marvin's tremelo, Link Wray's "Rumble" and Dick Dale's reverb-soaked, distorted tone didn't want to sound as if they'd sell soap suds to housewives; they sounded as if they'd rather get the housewife riding her ironing board out to sea.

Like the lifestyle that surfers favored, surf music was hard to take unless you were of the right mind. It was fast, imprecise, raw sounding, and as wild as the crashing waves. Or at least that was the intention. The loud, instrumental sounds of guitar-led combos were constantly pushing the sound-level meters into the red, making tiny radio speakers rattle. Bobby soxers who swooned over cookie-cutter crooners were not going to go for it, but guys like Dennis, who were discovering a music that moved as fast as they did, lapped it up.

The instrumental sounds of warped guitar and bubbling organs began to enter the mainstream charts in 1960. A particularly surprising hit at the time was the Bill Black Combo's instrumental version of "White Silver Sands." (Black was a former Blue Moon Boy and a bassist for the original Elvis Presley trio.) Originally a hit in 1957 for laid-back bass crooner Don Rondo, Black's version substitutes the smooth vocal with a popping, distorting staccato organ (played by Carl McVoy, Jerry Lee Lewis's cousin) and honking saxophone (played by Ace Cannon) against a chugging bass and guitar. The effect is to turn what was Rondo's beachside romantic rendevous between two lovers, into a scene for a teen party. In Black's version, the beach becomes a place purely for communing with the surf, where true love is a waxed board, and not a lover.

Black's foray into what sounded like a prototype surf music was not pursued, though. His combo followed it up with a frothy number titled "Josephine" before covering one of his old boss's hits, "Don't Be Cruel." However, the quality of the organ and sax sound on "White Silver Sands" plainly had an influence on later surf records.

In 1960, the biggest guitar act was the Ventures (whose huge hit of the year, "Walk, Don't Run," owed a lot to Britain's Shadows), but in California both Link Wray and Dick Dale were making their own guitar sound that was just as distorted and wild-sounding as McVoy's organ and Ace Cannon's sax. However, the guy who in 1960 sounded as if he were already the complete surf guitarist was a Scotsman named Joe Moretti. Anyone familiar with the opening few bars of Johnny Kidd and the Pirates' "Shakin' All Over" (1960) will recognize one of rock music's foundation pieces. Everyone from the Guess Who to the Who covered the song, as much for the guitar runs as for the inherent sexual tension of the lyrics. However, listen to the follow-up single from the same year, "Restless," and you hear the sound of the surf guitar par excellence. Sparse, distorted, and full of vibrato and reverb, the scorching runs and bending high notes of the disc's middle eight set a template for aspiring guitarists everywhere, but particularly in California, it seems. Listen to the Surfari's "Wipeout" (1963) and you can hear a guitarist trying to play "Shakin' All Over" or

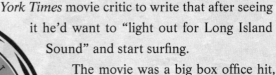

"Restless," only not being quite dextrous enough.

By the time Dennis was playing drums and Carl was taking to the guitar seriously in 1961, surfing had made an impact on Hollywood via a series of teen novels, not music. California's surfing scene saw its first worldwide exposure in the movie *Gidget* (1959) starring the 17-year-old Sandra Dee in the title role. Based on the novels of Frederick Kohner, which had been informed by and about his 16-year-old daughter Kathy, aka Gidget, the film was shot on location at Leo Carillo State Park at the foot of the Santa Monica mountains. The story is a typical one of girl meets boy (Moondoggie, played by James Darren), who ignores her before they finally find love. But the surfing and beach party scenes in the movie were original and inspired enough for the *New York Times* movie critic to write that after seeing it he'd want to "light out for Long Island Sound" and start surfing.

The movie was a big box office hit, and in 1961 Gidget made her way to the original birthplace of surfing to make *Gidget Goes Hawaiian*. The second screen Gidget was portrayed by twenty-year old Deborah Walley, but James Darren was still Moondoggie, and he got to sing lead on the Hawaiian guitar-washed pop-song title tune. *Gidget Goes Hawaiian* was an even bigger hit than *Gidget* had been, and surfing was on the rise.

Hawaii was particularly busy that year, because just before Gidget's crew arrived, in March and April another movie had been shot on the east coast of Kauai: *Blue Hawaii*, starring Elvis Presley. Because it was the only slightly "foreign" place he could visit due to manager Tom Parker's lack of a passport, the pair mixed business with pleasure and enjoyed it so much that they made two further movies on location there.

**Gidget (Kathy Kohner) loading
her board into the family car after
a day spent surfing, 1959.**

Left: Brian playing bass, with Carl (center), in a Carl
and the Passions show at Hawthorne High.
Opposite: Dick Dale–"King of the Surf Guitar"–performing
at the Rendezvous Ballroom in Balboa, July 1961.

Girls! Girls! Girls! of 1962 was originally supposed to be titled *Hawaiian Beach Boy*, but *Paradise Hawaiian Style* of 1965 was intended merely to play on the island's appeal. While Elvis never actually surfs in any movie, he posed for publicity photos for *Blue Hawaii* atop a surfboard. Its soundtrack includes a curious number titled "Almost Always True" that features a reverb-soaked staccato guitar, a Hawaiian slide guitar, and a rough(ish) honking saxophone behind one of Elvis's less inspired vocals. It's not exactly as raw and powerful as Dick Dale's "Jesse Pearl" (1960), but it sounds more "surf" than the future King of Surf Guitar's recordings had done until the summer of 1961.

However, because of events that summer, Dick Dale is credited with inventing the "surf sound." A left-handed guitarist who could play rapid scales on his upside-down Fender (he didn't restring it), Dale had recorded rockabilly and rock-and-roll songs for his own Deltone label (funded by his father, Jim Monsour, who is also credited as producer on Dale's records), but living and surfing in the Huntington Beach/Balboa area, Dale had made lots of surfer pals.

There's little in his late 1950s vocal discs to suggest that Dale would invent the surf guitar sound, but on getting hold of a new Fender Showman amp in 1960, Dale clearly found a new sound: reverb and tremelo-saturated staccato picking sounded great through the amp, especially when played real loud. He dropped vocals because guitar bands were the rage, gave new instrumental songs

"The one thing that kept our family together was music."

DENNIS *Wilson*

surf-related titles, and soon drew ever-expanding crowds to his local venue, an ice cream hut on the beach, which soon proved too small.

In July 1961, Dale and his Del-Tones began a residency at the 3,000-capacity Rendevouz Ballroom in Balboa. The summer residency became the hottest place to be on a Saturday night, and similarly minded musicians traveled there to see what they might learn. Among them were members of the Bel-Airs (who added a sax to the sound) and the Gamblers, as well as younger kids like Carl Wilson, who made it there as often as he could, and played as much like Dale as possible when back in Hawthorne.

Brian and Mike, who were not hip to that scene, learned about it from Carl and from Dennis, who was more vociferous in his appreciation of the surf sound than Carl. Brian and Mike, the pure pop followers, were still singing barbershop harmonies and supperclub jazz of the Four Freshmen kind, occasionally adding some white doo-wop and some hits like the Five Satins's "In the Still of the Night." According to David Marks, Brian, Mike,

and Al Jardine called themselves Kenny and the Kadetts and "weren't into surf music; they just played for parties and bar mitzvahs." Carl and he played something closer to surf music, he said—that was, until Brian decided that he liked the sound of Carl's guitar and called him into his band. "Brian was the big brother," Marks shrugged.

With Carl and Dennis raving about the summer's surf craze, Brian—the chip off the old block—recognized the potential and called the group the Pendletones after the Pendleton shirt-jackets that surfers wore. Not that he went totally for the Del-Tones sound. Carl later recalled that they practiced "Coasters songs and Freshmen arrangements, as Brian was high on their style of vocalizing." Naturally the Pendletones were going to be vocal-led, not instrumental, but the lyric content would be all about the scene.

Meanwhile Al Jardine and another school pal named Gary Winfrey had formed a folk music duo (the Islanders) and worked up a version of "Sloop John B." Al visited the Wilson house one day asking for Brian's assistance in shaping the song for them. Instead, though, Al met Murry, who gave the boys his professional opinion on what they were doing and suggested that they go to see "his publisher" Hite Morgan about making a demo recording. Al and Gary met with Hite and played him a version of an old poem they'd set to music. Morgan was unimpressed but took their number anyway.

In September 1960, Brian began attending El Camino Community College, majoring in psychology with music as a side, although he'd failed his senior year high school music course. He had handed in a melody that would become "Surfin'" rather than the requested sonata, leaving his professor no choice. By that time Al was

living in Michigan and attending Ferris State University, intending to become a dentist. Neglecting his psychology college work, Brian actually majored in music and tried out several different combinations of friends and family in order to get the right mix of voices for sporadic live performances, most of which were hits of the day.

Early in 1961, Brian's lineup included Dennis, who'd taken to the drums; Carl on guitar; and Mike singing and honking on a saxaphone. In June, Al Jardine finished at Ferris for the year, returned to Hawthorne, and played bass. In August, Brian and his band found freedom from the overbearing presence of Murry for five days when the Wilson parents traveled to Mexico on business, leaving the brothers $100 each to buy food. Instead, Dennis bought a drum kit, and Brian rented a PA and set the band up in the family home to rehearse a song he'd written called "Surfin'." He recorded their progress on the Wollensak, and they played almost nonstop for the whole time their parents were away. The recording

was rough, but it was good enough to calm an infuriated Murry on his return. He wasn't expecting his living room to be filled with instruments and food detritus, so he lit into the teenagers. Until he heard the tape.

Murry recognized his eldest son's smart thinking, and "Surfin'" sounded like a hit to him and to "his publishers," Dorinda and Hite Morgan, who had licensed some of his songs. They remembered Al when the Pendletones played "Sloop John B" for them, among a slew of other current hits. Not favorably, either. Just as it seemed their audition had failed, Dennis mentioned that they had an original song about surfing they hadn't quite finished yet, and the Morgans asked to hear it.

They dug "Surfin'" enough to pay for a recording session in October at a movie-dubbing studio. Naturally, Murry took charge of everything and ran the session like he did their home life.

It was the start of something—that much they all knew.

The first studio-based publicity shoot for Capitol Records in 1962. L-R: Brian Wilson, Mike Love, Dennis Wilson, Carl Wilson, David Marks.

2

SURFIN' USA

1962 · 1964

The Pendletones's first recording session outside of the Wilson family home took place in September 1961 at the home of the Morgans. Dorinda and Hite made demos of the songs that they liked with different songwriters, sometimes playing and singing numbers themselves, and sometimes, as with the Pendletones, getting the band in to lay down a basic recording. Because Brian and Mike (who had contributed the "bom-bom dip-dip-i-dip" to Brian's "surfin...surfin" as they originally worked it up back in August) had not written anything else, the Morgans had them record a song that their son Bruce had written with an almost surfing theme, the Hawaiian-ish "Luau," and another by Dorinda, titled "Lavender." "Luau" sounds like an outtake from *Blue Hawaii* (although its "loop-de-loop" refrain would be used later by the Beach Boys, most wittily on a Christmas song, "Santa's Got an Airplane"), while "Lavender" is an a capella number that the Four Freshmen would be proud of.

The September demo recording has only a guitar backing, finger clicks, and the voices of Brian, Mike, Carl, Al, and Dennis singing the familiar refrain. It's slower than the second recording, which was made at World Pacific studio in October 1961, and it's rough, but

Previous page: L-R: Al Jardine, Brian Wilson, Carl Wilson, Mike Love, Dennis Wilson, circa 1963.
Opposite: Dennis on drums, Mike with a saxophone, Brian on bass, and Al on guitar in the Wilson living room, 1963.

the catchy hook and fine harmonies are all there. It was unlike anything else that the Candix label had released thus far, which included rockabilly/rock-and-roll numbers by Lanny Duncan, Johnny Macrae, and Eddie Lamaire; novelty songs "I've Never Seen a Straight Banana" (The Hi-Tones) and "Speedy Gonzales" by Solid Jackson (a version of the same song by Pat Boone would become a million-seller in 1962). Candix also put out Lou Rawls's first two releases ("In My Little Black Book" and "80 Days"), Theola Kilgore's answer record "That's the Sound of My Man (Working on the Chain Gang)," and Scott Walker's brief dalliance with instrumental surf sound as a Moongooner, with the "Moongooner Stomp"—which became the "Moongooner Twist" in 1962.

At the band's second recording, this time in a professional studio, Murry insisted that Dennis couldn't drum—they were using a garbage can with a shirt thrown over it, according to Carl—so Brian beat out the tempo. Carl played the guitar, and Al an upright acoustic bass. All three, along with Mike (suffering from a head cold) and Dennis, added vocals while standing at the same microphone. It's a more up-tempo version than the demo, and it begins by going straight into a vocal line that declares "surfin is the only life, the only way for me" before the "bom-bom, dip-dip-i-dip" backing and the instruments come in. It's clear, clean, and sparse, and it sounded great on the radio.

"We got so excited hearing it on the radio that Carl threw up," Dennis later told *Disc* magazine. "Nothing will ever top the expression on Brian's face, ever. I ran down the street screaming, 'Listen, we're on the radio!'

SURFIN'

CANDIX, DECEMBER 1961, JANUARY 1962

B-side	"Lua"
Writers	B. Wilson/M. Love
	B. Morgan
Producer	Murry Wilson/Hite Morgan
Recorded	10/3/61
U.S. Chart	#76 *Billboard*

"Surfin'" had three separate releases with different catalogue numbers, Candix 331 and X-301, both in December 1961, and Candix 301, released in January 1962. It's likely that the X label was used for a small pressing done by Hite Morgan for promotional purposes. Candix was formed in August 1960 by twins Robert and Richard Dix with Bill Silva. They were Lou Rawls's first label and released the first version of "Speedy Gonzales" (by Solid Jackson) with minor success, but had more luck locally with "Underwater" and "Beware Below" by the Frogmen, an instrumental surf band. Candix A&R man Joe Saraceno and the label's distributor, Russ Regan, considered the name "The Pendletones" not strong enough to work, so told the pressing plant to use "The Beach Boys" instead. According to legend, the Wilsons didn't know about the name change until they received their copies of the disc. Regan promoted the single to L.A. stations KFWB and KRLA, whose listeners liked it enough to make it a local hit. It went national following the January release, entered the chart that month, and made it to #76 in March.

SURFIN' SAFARI

CAPITOL, JUNE 1962

B-side	"409"
Writers	B. Wilson/M. Love;
	B. Wilson/G. Usher
Producer	B. Wilson
Recorded	4/19/62
U.S. Chart	#14 *Billboard*

There was a big trend for dance-related hits in the early 1960s that called for participation from listeners in their lyrics. Surfing wasn't a dance, but Mike was determined to teach everyone how to do it anyway, and so wrote this all-inclusive shoutout for everyone to join in on a surfin' safari, inviting the listener to take a safari with him. Chubby Checker's "The Twist" and "Pony Time" of 1961 had both been #1 hits; "The Watusi" by the Orlons would make #2 later in 1962, and James Brown, credited as Nat Kendrick for legal purposes, had enjoyed an R&B hit in 1960 with "(Do the) Mashed Potato," while early in 1962 Dee Dee Sharp had a huge hit with "Mashed Potato Time." A couple of months later

Little Eva had everyone doing "The Loco-Motion" ("with me"), and it wasn't long before Chubby and Dee Dee were "Slow Twistin'" together. So, inviting listeners on a surfin' safari seemed like a smart commercial move. Not that the record company agreed, according to Murry, who always insisted that Capitol had made "409" the A-side, even though he and the band knew that "Safari" would be the hit. However, there's no evidence to support Murry's claim, and the original DJ demo release has a large red letter *A* imprinted over the "Safari" side of the disc, which was given a catalogue number (37735) one digit lower than 409 (37736), suggesting that it's the first side. Both sides charted, but "Safari" was the big hit.

That started it." It won a phone-in competition on a station that asked listeners which of six discs should be played every day for a week, much helped by the Boys calling up repeatedly and using different voices to ask for their song. It went on to sell somewhere between 30,000 and 50,000 copies. Actual sales figures were hard to come by, and the band was reportedly only paid $900 in royalties for it.

With a Los Angeles–area radio hit to their name, the Beach Boys began to meet their public in the region. Their first ever live performance came at the Rendezvous

Ballroom, where Dick Dale was the headliner (of course). It was two days before Christmas 1961, and they played "Surfin'" and "Luau" during the intermission while wearing, Dennis later recalled, "Pendleton shirts and tennis shoes." Their payment was $10.

On New Year's Eve 1961, the Beach Boys made their second live appearance, and performed three songs at the annual Ritchie Valens Memorial Dance, sponsored by radio station KFBW—which had placed "Surfin'" on their top forty chart that week—in Long Beach. This time they made $300 and got repeat bookings from the radio station. That second gig was notable for being the first time that Brian played bass on stage. Al's double bass was proving too big and cumbersome for them to carry around, and Murry thought it best if Brian took over, so bought him an amp and Fender Precision bass guitar on December 26. Brian learned to play in three days. Al and Carl both played guitar from then on.

As "Surfin'" gained radio play farther afield than just the greater Los Angeles area, paying gigs increased in number and the Beach Boys had to extend their repetoire to include hits of the day. Al, perhaps annoyed at being replaced as bassist by Murry, but just as likely because he didn't think there was a future in the music business, decided to leave the band and returned to his college studies at El Camino.

He was present at the Beach Boys' first two recording sessions of the year, though, both once again paid for by the Morgans. In February, Brian, Al, and Dennis, eager to keep the surf craze growing, went into a demo studio to record a version of a new song written by Brian and

Dick Dale (left) and his Del-Tones on the set of *Muscle Beach Party* (1964).

Mike titled "Surfin' Safari." It was recorded as a demo along with "Surfer Girl," "Judy," and "Karate"—the last being the Boys' first recorded attempt at a surf instrumental. "Karate" lacks the dynamism and cutting edge of any of Dick Dale's work, but uses the by-then essential staccato, damped rhythm, and reverb-soaked lead guitar; flat-sounding drums; and swinging bass line of true surf numbers. "Judy" is a very average doo-wop-influenced ballad that, like "Karate," wouldn't be released under the Beach Boys name.

Just in case the surfing craze passed quickly, the Morgans also had Kenny and the Kadetts (Brian's previous prom-playing band name) record a couple of songs for them, both written by their son Bruce. Brian and Carl persuaded their mother to join them in singing backing vocals, which she did along with Val Poliuto, formerly of the mixed-race doo-wop act the Jaguars (whose biggest hit had been a version of "The Way You Look Tonight," in 1959). The first Kadetts number, titled "Barbie," could have been released at any time between 1952 and 1962, and is a fairly unremarkable doo-wop love song, with only Brian's falsetto making it of interest. The B-side, "What Is a Young Girl Made Of" is slightly more up-tempo, but it's another largely forgettable number. It sank without a trace on release in April 1962.

With Al gone, the Boys performed as a four-piece a few times before deciding that Carl's friend David Marks could be an extra (rhythm) guitarist, allowing Carl to play the lead lines on stage. Marks was 13 years old when Murry persuaded his parents to let him perform with the band. "We all begged my Mom and Dad to let me join," Marks later explained to a magazine.

Murry the manager then persuaded the Morgans to sign an agreement that they'd arrange a recording that would be used to get a major record label deal. Despite the success of "Surfin'," as Murry later told *Rolling Stone*, the music business thought that "The Boys were a one-shot" act, and there had been no approaches to them

Dennis Wilson in uniform, 1962.

from any major label following the success of "Surfin'." Candix had proven incapable of breaking them into the big time as far as Murry and his charges were concerned (and would soon go bust anyway). So, he thought, with a proper demo recording and the guidance of Hite Morgan, they'd doorstep the major labels and get a deal for the Beach Boys.

At least one person in the music industry had noticed the Beach Boys, though, and Brian in particular. He wasn't exactly a big shot, but Gary Usher knew plenty of people in the business. An aspiring pop star himself, he had grown up in L.A. and released a couple of singles with limited success. Then he discovered the surf scene and released the distinctly weird-sounding "Driven Insane" (b/w "You're the Girl," Titan, 1961). The single's heavily reverb-soaked guitar, slow dampened drumbeat, and ethereal wailing backing vocals appealed to KRLA and KFWB DJ Roger Christian, who played the record, although with little resultant success. Christian met Usher through Carol Connors, mostly because all three shared a love of hot rod cars. Connors was the female vocalist in Phil Spector's first hit group the Teddy Bears in 1958 (Spector sang as well as produced), and she'd go on to write the hot-rod classic "Hey Little Cobra," produced by Usher and the future Beach Boy Bruce Johnston with Terry Melcher, in 1964.

Usher's second solo single release, "Tomorrow" (b/w "Lies," Lancet, 1961) fared little better commercially, and its slightly warped, double-tracked vocals, rushed beat, and Dale-like trebly lead guitar was a fair distance from the commercial rock-and-roll sound popular at the time. It had something of the sound of a near future, though.

Usher met Brian in Hawthorne (his uncle was one of the Wilsons' neighbors), saw the Boys perform, and got on well with Brian. A shared love of cars and the burgeoning California custom and drag-car craze helped cement their friendship. They started to hang out at Brian's house, or drive around, writing songs.

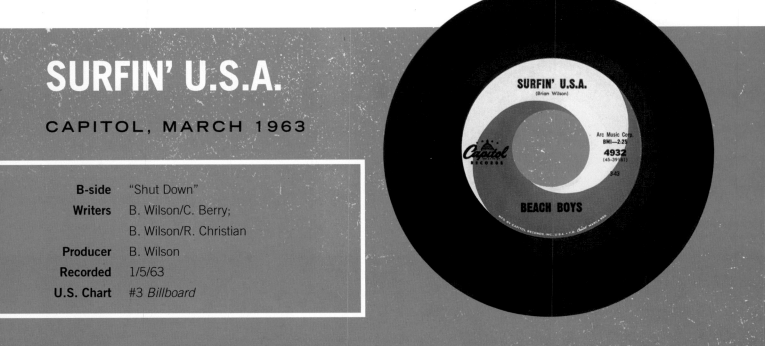

SURFIN' U.S.A.

CAPITOL, MARCH 1963

B-side	"Shut Down"
Writers	B. Wilson/C. Berry;
	B. Wilson/R. Christian
Producer	B. Wilson
Recorded	1/5/63
U.S. Chart	#3 *Billboard*

The tune is directly inspired by Chuck Berry's "Sweet Little Sixteen" (1958)—Brian admitted as much when Berry's publishers sued for copyright infringement, settling out of court. The idea for the lyric is possibly inspired by Karl Mann's "Twistin' USA," which had been a #27 hit for Danny and the Juniors in 1960 and the B-side to Chubby Checker's #1 hit "Twistin'" in 1960 and '61. For any pop or dance craze to be a true American success, it has to travel across the country, state by state, city by city. If only, thought Brian, everyone had an ocean across the country. Just as "Surfin' Safari" had crammed as many surf terms into the verses as possible, this song namechecks the proper attire (baggies and huarache sandals), while also naming some of the best surf beaches in California, plus one in Australia (he knew his market). The B-side is notable for being the first release co-written with DJ and auto nut Roger Christian. Like the surfing songs the Beach Boys had released, "Shut Down" is packed with hip auto jargon, from the opening "tach it up" through the "413," "slicks," and "dual quads" to the repeating chorus—all taken from a poem by Christian. A shut down is a win in a street drag race.

L-R: Mike Love, David Marks, Dennis Wilson, Brian Wilson, Carl Wilson at Paradise Cove, 1962. Photographed by Ken Veeder for Capitol Photo Studio.

SURFIN' SAFARI

CAPITOL, OCTOBER 1962

Producers	Brian Wilson/Murry Wilson/Nick Venet
Engineer	Chuck Britz
Recorded	8/18/62, 9/5, 6/62, Capitol Studio, Hollywood
U.S. Chart	#32 *Billboard*
Singles	"Surfin'," "Surfin' Safari," "Ten Little Indians"

Side 1

1. SURFIN' SAFARI
B. Wilson/M. Love

2. COUNTY FAIR
B. Wilson/G. Usher

3. TEN LITTLE INDIANS
B. Wilson/G. Usher

4. CHUG-A-LUG
B. Wilson/G. Usher/M. Love

5. LITTLE GIRL (YOU'RE MY MISS AMERICA)
H. Alpert/V. Catalano)

6. 409
B. Wilson/G. Usher/M. Love

Side 2

1. SURFIN'
B. Wilson/M. Love

2. HEADS YOU WIN–TAILS I LOSE
B. Wilson/G. Usher

3. SUMMERTIME BLUES
E. Cochran/J. Capehart

4. CUCKOO CLOCK
B. Wilson/G. Usher

5. MOON DAWG
B. Wilson/G. Usher

6. THE SHIFT
B. Wilson/M. Love

Despite the Pendleton shirts, surfboards, and location of the cover shoot (Paradise Cove), the Beach Boys who wrote and sang on their first album were not surfers. They helped to build the wave of popularity for surf songs that they alone mastered like no others, but they did so with just enough knowledge about it to be able to exploit it in sub-three-minute songs. They emerged at a time when the pop music business was still young and the men who ran it (there were few women in positions of power) were eager to create and milk all and any youth markets that came along. Capitol producer Nick Venet, the young man who signed the Beach Boys to the label, had to threaten to quit unless his middle-aged boss paid $300 for the right to release the second single, "Surfin' Safari," but he understood that they had the potential to be more than a one-hit wonder. What he didn't know until he began recording this, their debut long player, was the extent to which the overbearing manager and father of the Wilsons was in danger of destroying his eldest son's confidence and stifling his productivity. During the three sessions in which these twelve songs were recorded, Murry was ever-present—and ever-annoying to Brian, who, it was clear, was the man with the vision and talent to make some great commercial pop songs. Venet spent as much time in the studio distracting Murry as he did addressing the production, which was fine as it turned out, because Brian quickly learned how a studio worked. Although sometimes the guitars are lost in a murky swamp of vocals and the drums sound as if they're being played underwater, this is still a very fine debut album.

Although Brian had started to miss tour dates by mid-1963, he still made important live appearances with the band, such as this one for the *T.A.M.I.* TV show in 1964.

One of the first songs Brian and Usher wrote together was about a car that Usher wanted. "We wrote the song about a car that Brian wanted, too," Usher said in an interview with Roger Christian (found in the excellent *Hot Rods and Custom Classics* four-CD box set, Rhino, 1999). "We were on our way to a speed shop to buy some equipment for my car [a Chevvy 349] and we started talking about the new 409. We made some comments about 'Giddy up, giddy up,' and Brian started humming a little song. I threw some more lines out and it evolved."

He and Brian dragged the Wollensak tape deck into the road back in Hawthorne that night in order to record

Usher's car dragging up and down the street. Which you can hear on the opening of the recording.

In April 1962, the Boys twice worked at Western Recorders studio in Hollywood. The first time they and Usher, who knew the place, met the engineer Chuck Britz (real name Charles Dean) and demo'd "The One Way Road to Love," "Beginning of the End," "Visions," and "My Only Alibi," all with Usher on lead vocals. They neither sound like the Beach Boys of "Surfin'" or "Surfin' USA," nor do they have the unhinged edge of Usher's previous single releases. The results are horribly banal and uninspired, but the band and Usher returned to Western a few days later to record two other songs written by he and Brian, "Lonely Sea" and "409." They also re-recorded "Surfin' Safari" and "Judy."

Murry was impressed enough with "Safari" and "Lonely Sea" that he included them, along with "409," on a demo tape that he then carried around to the offices of Dot and Liberty record labels. Accompanied by Hite Morgan, Murry was left sitting in the foyer at both places with no one willing to meet with him or hear his tapes. Morgan, according to a story Murry told to a newspaper later, gave up at that point and walked away forever.

Murry didn't give up, of course, and managed to make an appointment in May to meet with a 23-year-old A&R man at Capitol Records named Nick Venet. Murry played "Surfin' Safari" in Venet's office, and the A&R man was dancing before the disc got to the middle eight. He rushed out to his boss's office and asked Voyle Gilmore (most famous for arranging and producing many of Sinatra's first Capitol-release records) to hear it.

Brian Wilson's first non-family co-songwriter, Gary Usher, photographed in 1962 when he was trying to make it as a solo singing star.

"LIKE WOODSTOCK ON A WAVE"
—ENTERTAINMENT TODAY

"SPECTACULAR"
—SAN CLEMENTE SUN POST

"GORGEOUS"
—DAILY VARIETY

"A DAZZLER"
—L.A. TIMES

"STUNNING"
—UNIVERSITY OF CALIF.

pacific vibrations

Featuring the sounds of...CREAM...THE STEVE MILLER BAND
WOLFGANG...RY COODER...AND MANY OTHERS

G ALL AGES ADMITTED General Audiences

A FILM BY JOHN SEVERSON · COLOR BY MOVIELAB · AN AMERICAN INTERNATIONAL RELEASE

71/179

Ace surf photographer John Severson played on his connection with
the Beach Boys' second album in titling his 1970 documentary.

SURFIN' USA

CAPITOL, MARCH 1963

Producers Brian Wilson/Murry Wilson/Nick Venet
Engineer Chuck Britz
Recorded 1/2, 31/63, Capitol Studios, United Western Recorders, Hollywood
U.S. Chart #2 *Billboard*
Singles "Surfin' USA"

Side 1

1. SURFIN' USA
B. Wilson/C. Berry

2. FARMER'S DAUGHTER
B. Wilson/M. Love

3. MISIRILOU
N. Roubanis

4. STOKED
B. Wilson

5. LONELY SEA
B. Wilson/G. Usher

6. SHUT DOWN
B. Wilson/R. Christian

Side 2

1. NOBLE SURFER
B. Wilson/M. Love

2. HONKY TONK
B. Doggett/C. Scott/B. Butler/H. Glover/S. Shepherd

3. LANA
B. Wilson

4. SURF JAM
C. Wilson

5. LET'S GO TRIPPIN'
D. Dale

6. FINDERS KEEPERS
B. Wilson/M. Love

No Beach Boys were sent out on a board in order to get the cover photograph for this album. It was brought in by Capitol from John Severson, who'd shot Leslie Williams in action on Oahu, Hawaii, in January 1960, intending to put the photo on the cover of his *Surfer* magazine, but the negative was damaged, so he put it aside. But when Capitol called asking for a shot for an album of surf songs, Severson dug around his darkroom, found it, and touched it up enough for use. Capitol, eager to make the most of the surfing craze, had made Venet rush the band into the studio in order to get a new album out within six months of the first. Still working at the label's studio, Brian put together a collection of surf-related cover versions, including two key surfing instrumentals, Dick Dale's "Let's Go Trippin'," and "Misirilou," an old Greek song that Dale made his signature tune and he played in the movie

A Swingin' Affair (1963). Both are adequate versions but lack the punch of Dale's. "Stoked" is Brian's attempt at a similar surf instrumental and "Surf Jam" is Carl's—the latter is more frenetic and authentic-sounding. "Honky Tonk" is a take on Bill Doggett's 1956 instrumental given an unhappy surf makeover. "Farmer's Daughter" is possibly inspired by Don and Dewey's "Farmer John" of 1959, which became a hit in 1963 in a raw cover version by the Premiers (now considered a classic of the garage scene). The standout tracks are the title song and "Shut Down." "Lonely Sea" is an affecting and enduring doo-wop ballad, and will gain more attention when Brian and the Boys perform it in the movie *The Girls on the Beach* (1965). Not long after this release Jan and Dean became the #1 surf group though, when they made the top spot on the singles chart with a song co-written by Brian ("Surf City").

SURFER GIRL

CAPITOL, JULY 1963

B-side	"Little Deuce Coupe"
Writers	B. Wilson/M. Love
	B. Wilson/R. Christian
Producer	B. Wilson
Recorded	6/5,12/63
U.S. Chart	#7 *Billboard*

The first ballad from the Beach Boys is a classic post-doo-wop hymn of objectification and remote admiration. The surfer girl that Brian so idolizes could be Gidget, or Carol Mountain (a girl admired from afar in high school), or Marilyn Rovell, his latest love—and no matter that only Gidget surfed. In 1962 Bob Halley had slowed down the Twist for a minor hit about "That Twistin' Girl of Mine," but the dance fad hadn't stretched to ballad form. However, Phil Spector's "Be My Boy" (co-written with his sister Shirley, aka Cory Sands), produced for the Paris Sisters in 1961, is a significant influence on Brian's writing here. That song and the Sisters' "I Love How You Love Me"

were the kind of ballads that tugged at Brian's emotions (and were almost as influential on him as the Ronettes' "Be My Baby" would be). Spector's work at Gold Star Studio with numerous acts—especially girl groups like the Paris Sisters, the Crystals, and the Ronettes—was impressing and inspiring Brian. He'd tried out the same studio (although this was recorded at Western Recorders) and was employing some of the same musicians favored by Spector. Brian produced a session for Marilyn's girl-group, the Honeys, in March 1963 ("Shoot the Curl") that hinted at a Spector-like sound. More would follow.

Gilmore liked what he heard, so Venet ran back to his office and asked Murry what he wanted for the demo tapes. He told him that Capitol would like to release a single of "Safari."

Murry asked for $300 for all three recordings. Venet ran back to Gilmore and was told by him it was too much, but ignoring his boss, Venet returned to Murry and did the deal. Within a month Capitol had pressed "409" and "Surfin' Safari" and released them. The same L.A.-based DJs who'd loved "Surfin'" took to "Safari" and played it loud and long. Roger Christian played both sides loud and long, because he really liked "409."

California car culture and surf culture were, and

remain, intricately linked. Surfers need their cars in order to get to the beach, and they need them to pose in at night when surfing's out. Just as surfers customized their boards, so they cut, cropped, dropped, candy-colored, and polished their cars, too.

Gary Usher, like a multitude of young California males including the Wilsons, loved his car and hung around with like-minded enthusiasts. One of them was Roger Christian, a DJ who spoke the language of cars, which fascinated Brian in a similar way to how surf jargon had. In a radio interview of 1973, Christian reckoned that he'd owned 100 cars, and his best ideas for songs came while driving around. Late that summer of 1962 the DJ had Brian Wilson in his passenger seat, and they were writing songs together, among them "Little Deuce Coupe" and "Shut Down."

As "Surfin' Safari" spread across America from radio network to network it became a hit and then a full-fledged phenomenon. It started in Phoenix, of all places. Then it spread to Detroit and "broke all kinds of records for us [at Capitol] in New York," claimed Venet. Demand for the Beach Boys to play gigs around the country, combined with radio play and sales, persuaded Capitol to sign them to a longer and more binding contract. They signed in mid-July 1962.

BE TRUE TO YOUR SCHOOL

CAPITOL, SEPTEMBER 1963

B-side	"In My Room"
Writers	B. Wilson/M. Love; B. Wilson/G. Usher
Producer	B. Wilson
Recorded	9/2/63
U.S. Chart	#6 *Billboard*

The tune is based on the Hawthorne High School fighting song, which Brian would hear every time he (and Al) took to the football field for their old alma mater. That, in turn, had been based on "On, Wisconsin," the fight song of the University of Wisconsin Badgers (written in 1905 by William Purdy for the University of Minnesota; he was persuaded to switch allegiance). How it got to Hawthorne is unknown, but probably via an alumnus of Wisconsin who was employed there. Brian and Mike may have turned it into a Beach Boys song because they were performing at high schools and universities at the time, and the sentiments of the song are applicable to every American institute of learning, so it would have been a real crowd pleaser. It is strictly conformist and parochial, a rousing jock anthem, and it naturally was a big hit in America. Oddly though, it was also a hit in Sweden and Australia, too. The B-side is far more interesting. "In My Room" is the opposite of the macho "School," being personal and private, and it has the singer "crying," "sighing," keeping "secrets," "safe," etc. That would have been considered the sole territory of a female singer at the time, but it's Brian, who'd retreat to his bedroom for days and weeks later in life, who's singing.

Brian (left) in charge in the studio, with Carl (seated) and Mike.

In late summer, Brian—fed up with having to share a bedroom with his brothers and having to use the garage as a studio, and constantly at war with Murry over new friends he'd made who were hanging around the family home—moved out. He relocated to a shared apartment around the corner with Bob Norberg, a man Murry considered a bad influence on Brian, according to biographer Steven Gaines. Brian moved house in between producing at recording sessions. He was 20 years old.

For the rest of the year the band played numerous dates around and across California in between recording sessions. In August 1962, they spent three days at the Capitol studio to begin recording their first album (they had re-recorded "Surfin' Safari" in June). From the beginning, Murry and Nick Venet competed with Brian at the soundboard. Brian would set things up perfectly only to have Murry reset levels when his son returned to the sound booth. Brian was certain that he knew how to run things. He came to hate the Capitol studios, which were designed to house orchestras, and after making the first two albums there, persuaded Venet to let him produce future Beach Boys records in studios of his own choosing—mostly presumably because he (and manager Murry) agreed to do so at their own cost. Murry thought that was a good idea because it meant Venet couldn't walk in to the studio and take charge whenever he liked.

In October 1962, "Surfin' Safari" peaked at #14 on the *Billboard* pop charts and *Surfin' Safari* was released. More importantly (to him, at least) that month Brian met 14-year-old Marilyn Rovell, the cousin of Gary Usher's girlfriend. It was love at first sight for him. Marilyn, who sang in a group with her older sister, Diane, called the Honeys, was bemused when she became his muse.

As 1963 began the first Beach Boys album was doing OK, but the single "Ten Little Indians" had failed to crack the Top 40. January and February were spent recording the new album at Western Recorders in between playing live shows, and then in March, "Surfin' USA" b/w "Shut Down" was released.

FUN, FUN, FUN

CAPITOL, FEBRUARY 1964

B-side	"Why Do Fools Fall in Love"
Writers	B. Wilson/M. Love; F. Lymon/H. Santiago/ J. Merchant
Producer	B. Wilson
Recorded	1/1, 8, 10/64
U.S. Chart	#5 *Billboard* Hot 100

Almost as if they wanted to cheer up America, in writing "Fun, Fun, Fun" Brian and Mike looked back to the days when they were cruising around in their car, looking for girls and listening to Chuck Berry. Like a Berry story song, it tells of a girl who borrows her father's car, promising to visit the library but instead heading for the hamburger stand, where she can show off her wheels, race the guys (who'll never catch her), and have fun, fun, fun—until the ultimate patriarchial power removes the source of her enjoyment. It's a mini-feminist tract and an auto fetishist's dream. It wowed America and lit up some of the post–Kennedy assassination gloom that still hung over the country three months later. Innately understanding of the power of nostalgia, Brian chose a great Frankie Lymon and the Teenagers' 1956 hit for the B-side. It would remind people of how great America had been, just a few years back. Choosing Gold Star as the venue, and working with a handful of the Wrecking Crew backing musicians, Brian created a version of the Wall of Sound on it that could easily be mistaken for the work of Phil Spector. He even used a pseudo-Spector intro, complete with echoing piano, tinkling bells, and a cavernous reverb. It would be their last chart hit before the Beatles arrived in America.

SM-1981

Capitol ®

SURFER GIRL
THE BEACH BOYS

LITTLE DEUCE COUPE · SURFER GIRL · CATCH A WAVE · THE SURFER MOON · SOUTH BAY SURFER · HAWAII
IN MY ROOM · THE ROCKING SURFER · SURFER'S RULE · OUR CAR CLUB · YOUR SUMMER DREAM · BOOGIE WOODIE

SURFER GIRL

CAPITOL, SEPTEMBER 1963

Producer Brian Wilson
Engineer Chuck Britz
Recorded 6/12,14,16/63, United Western Recorders, Hollywood
U.S. Chart #7 *Billboard*
Singles "Surfer Girl"

Side 1

1. SURFER GIRL
B. Wilson

2. CATCH A WAVE
B. Wilson/M. Love

3. THE SURFER MOON
B. Wilson

4. SOUTH BAY SURF
B. Wilson/D. Wilson/A. Jardine

5. THE ROCKIN' SURFER
trad. arr. B. Wilson

6. LITTLE DEUCE COUPE
B. Wilson/R. Christian

Side 2

1. IN MY ROOM
B. Wilson/G. Usher

2. HAWAII
B. Wilson/M. Love

3. SURFER'S RULE
B. Wilson/M. Love

4. OUR CAR CLUB
B. Wilson/M. Love

5. YOUR SUMMER DREAM
B. Wilson/B. Norberg

6. BOOGIE WOODIE
trad. arr. B. Wilson

There were six months between album releases from the Beach Boys. Unsurprisingly, the formula is the same for both. Later, Brian would say, "there was a compulsion involved. We did it out of compulsive drive. You see so many pressures happening at once, and you grit your teeth…I was in a state of creative panic." Still, the songs are wrapped in swooping harmonies, with lots of surfing commentary. There are two strong anthems—"Surfer's Rule" and "The Rockin' Surfer"—and as with the previous releases there are also a couple of hot-rod numbers. "Little Deuce Coupe" is a better song than "Shut Down." Although originally released as the B-side of the title track, "Little Deuce Coupe" became the first of the Beach Boys tracks to reach a million radio plays (it also scored higher than any other B-side for them,

making #15). Three of the six directly surf-related songs are filler, although the title track (based on "When You Wish Upon a Star"), "In My Room," and "Catch a Wave" stand repeated listening. This was the first album to be wholly recorded somewhere other than Capitol Studios. Brian was paying his own recording costs—the success of the last album and single had made enough money that they could afford it—and he paid to take engineer Chuck Britz with him to Western Recorders. He also paid to employ some outside professional session musicians. This was the start of a long association with drummer Hal Blaine, a founding member of the Wrecking Crew of musicians who'd provide backing on some of the world's most successful pop-and-rock records and for a number of legendary producers, albeit anonymously.

"We sang "Surfin'" and it was done in two takes. We've been going ever since."

MIKE *Love*

From a publicity photo shoot by Ken Veeder at Paradise Cove, 1962, which would produce the image for their first and third album releases, and for many singles bags, too. L-R: Mike, David, Brian, Dennis, Carl.

Brian, Mike, and Carl in New York outside Capitol Records' office
on West 54th Street, for a party held in their honor, 1964.

Brian worked nonstop through the summer and fall of 1963, recording *Little Deuce Coupe* with the Boys and other songs for the Honeys. At the end of the summer Nick Venet left Capitol to start his own company, and Murry felt as if he'd won a personal war.

When *Little Deuce Coupe* made #4 on the charts, it became their third straight Top 10 LP release. They'd had three Top 10 singles that year, too, and when their first Christmas single "Little Saint Nick" made it to #3 on *Billboard*'s special Chrismas chart, it seemed that the Beach Boys were the hottest pop act in America. Only the Four Seasons came close to matching them. For now.

WHEN I GROW UP

CAPITOL, AUGUST 1964

B-side	"She Knows Me Too Well"
Writers	B. Wilson/M. Love (both)
Producer	B. Wilson
Recorded	8/5,10/64
U.S. Chart	#9 *Billboard*

Brian was 22 years old and Mike Love 23 when they came up with this philosophical problem prettified by a harpsichord and four-part harmonies. In it they ponder the future and what they'll be like when they eventually become men. Most of their imagination is spent on matters of sex, such as if they'd look for the same things in a woman as they do a girl (in Mike's lead part), and if they'll love their wife for the rest of their life (Brian's). The dumbness of the lyrics is either very smart in communicating all the emotional depth of a 14-year-old or genuinely naïve and well intentioned. Brian was, after all, dating a 16-year-old (Marilyn). It was musically inventive, though, and the harpsichord lends the recording an air of the baroque that was about to become more common in rock music. Brian had undoubtedly heard it in Henry Mancini's recording of Cy Coleman's "Playboy's Theme" of 1960, but he might also have heard it used on "If You Ever Need Me," by Margaret Mandolph, written and produced by David Gates (released May 1964). The B-side, "She Knows Me Too Well," has a lead vocal by Brian (and no harpsichord), and it sounds as if it's a private recording for Marilyn's ears alone. The singer's perspective is strangely detached, but it lends a sense of loneliness to the song, and gives it an air of real teenage yearning.

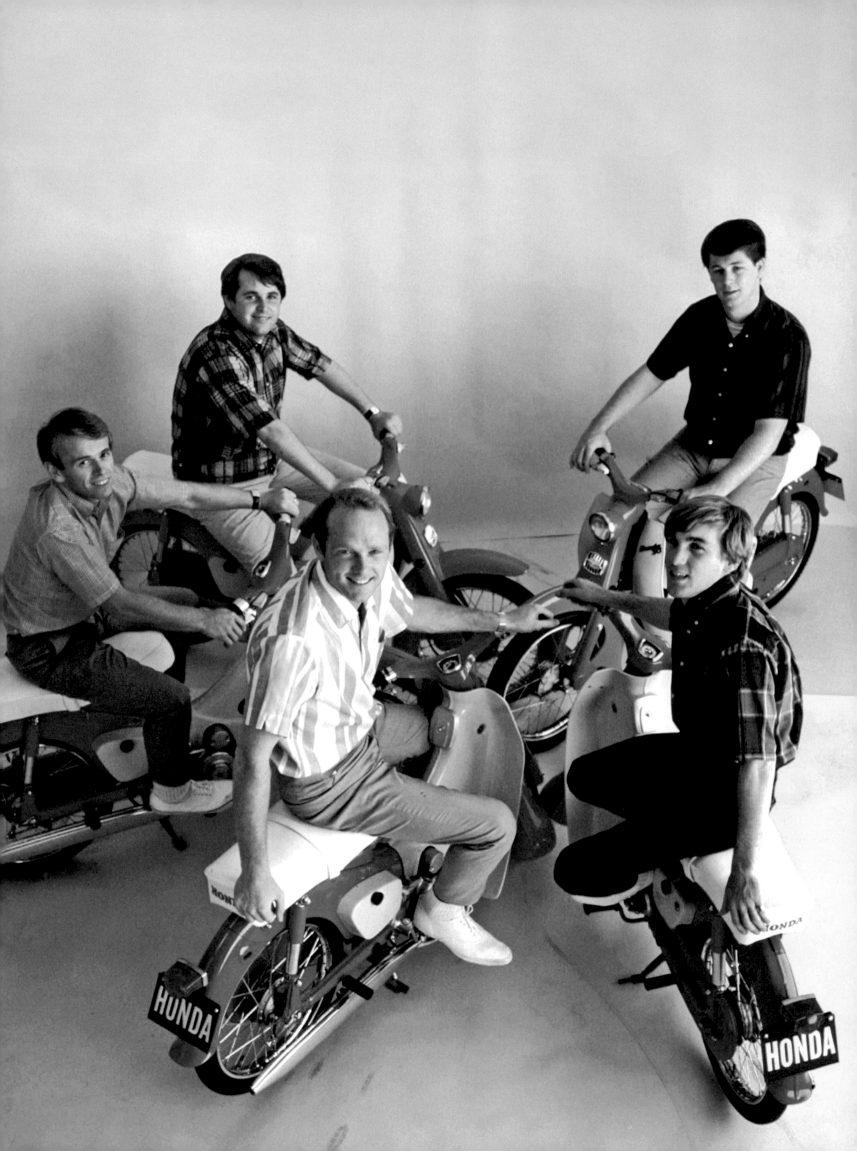

3

BEACH BOYS TODAY!

1964 · 1965

From surfboards and matching Pendleton shirts to a Stingray and matching car jackets. From the photo session for the *Shut Down Volume 2* album sleeve.

SHUT DOWN VOLUME 2

CAPITOL, MARCH 1964

Producer	Brian Wilson
Engineer	Chuck Britz
Recorded	1/1/64, United Western Recorders, 1/7–8/64, Gold Star Studios Hollywood
U.S. Chart	#13 *Billboard*
Singles	"Fun, Fun, Fun"

Side 1

1. FUN, FUN, FUN
B. Wilson/M. Love

2. DON'T WORRY BABY
B. Wilson/R. Christian

3. IN THE PARKIN' LOT
B. Wilson/R. Christian

4. "CASSIUS" LOVE VS "SONNY" WILSON
B. Wilson/M. Love

5. THE WARMTH OF THE SUN
B. Wilson/M. Love

6. THIS CAR OF MINE
B. Wilson/M. Love

Side 2

1. WHY DO FOOLS FALL IN LOVE
F. Lymon/M. Levy

2. POM-POM PLAY GIRL
B. Wilson/G. Usher

3. KEEP AN EYE ON SUMMER
B. Wilson/B. Norberg/M. Love

4. SHUT DOWN, PART II
C. Wilson

5. LOUIE, LOUIE
R. Berry

6. DENNY'S DRUMS
D. Wilson

By the time this was released, America had come firmly under the spell of Beatlemania. At the time of recording though, Brian had no idea of what was about to happen to the American music scene. Somehow the Beatles made all of this album sound incredibly old-fashioned, even though the Liverpudlian quartet drew on many of the same musical influences as Brian. The difference perhaps was that Lennon and McCartney didn't show their inspirations quite as clearly as Brian—a Little Richard–style "woooh!" in a song about seeing a girl across a dance floor ("I Saw Her Standing There") isn't as blatant as using a Chuck Berry tune to carry a song about surfing. Here, Brian covers a Frankie Lymon song from 1956 ("Fools") pretty faithfully, but Richard Berry's "Louie, Louie" from 1955, is a pale shadow of the Kingsmen's reductive thrash of 1963, which had changed the way that guitar bands practiced in their garage forever. The ballads "Keep an Eye on Summer" and "The Warmth of the Sun" (written the night of JFK's assassination) are lovely, classic Beach Boys songs, but they're nothing new. Brian knew the surf and car crazes would eventually pass; the arrival of the Beatles had just hastened their end. And while the Beach Boys still awaited their first U.S. #1 hit single, the Beatles had managed two in just a couple of months.

ALL SUMMER LONG

CAPITOL, JULY 1964

Producer	Brian Wilson
Engineer	Chuck Britz
Recorded	10/18/63, 4/2/64–5/19/64, United Western Recorders, Hollywood
U.S. Chart	#4 *Billboard*
Singles	"I Get Around," "Little Honda," "Wendy"

Side 1

1. I GET AROUND
B. Wilson/M. Love

2. ALL SUMMER LONG
B. Wilson/M. Love

3. HUSHABYE
D. Pomus/M. Shuman

4. LITTLE HONDA
B. Wilson/M. Love

5. WE'LL RUN AWAY
B. Wilson/G. Usher

6. CARL'S BIG CHANCE
B. Wilson/C. Wilson

Side 2

1. WENDY
B. Wilson/M. Love

2. DO YOU REMEMBER?
B. Wilson/M. Love

3. GIRLS ON THE BEACH
B. Wilson/M. Love

4. DRIVE-IN
B. Wilson/M. Love

5. OUR FAVORITE RECORDING SESSIONS
B. Wilson/C. Wilson/D. Wilson/A. Jardine/M. Love

6. DON'T BACK DOWN
B. Wilson/M. Love

More perhaps than any other American pop band of the time, the Beach Boys were shocked into action by the success of the Beatles in their homeland. When the Liverpudlians arrived in New York, the Beach Boys were in Europe, making TV and live appearances. On their return Stateside the music scene had changed enormously, but Brian Wilson took inspiration from the guitar-led, fast-paced and rougher sounds of the Beatles. He began writing and demoing new songs at the end of April 1964, with "I Get Around" being the first song finished. It was released as a single in May, and swiftly became the band's first U.S. #1 hit. During the recording Brian sacked his father Murry as manager, and the songs on this album sound as if they're making a new beginning. The familar themes of summer, surfing, and cars are still present, as are the by now standard swooping harmonies, but as if to show that just like John, Paul, George, and Ringo, the Beach Boys could—and did—fool around while at work, there's "Our Favourite Recording Sessions." It predates The Monkees' similar schtick by two years and is not just a "filler" track because the job it's designed to do is to show fans that they are a group of guys just like any others who get things wrong, joke around, and disobey the voice of authority—in this case Murry's. The barely disguised antagonism beneath the surface of the previous album's scripted "'Cassius' Love Vs 'Sonny' Liston" is absent, and here the mistakes are genuine. The inclusion of fluffed notes and lines should have been embarrassing, but instead they're humanizing. The Fab Four cracked great jokes on TV, radio, and in newsreels, it was a big part of their appeal. Other bands had to show the same wit; Brian's Boys were the first.

Date number 20 of the 1964 *Summer Safari* tour,

on which the Boys played two shows.

**Left: An increasingly rare live performance featuring
Brian, on the *Andy Williams Show*, October 22, 1965.**

The Beach Boys made appearances on the *Steve Allen
Show* and then taped a live concert for NBC in March,
before miming to "Don't Worry Baby" on *American
Bandstand*—as one of two acts on the show (broadcast
April 18). The rest of that 45-minute *American Bandstand*
was given over to the Beatles. It was becoming clear to
Brian that the surf and car scenes had finished.

Most of Brian's collaborators at the time didn't want
to believe it, of course. Roger Christian wasn't ready
to give up on hot-rod songs. The Rip Chords had their
biggest hit with Carol Connors's "Hey Little Cobra" in
February, b/w one of his and Jan Berry's songs titled
"Three Window Coupe" (which was not too dissimilar to "Little Deuce Coupe"). Gary Usher was busy
producing other hot-rod and surfing acts, such as the
Hondells, who'd score a hit later in 1964 with a version of "Little Honda," written by Brian. Jan and Dean's
"Dead Man's Curve," "Drag City," and "Little Old Lady
from Pasadena" would all make the Top 10 in 1964. As
prolific as the Beatles were, they couldn't fill every spot
in America's singles and albums charts, every week.

But, as Brian told a teen magazine about the next
Beach Boys album of 1964, "We needed to grow. We
had done every angle about surfing and then we did the
car thing." Part of that growing involved not just finding
new musical inspirations and sources, but also breaking
free from the ties that bound them to the old way
of doing things—the strongest one of which was Murry,
of course, who was still their manager.

As Gaines tells the story in his biography of Brian
and the Beach Boys (*Heroes and Villains*), the big break
with Murry came at an early April recording session at
Western Recorders, where Brian, Al, Carl, and Dennis
were beginning to record "I Get Around." At some prior
point Murry had been fooled into thinking that the
section of a mixing desk ascribed to him at Western was
functional, when it was a dummy, rigged on the instructions of Brian to stop the old man screwing with his
levels when he went into the sound booth.

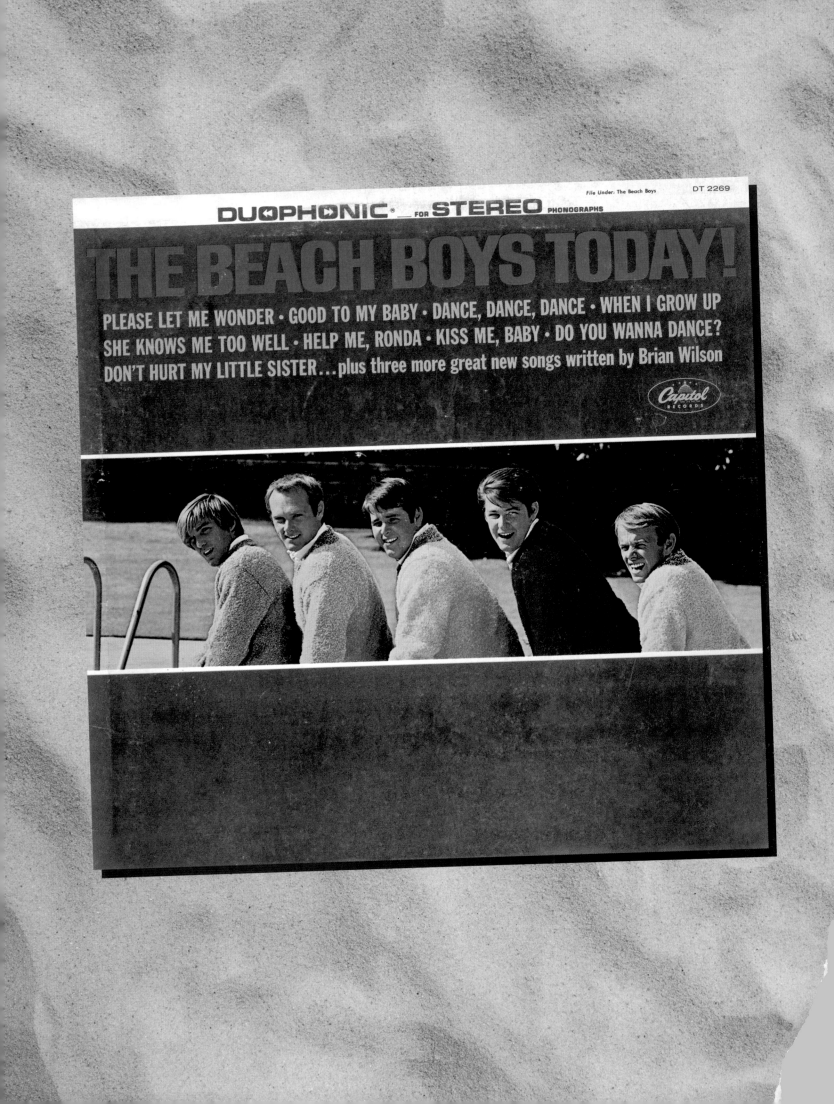

THE BEACH BOYS TODAY!

CAPITOL, MARCH 1965

Producer	Brian Wilson
Engineers	Chuck Britz, Larry Levine
Recorded	8/5, 8, 10/64, 10/9/64, 12/16/64, 1/7–19/65, United Western Recorders, Gold Star, RCA Studio, Hollywood
U.S. Chart	#4 *Billboard*
Singles	"When I Grow Up (to Be a Man)," "Dance, Dance, Dance," "Do You Wanna Dance?"

Side 1

1 DO YOU WANNA DANCE?
B. Freeman

2. GOOD TO MY BABY
B. Wilson/M. Love

3. DON'T HURT MY LITTLE SISTER
B. Wilson/M. Love

4. WHEN I GROW UP TO BE A MAN
B. Wilson/M. Love

5. HELP ME, RHONDA
B. Wilson/M. Love

6. DANCE, DANCE, DANCE
B. Wilson/C. Wilson/M. Love

Side 2

1. PLEASE LET ME WONDER
B. Wilson/M. Love

2. I'M SO YOUNG
W. H. Tyus Jr.

3. KISS ME
B. Wilson/M. Love

4. SHE KNOWS ME TOO WELL
B. Wilson/M. Love

5. IN THE BACK OF MY MIND
B. Wilson/M. Love

6. BULL SESSION WITH BIG DADDY
The Beach Boys

This is the first album Brian created while regularly smoking marijuana. He suffered at least three breakdowns during recording and writing, but strangely, little of that can be heard on the record. The songs' subject matter are not soaked in surf or engine oil, but neither are they deeply personal or revelatory. There are plenty of ballads that teem with self-pity and lovelorn pining, as well as standard teen-pop rock and roll bluster. They sound fantastic, of course. Almost all of the 30+ musicians employed on this album were regularly used by Phil Spector. "Do You Wanna Dance?" was recorded at Gold Star, Spector's favored studio, so it's little surprise that it sounds like a Spector production. Brian's musical influences haven't changed much since the recording of "All Summer Long," although Lennon and McCartney have been joined to the list of songwriters and arrangers that he gains inspiration from. The electric guitar makes more noise on this album than it had on previous Beach Boys releases, and not just as a backing instrument. It carries melody and inserts hooks (particularly on "Don't Hurt My Sister" and "Dance, Dance, Dance"); it chimes and drives the beat along. The layers of horns scattered across the tracks are pure Spector; the harpsichord ("When I Grow Up") is a new touch. Previously mostly used by film score composers (Henry Mancini was fond of it in the early '60s) it will become more common on rock and pop songs after this. The cover versions, as was becoming usual on Beach Boys albums, date from 1958 and were by doo-wop artists, Bobby Freeman's "Do You Wanna Dance?" and the Students' "I'm So Young."

Al and Brian at the piano, 1965.

As was often the case, throughout the fateful session Murry thought he was producing, and kept projecting his voice and opinion into the sound booths from the control room. His opinion was that the song was poor, Brian was a loser, and Murry knew how to make a hit song better than he did.

After a while, when Murry stopped the tape because he thought the bass (that Brian was playing) was wrong, the eldest son simply stated, "You don't know what you're talking about, Dad." Murry, says Gaines, screamed, "Don't you ever speak to me that way! I made you and the Beach Boys! Hear me? You'd be nothing without me!" In response, as Gaines tells it, Brian pulled his father from his chair and threw him up against the wall. H shouted, "Get out of here! You're fired!"

Murry left without a fight. Brian was physically much bigger than him at this point, and there were witnesses in the room, people who were not family and shouldn't see physical violence between father and son, so the old man let it slide—for now. It transpired that Murry would have a kind of revenge that he relished more than feeling the smack of his fist on his son's head. Years later, Murry would refer to the scene in a letter to Brian in which he set out the reasons, as he saw them, that the Beach Boys were "finished."

Audree, talking to *Rolling Stone*'s David Felton in 1976, said that the sacking "destroyed" her husband. She understood why it destroyed him, she explained, and went on: "That was a horrible time for me. He was just destroyed by that and yet he wasn't really up to it. He'd already had an ulcer and it was really too much for him; but he loved them so much, he was overly protective, really. He couldn't let them go, he couldn't stand seeing anyone else handling his kids. Those were terrible days, frankly, and he was angry with me. You always take it out on the closest one. He was angry at the whole world....He stayed in bed a lot."

An accounting firm was called in to take care of business while Murry sulked at home in bed. Only Carl remained resident at the Hawthorne house at that point, Dennis having left a few months earlier. Carl stuck posters of the Beatles on his walls, according to Murry some years later, and played the first two U.S. Beatles LP releases almost nonstop.

In between recording sessions in April, the Boys spent two days filming *Girls on the Beach* (aka *Summer of '64*, 1965), a B-movie about a sorority house trying to get the Beatles to perform at a benefit gig for them, but having to settle for the Beach Boys instead. In a scene that calls for Brian to sing the title song while seated on the beach, surrounded by girls in bikinis and the rest of the Boys, he looks as if he's sitting on an ant hill.

As if Hollywood wasn't content with making them suffer the indignity of being a Beatles surrogate on screen, in May the band mimed being the backing band for former Mouseketeer Annette Funicello in a flop Disney movie titled *Monkey's Uncle* (1965). The Beach Boys only appear in the opening scene as the credits roll, playing and singing backing (with characteristic Wilson

DO YOU WANNA DANCE?

CAPITOL, FEBRUARY 1965

B-side	"Please Let Me Wonder"
Writers	B. Freeman; B. Wilson/M. Love
Producer	B. Wilson
Recorded	1/7, 11/65
U.S. Chart	#12 *Billboard*

This was the first time that Dennis had been given lead vocal duties on a single release—he'd led on album tracks "Little Girl (You're My Miss America)" on *Surfer Girl*, and on "This Car of Mine" on *Shut Down Volume 2*—and he was a natural choice for it. Where Brian's falsetto and Mike's sweet tone would have created a version closer to the anondyne, fluffy pop thrill of the UK's Cliff Richard (a milksop Elvis impersonator), Dennis's rawer tone gets closer to that of the song's writer Bobby Freeman. As with Freeman's original there's a hint in the delivery that the invitation onto the dance floor is as a precursor to something to follow that would involve a different kind of dance. Unlike the 1958 original, which is sparsely orchestrated, Brian fills his recording with Dennis's deep pounding drums, a piano that sounds as big as a cathedral organ, a highway full of honking horns, and a choir of backing voices that only Phil Spector could match. The B-side is a lovely ballad with Brian's lead vocal sounding totally sincere. It's notable for the inclusion of a clearly audible guitar riff that has the ring of George Harrison's work with the Beatles, and an organ break that would sound in place on one of their releases, too. Brian was listening closely to the competition.

Copyright © 1965 by Paramount Pictures Corporation. Permission granted for newspaper and magazine reproduction. (Made in U.S.A.)

"THE GIRLS ON THE BEACH"

PARAMOUNT RELEASE

falsetto harmonies) on a Richard and Robert Sherman title song that would never be found on any Sherman Bros. greatest hits collection (which would include "I Wanna Be Like You," "Chim-Chim-Cheree," and "Hushabye Mountain" among many others).

Annette would have much more success in *Beach Blanket Bingo* (1965), starring alongside Frankie Avalon. A mildly exploitative surf pic, it's the fifth in a series of seven "beach party" pictures that began in 1963 with *Beach Party*, also starring Annette and Frankie. Gary Usher and Roger Christian managed to squeeze three songs into *Blanket*, two performed by the Hondells and one by Annette. They'd had three songs in *Beach Party*, two performed by Dick Dale, and six in *Muscle Beach Party* (1964), all those songs co-written with Brian Wilson, with four performed by Dick Dale and two by Frankie Avalon and the cast. Little Stevie Wonder's in on the Muscle Beach party, too, performing "Happy Street" with Dick Dale and the Del-Tones.

However, as with the pop-music charts, the whole idea and concept of movies starring or featuring music

Above: The script called for a band to take the place of the Beatles.
Opposite: The poster gave them a big billing, but the
Beach Boys only appeared in a couple of scenes.

acts was about to change radically, and all because of the Beatles. When *A Hard Day's Night* opened in August the band was already the biggest music act in America (if not the world), so despite the movie being shot in black and white, and having no glamorous or exotic locations, it was an immediate box-office hit. The Beatles play themselves in the film, which was unusual, since even Elvis never got to play Elvis, only weak caricatures of an Elvis-style figure.

A Hard Day's Night doesn't depend on the presence of scantily clad girls to sell it. The dialogue is quick-witted and slangy, and the Beatles' accents are barely softened, making it difficult sometimes for non-Scouse-speaking viewers to fully understand what they're saying. But the spontaneity and naturalness and those great songs made the movie hugely appealing. After that, all

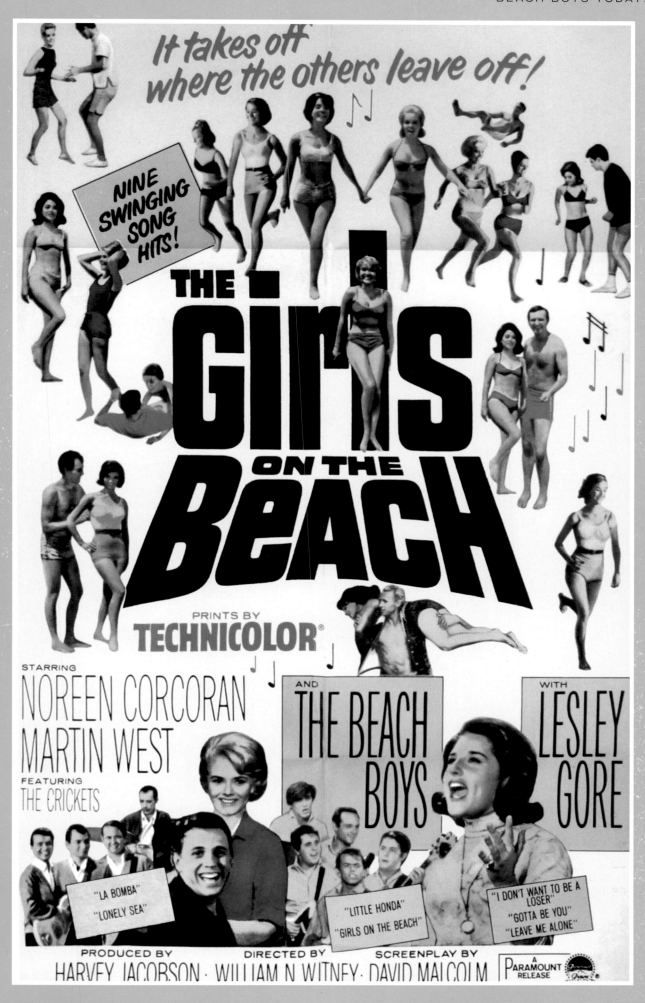

HELP ME, RHONDA

CAPITOL, APRIL 1965

B-side	"Kiss Me, Baby"
Writers	B. Wilson/M. Love
Producer	B. Wilson
Recorded	1/19/65, 2/24/65
U.S. Chart	#1 *Billboard*

The first release of this song appeared on the *Today!* album with the spelling as "Ronda," but the single version was a reworking (at which Murry made his now infamous intervention, telling them to sing "from the heart"). It's the first single to feature Al as lead singer (he'd previously only sung lead on "Christmas Day" for the 1964 Christmas album), and it uses a re-recorded vocal and backing vocals. As with "Do You Wanna Dance?" the guitar (played by Glen Campbell) is high in the mix and has a circular, ringing quality to it, this time backed by a strummed ukulele. Where the original album version begins with a counted intro and ukelele, the single goes straight into

the vocals. The piano that leads the instrumental break is played by Leon Russell. The harmonica lines played by one-time Sun label artist Billy Lee Riley on the original recording is missing on the single release version, which can also be found on the *Summer Days (And Summer Nights!!)* LP. As was becoming something of a habit, the B-side is a ballad, the lead vocals shared between Mike and Brian. The bass on "Kiss Me, Baby" was played by Carol Kaye, a familiar Wrecking Crew member who'd sat in on a lot of Spector sessions, and the guitar was played by Nancy Sinatra's arranger, Billy Strange, both musicians who were at the top of their game

the bikini-clad figures and hunks in trunks in California were not going to have audiences rushing to cinemas to watch surf movies. Instead, pop music acts would have to be naturals in front of a camera in order to star in something as corny as a formulaic B-movie.

After the Beach Boys' movie-making experiences, in June 1964 they recorded a whole album's worth of Christmas-themed songs, ready for a November release. In July they went out as the headline act on the *Surfin' Safari* tour, beginning on the third in Honolulu. One of the support acts that night was Bruce and Terry (Johnston and Melcher), two men who would come to figure largely in the Beach Boys' future. They were also

joined by old friends Jan and Dean plus, at the bottom of the bill, Peter and Gordon, two English guys who were about to steal the hearts of former Jan and Dean and Bruce and Terry fans, as much because of their English accents as for their having Paul McCartney write songs for them (Peter was an Asher, brother to Paul's girlfriend of the time, Jane). The Beatles influence was everywhere, even in Hawaii.

The Beach Boys played four shows in Hawaii before flying to Arizona, where the duos all dropped out of the tour. Unusually for Brian, he played 33 straight dates without a visit to a recording studio, but on August 5 he and the Boys recorded "When I Grow Up to Be a Man," which was released less than three weeks later. The *All Summer Long* album had been released in mid-July and, helped by the success of "I Get Around," made it to #4 on the U.S. album charts.

The seemingly interminable *Safari* tour hadn't ended, though, and early September 1964 saw them on the East Coast, following which was a crawl south to Florida, before heading back to New York for shows in late September and an appearance on the *Ed Sullivan Show*. October 27 found the band back in California and laying tracks for the next studio album just as their first live album was released. *Beach Boys Concert* amazingly went to the #1 position on the *Billboard* U.S. national charts— becoming the first Beach Boys LP release to do so.

When the Beach Boys landed in London in November, nine months after the Beatles had conquered America, it felt as if the California boys were taking over Britain. Girls screamed at them when they landed and from outside of their hotel. TV and radio stations wanted to interview them, and the press seemed to be genuinely appreciative of their music. All of which was pleasing, but to Brian it was only vaguely reassuring. After so long touring, and on the eve of another long transatlantic flight, he'd suffered huge insecurities about his relationship with Marilyn again. As they had when he was in the Antipodes, they spoke for hours on the telephone. He proposed again.

While in London Brian made a public disavowal of his musical past, telling a reporter, "We don't play surf music. We're tired of being labelled as the originators of the surfing sound. We just produce a sound that the teens dig, and that can be applied to any theme. The surfing theme has run its course. Cars are finished now, too. And even Hondas are over. We're going to stay on the life of the social teenager."

After Britain the Boys flew to Paris for a live performance on a TV show before heading to Italy and then West Germany, before another show in Paris and then on to Scandinavia. They flew back to the USA in time for Thanksgiving and another five performances in the Northeast before they could get to California and Brian could reunite with Marilyn.

Although not yet 17, Marilyn's parents gave their consent, and she married 22-year-old Brian on December 7, 1964. He went back to work at Western Recorders on a new album (*Beach Boys Today!*) nine days later, and on December 17, the Beach Boys recorded six songs for British TV producer Jack Good's *Shindig! Christmas Special*. The producer told them that they "sing like eunuchs in the Sistine Chapel," which Brian liked. Six days later he really didn't like hearing "here's your meal Mr. Wilson" from a stewardess on a flight to Houston, though. It was supposed to be the beginning of another 25-date tour, but Brian had had enough.

As he said to magazine writer Earl Leaf (who'd become the editor of the Beach Boys' fan magazine), "I told the stewardess, 'I don't want any food. Get away from me.' Then I started telling people that I'm not getting off the plane. I was getting far out, coming undone, having a breakdown, and I just let myself go completely. I dumped myself out of the seat and all over the plane. I let myself go emotionally....The rubber band had stretched as far as it could go." It took some time to get him off the plane in Texas, but eventually Brian calmed himself enough to disembark and play the gig.

The next morning Brian couldn't stop crying and wouldn't talk to anyone, not even his brothers. Al Jardine would later tell a British music paper that, "We were really scared for him. He obviously had a breakdown. None of us had ever witnessed something like that." That evening, accompanied by a member of the road crew, Brian flew back to L.A., and his mother collected him from the airport. Brian told Earl Leaf that he

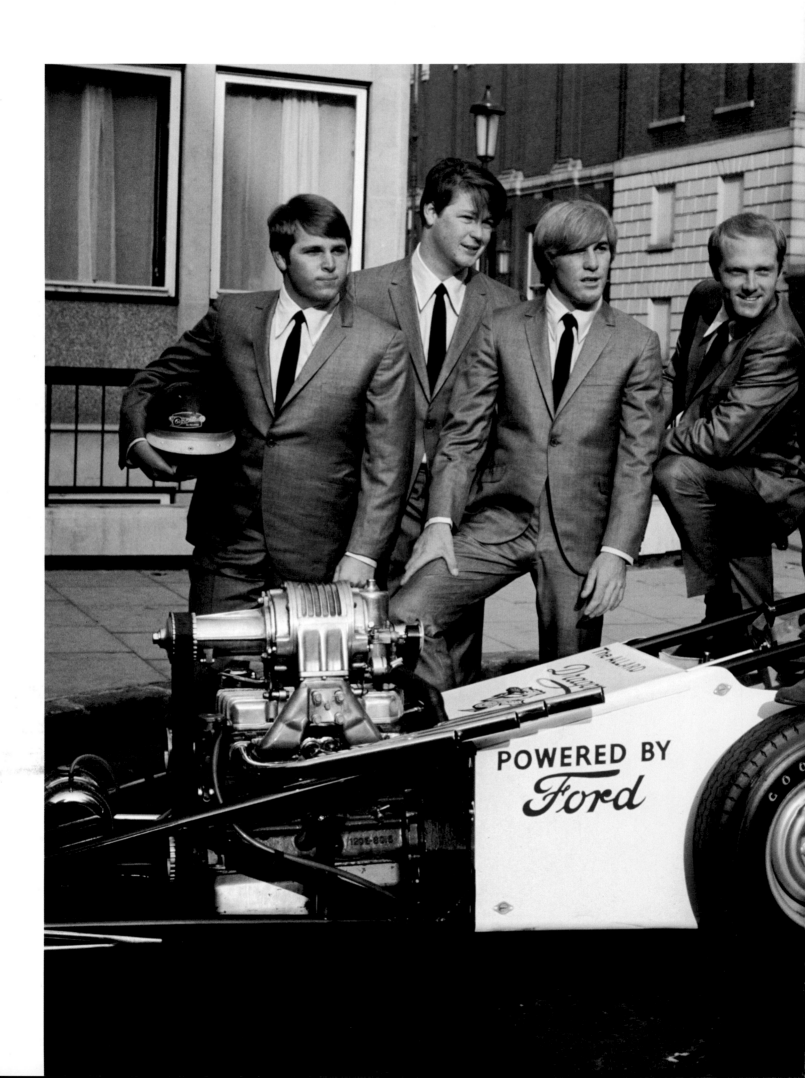

asked Audree to drive them to the old family home in Hawthorne, which was standing vacant.

"We went over to our old house and we had a three hour talk. I told her things that I hadn't told anyone in my life. She sort of straightened me out." It was clear that Brian wouldn't be playing the rest of the tour, and so Glen Campbell flew out to Texas, put on the same striped shirts that the band had been wearing on stage for two years, and became the fifth Beach Boy for the last four shows of 1964.

With his mind made up that he would no longer tour with the band as well as write and record their music (but without telling them that), Brian spent the first two weeks of 1965 recording material for the next Beach Boys album (*Today!*). Glen Campbell continued to perform with the band and also to play guitar on the recording sessions.

Some time around the middle of January, Brian told the rest of the band that he wouldn't be touring with them again. It couldn't have been an enormous surprise, but apparently they all took it badly. Brian told Earl Leaf that, "They all broke down. Mike had a couple of tears in his eyes...he lost his cool. Dennis picked up a big ashtray and told some people to get out of there or he'd hit them. Al Jardine broke out in tears and stomach cramps, and my mother, who was there, had to take care of him. Good ol' Carl was the only one who never got into a bad emotional scene." The next day recording continued and tour dates were set up as usual. It was decided that Glen Campbell would continue to fill the fifth striped shirt on stage, although Brian did appear at their first week's gigs after the announcement, beginning January 27 in Portland Oregon, because Campbell couldn't make

The Beach Boys in Manchester Square, London, 1964. Outside EMI HQ, with a drag car, presumably because the press office couldn't get a beach and surfboards.

those dates. Brian returned to the studio in February, and on the twenty-fourth he was in Western Recorders re-recording "Help Me, Rhonda" for release as a single.

Remarkably, given what had happened in April of the previous year between Brian and Murry in the recording studio, tapes of the "Rhonda" session contain the voice of Murry attempting to direct the boys as they harmonize on the chorus. Clearly under the influence of alcohol, Murry keeps repeating himself, telling them that they have to "sing from the heart" or it won't work. He makes various cutting remarks about how just because they've "sold a few records" and "made enough money" that they aren't "hungry enough for more success."

At one point Murry is heard scat singing and explaining to Al how to sing "Rhonda" "sexy," and to loosen up. He keeps telling Dennis, Carl, and Mike that they're flat while Brian is sharp. As the session drags on he veers between self-pity, whining "mother and I can leave now if you want" more than once (Audree may have driven him to the studio), and astounding arrogance, telling Brian, "I'm a genius too." Eventually Brian addresses his father directly and asks him to say what he wants and then leave. After apologizing to Audree ("Sorry dear, we'll never come to another recording session"), Murry sneers at his son, "Chuck [Britz] and I used to make hit after hit for you in thirty minutes and now you take five months over it." Brian simply states, "Times are changing...times are changing."

In May 1965, Murry wrote to Brian on Sea of Tunes headed notepaper (the publishing company that he managed and which administered all of Brian's songs) an eight-page letter in which he sets out to explain how sorry he is that things have turned out the way they have between them. "I am over the big hurt of losing my three sons as a manager for their benefit and good fortune," Murry wrote, "but I am not over the fact that I have lost my three sons' love, and I mean real love, because you are all in a distorted world of screams, cheers and

Left: Bruce Johnston, soon to be a Beach Boy.
Above: Poster for the Hollywood Bowl gig for which Brian rehearsed but didn't appear.

CALIFORNIA GIRLS

CAPITOL, JULY 1965

B-side	"Let Him Run Wild"
Writers	B. Wilson/M. Love
Producer	B. Wilson
Recorded	4/6/65, 6/4/65
U.S. Chart	#3 *Billboard*

This is where the next phase of Beach Boys music begins to show itself. In "California Girls" can be heard the sound that was to dominate Brian's musical output over the next two years. He later claimed that the inspiration for the see-sawing rhythm that sounds almost like a fairground organ on this, came to him when "I was thinking about the music from cowboy movies." He also said that taking LSD had an effect on it, too. There's no doubt that echoes of the repeating, churning organ on "California Girls" can be heard in the theme tunes of cowboy TV shows such as *Maverick* (1957–62) and *Colt 45* (1957–60), which he would have watched when a kid, but there's also something of Johnny Tillotson's "Poetry in Motion" (1961) in there, too. The lyrics are a crass sexist objectification of women, but importantly American women, who are better than all the "girls" the singer (Mike) has met around the world. It has a nationalistic fervor that would appeal to all red-blooded U.S. high school jocks, and became the regular show opener of touring Beach Boys for decades after. The ballad on the B-side has Brian telling an object of his adoration that her boyfriend's a liar but he (Brian) would be a truer lover. He'd later state that he hates his singing on the B-side for being too shrill, but the layered horns, electric piano, and voices are perfectly balanced.

financial success. The money will not mean a damn thing to any of my sons if they are not happy when the job is done and it is a sad thing for three young beautiful sons to place their life's success on the success of a record album or a 45 RPM disc or to how successful they are in the eyes of the music world from how many seats they sell in a live concert. I hope to God that you and your brothers review your thinking now before it is too late, because only more damage can arise from this temporary, fleeting image of success known as The Beach Boys."

The letter suggests that it's all Audree's fault because she undermined his authority while they were growing up. Despite his best efforts to instill moral correctness and honesty in them, Murry writes, "when I gave an order for my sons to do a job, even though my wife didn't actually say something against me, the look of resentment against authority was there."

Furthermore, he wrote, "Although Audree did not realize what she was doing, she was trying to raise you boys almost like girls." He goes on to admonish Brian for taking all the credit for producing Beach Boys records when it was actually done by Murry, and says that he is sorry that Brian believes he did it all "single-handed." He then not so subtly threatens to expose members of the band for their "lascivious, felonious and unlawful behavior," which had been kept out of the public eye.

Murry ends the letter by telling Brian to get their attorneys together with him and "dissolve yourselves as a group," while he ensures that Brian gets his dues from Capitol, and not have to pay too much income tax.

Brian leads the Boys in rehearsal at the Hollywood Bowl on July 3, 1965. He wouldn't play, though.

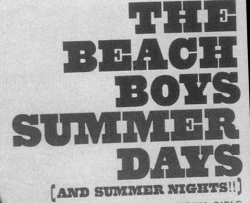

THE BEACH BOYS SUMMER DAYS

(AND SUMMER NIGHTS!!)

CALIFORNIA GIRLS
SALT LAKE CITY
THE GIRL FROM NEW YORK CITY
AMUSEMENT PARKS U.S.A.
GIRL DON'T TELL ME
THEN I KISSED HER
...and other great songs

Capitol
RECORDS

SUMMER DAYS (AND SUMMER NIGHTS!!)

CAPITOL, JULY 1965

Producer	Brian Wilson
Engineer	Chuck Britz
Recorded	2/24/65, 3/4–20/65, 6/4/65, United Western Recorders, CBS Columbia Studio, Hollywood
U.S. Chart	#2 *Billboard*
Singles	"Help Me, Rhonda," "California Girls"

Side 1

1. THE GIRL FROM NEW YORK CITY
B. Wilson/M. Love

2. AMUSEMENT PARK USA
B. Wilson/M. Love

3. THEN I KISSED HER
B. Wilson/M. Love

4. SALT LAKE CITY
B. Wilson/M. Love

5. GIRL, DON'T TELL ME
B. Wilson

6. HELP ME, RHONDA
B. Wilson/M. Love

Side 2

1. CALIFORNIA GIRLS
B. Wilson/M. Love

2. LET HIM RUN WILD
B. Wilson/M. Love

3. YOU'RE SO GOOD TO ME
B. Wilson

4. SUMMER MEANS LOVE
B. Wilson

5. I'M BUGGED AT MY OL' MAN
B. Wilson/M. Love

6. AND YOUR DREAM COMES TRUE
B. Wilson/M. Love

It wasn't as if *Today!* had failed to sell, but for the follow-up album the Boys had "summer" in the title and a cover photograph of them in the sun, albeit also all at sea. Or not quite all, because Al is missing, and as he explains in person on the sleeve notes, "The very day the pictures were taken I had to spend in bed with flu." Bruce Johnston isn't in the cover photo, either, although he does sing and play on the album; "California Girls" was the first song he recorded with them, at Columbia Studios, which had an eight-track tape recorder, and neither Gold Star nor Western then had one. Brian's sleeve notes are revealing. As he writes, his notes state, people are "sitting around a coffee table singing Beatles songs. But," he continues, "my mind is somewhere else right now." Which is a little disingenuous, when "Girl, Don't Tell Me" owes so much to Beatles guitars and melodies. What is

on Brian's mind as he wrote, performed, and produced the songs on this album are Phil Spector (the cover of "Then I Kissed Her" is almost a mirror of the Crystals' original); the then current pop chart ("Girl from New York City" is an answer to the Ad Libs' "Boy from New York City," a Top 10 hit in February 1965); amusement parks, a part of the American summer the Boys hadn't covered in song before; Marilyn Wilson ("You're So Good To Me"); unrequited love ("Let Him Run Wild"), and Murry. "I'm Bugged at My Ol' Man" runs through an almost comic catalogue of wrongs that the singer's father has done to him, with Brian sneer-whining about how he's so square and he don't know it. The song is childish and insulting, but although no longer the band's manager, Murry still sought to tell them how to succeed in the business. It's a public brush-off to Murry, and it hurt his pride.

After being fired by his sons Murry Wilson became
manager (and producer) of the Renegades and changed
their name to the Sunrays (above). Their biggest hit
was "Andrea" in 1966 (#41 on the *Billboard* singles
chart). The woman is a model, the band was all male.

Elsewhere, Murry's letter hints at a separation
between he and Audree, which proved to be prophetic:
they split before the year's end.

The letter arrived just as Brian was making *Summer
Days (And Summer Nights!!)*, and just as "Help Me,
Rhonda" made the #1 spot on the charts. A couple of
weeks later Brian wrote, played, and sang "I'm Bugged
at My Ol' Man," in which he pokes very public fun at
Murry and tells the world that his ol' man kept him pris-
oner in his room, cut his hair off as he slept, sold his surfboard, and pulled the phone from the wall when he tried

to call his girl. None of it was actually true, but the world
wouldn't have been able to handle the truth about what
Murry did do to Brian when he was a kid.

Earlier in April, Glen Campbell told the Boys that
he couldn't make the early dates on an upcoming U.S.
tour and while he'd make most of them later, it would be
his last tour with them. Mike called Bruce Johnston (b.
June 27, 1944), formerly of Bruce and Terry and the Rip
Chords, and asked if he had any ideas about a replacement. Johnston offered to stand in, and although he
can't play bass, he told Mike, "I suppose I could sing all
the high parts if you show me what to do."

At the start of the tour Al played bass and Bruce piano,
but he spent time between gigs learning the bass parts.
After Glen joined the band Johnston stayed on the tour,
not performing but learning how to become a Beach Boy.

While the Boys toured, Brian created "California
Girls" and discovered what LSD could do for him. He'd
later recall that it was "What I would call a very religious
experience. I took LSD, a full dose of LSD and later,
another time, I took a smaller dose. And I learned a lot
of things like patience, understanding." In a different
interview Brian would say, "My mind was blown."

Brian had been smoking cannabis for a while with
the guys that Murry in his letter called "phoneys": Gary
Usher, Bob Norberg, Jan Berry, and Loren Schwartz. It
may have contributed to some of his erratic behavior
and breakdowns, but it went uncommented upon at the
time. LSD was another matter. It was legal to have and
take at the time, and there were eminent pro-LSD advoc-
ates on both coasts. Timothy Leary in the East and Ken
Kesey and various Beats and San Francisco artists in the
West argued for its use as a recreational and creative aid.
Artists who wanted to see, hear, and imagine the world
in a different way were experimenting with LSD and creating art of all kinds. Brian had believed that taking it
would be beneficial to him as an artist. "I have a very
bright mind and this LSD will really expand my mind,"

he is reported as saying, "and make me write better."

The album *Beach Boys Party!* didn't sound as if it was created by a man who was on any drugs, though. It sounds like a rushed contract filler, which it kind of was. Capitol demanded another album before Christmas 1965, and Brian suggested a "live" recording of a family sing-along, a "party" where everyone joins in on songs they all know. So Brian packed the studio with spouses, cousins, and friends, and over three days in September, let the tape run as they all sang along with him. He edited it down, and the LP was on sale in early November.

BARBARA ANN

CAPITOL, DECEMBER 1965

B-side	"Girl Don't Tell Me"
Writers	F. Fassert;
	B. Wilson/M. Love
Producer	B. Wilson
Recorded	9/23/65; 4/30/65
U.S. Chart	#2 *Billboard*

Something of a step backward musically, this was the third version of the song originally written by Fred Fassert from the Bronx for his band, the Regents. They cut it in 1958, but it wasn't released until 1961, when it became a national hit (making #13 on the chart). In 1962, Jan and Dean recorded a pretty straight imitation of the original for their *Golden Hits* album. It was Dean Torance who suggested the Boys record the song, when he dropped into a recording session for their *Party!* album. "They were all drunk," he later recalled, "and scratching around for another track." He suggested this and led it off—he can be heard alongside Brian's falsetto. The loosely sung backing vocals, handclaps, laughter, and acoustic guitar are supposed to replicate a house party atmosphere. The B-side features a lead vocal by Carl on a very Beatle-ish "Girl Don't Tell Me." A strummed acoustic supplies the rhythm as a glockenspiel plays a single note repeating pattern alongside it. A middle-eight chorus of "girl don't tell me you ride" complete with sparkling 12-string Rickenbacker clearly shows the influence of the Beatles' "Ticket to Ride," which had hit the charts a couple of weeks before this was recorded on April 30, 1965. The contrast between the A and B-sides is marked, and marks a change in direction that the Boys would briefly take.

In October Brian and Marilyn moved into a new house in Beverly Hills, and he set about decorating it. "He wanted a sandbox," Marilyn later explained. "So we got a sandbox. He said, 'I want to play in the sand. I want to feel like a little kid. When I'm writing songs I want to feel what I'm writing.'" A grand piano stood in the middle of the sandbox. Brian later had a huge purple tent draped over the living area in which he'd meditate, hold meetings with his bandmates, and listen to music. The sense of space must have been wonderful to a man brought up sharing a bedroom with two brothers.

Later in October, Brian called a full orchestra into United Recorders Studio A, under the guidance of journeyman arranger Dick Reynolds, and they recorded two American songbook classics, "Stella by Starlight" and "How Deep Is the Ocean," plus, "Three Blind Mice." Exactly why he did it is unclear (they've never been released, and Brian's not present musically on the recording), but perhaps he wanted to see what it'd take to conduct and record such a huge bunch of musicians.

In November, Brian booked horn players and the Wrecking Crew and laid down an instrumental track that was originally titled "Run James Run" (a few months later it was retitled "Pet Sounds"). It was intended to accompany the opening credits of a James Bond movie, claimed Brian, and 50 years later an enterprising fan dubbed it over the opening credits to *You Only Live Twice* on YouTube. It works surprisingly well, although Nancy Sinatra's interpretation of John Barry and Leslie Bricusse's title song is pretty good, even if it wasn't a hit.

Perhaps the orchestra session with Dick Reynolds was an attempt by Brian to gauge how he might work with a full orchestra, possibly even with an eye to composing cinematic scores in the future. The movies seemed to be on his mind around that time, and the immersive sense of the cinema, enhanced by watching while under the effects of LSD, can only have influenced his work.

Murry's constant carping about working hard to

Fooling around for the camera, Brian eating his words while seated at the dining table in his recently bought Beverly Hills home.

find the "new" thing may have contributed to Brian's apparent all-consuming sense of musical competition—and lack of self-worth. While his father was always praising Brian's ability to make music, particularly harmonies and melodies, he'd never congratulate his eldest son on a lyric. "I've always been insecure about my lyrics," Brian stated in the 1980s. "I always felt that what I wanted to say was never imparted in my lyrics... that the message just wasn't there." Which is why he seemed constantly on the look-out for new writing partners, especially while Mike was away on tour.

Naturally, Brian's constant search for similarly minded musical partners would inevitably lead him to consider what other musicians and bands were doing. Earlier in 1965 he revealed his driving compulsion to compete with other acts. "When I hear really fabulous material by other groups I feel as small as the dot over the *I* in nit. Then I just have to create a new song to bring me up on top. That's probably my most compelling motive for writing new songs—the urge to overcome an inferiority feeling."

He goes on to explain that he isn't solely driven by commercial forces, though: "I've never written one note or word of music simply because I think it will make money." Rather, he states, "My ideas for the group are to combine music that strikes a deep emotional response among listeners and still maintains a somewhat untrained and teenage sound." He was doing that, he explained, by "Using harmonics more than before and fusing it with a 1964 to 1965 approach to production."

That approach to production was to be found at its peak in Phil Spector's preferred Gold Star recording studio, and using the Wrecking Crew studio session players. But Brian was intending to take all that Spector knew and build upon it to create his own "sound."

The Beach Boys at Brian's home, L-R
behind sofa; Bruce Johnston, Al Jardine,
Brian Wilson, Mike Love. On sofa;
Carl Wilson, unknown, Dennis Wilson.
On floor; Brian's Beagle, Banana.

At the end of 1965 the Beatles released a new album titled *Rubber Soul*. It didn't look like other pop albums at the time, with its cover image taken from an odd angle and stretched, almost disfiguring the band—whose name was missing from the front. The title's cartoonish, soon-to-be-clichéd psychedelic font was an invention of illustrator Charles Front. There was no escaping the fact that, if you knew about such things, the cover screamed, "Cannabis! LSD!"

Brian would later remember that he was smoking when he first heard the record, in December 1965. "I was sitting around a table with some friends when we heard the disc for the first time. I smoked a joint and then I listened to it. It blew my mind because it was a whole album with all good stuff. It was definitely a challenge for me. I saw that every cut was artistically interesting and stimulating." It wasn't only that the songs dealt with things other than just girls, love, and relationships—there were taxes, drug-dealing doctors, and submarines, too— but it was also the range of instruments being used.

"I realized that the recording industry was getting so free and intelligent," Brian recalled. "We could go into new things—string quartets, auto-harps, and instruments from another culture. I decided right then: I'm gonna try that, where a whole album becomes a gas, I'm gonna make the greatest rock 'n' roll album ever made!" The sense of competition was strong enough to overcome reservations about his ability, and he set about working up new material while searching for a lyric writer.

However, as Brian was contemplating his new direction, Capitol Records took the decision to edit the recording of "Barbara Ann" from the *Party!* album down to two minutes and release it as a single into the Christmas market. Although it was a hit, making the #2 position behind the Beatles' "We Can Work It Out," the sound was old-fashioned and the production deliberately low-fi, not at all how Brian wanted his band to be heard in the immediate wake of the Beatles' new album.

Opposite: How the vocals were always done: all around one microphone in Western Recorders Studio. L-R: Dennis, Al, Brian, Carl.

Apparently a DJ on an East Coast radio station had taken a liking to the Boys' version of the old Jan and Dean (via the Regents) hit, and played it enough that other stations picked up on it, too. Most bands would have been delighted with a naturally occurring radio hit forcing their record company to release a track as a single, and then for it to do so well. Brian wasn't happy though. "That's not the Beach Boys!" he insisted in an interview at the time. "It's not where we're at, at all. Personally, I think the group has evolved 800 percent in the past year. We have more conscious, arty production now that's more polished."

Not that anyone had yet heard any of the arty, polished production. In what may have been a deliberate ploy to show Capitol what could be done with old songs, Brian went to work on recording a new version of "Sloop John B" before Christmas. Using backing tracks recorded in July, he assembled his brothers and cousin at Western Recorders and produced layered and over-dubbed vocals.

For his final session of the year Brian called in Wrecking Crew guitarist Billy Strange to play 12-string guitar on "Sloop John B." The 35-year-old guitarist was also a song arranger, and in fact had played on and arranged Nancy Sinatra's single-release version of "You Only Live Twice" earlier that year. As well as working with Nancy Sinatra (and Lee Hazelwood) over the coming years, Strange would work with Brian on *Pet Sounds* and write songs (with Mac Davis) for that other non-surfing superstar of the beach, Elvis Presley.

Brian was working with the very best in his studios, as befitted his skills as a producer.

A poster for a show that never happened—
a piece of fake memorabilia.

BEACH BOYS' PARTY!

CAPITOL, NOVEMBER 1965

Producer	Brian Wilson
Engineer	Chuck Britz
Recorded	9/8–27/65, United Western Recorders, Hollywood
U.S. Chart	#6 *Billboard*
Singles	"Barbara Ann"

Side 1

1. HULLY GULLY
F. Smith/C. Goldsmith

2. I SHOULD HAVE KNOWN BETTER
J. Lennon/P. McCartney

3. TELL ME WHY
J. Lennon/P. McCartney

4. PAPA-OOM-MOW-MOW
C. White/A. Frazier/S. Harris/T. Wilson Jr.

5. MOUNTAIN OF LOVE
H. Dorman

6. YOU'VE GOT TO HIDE YOUR LOVE AWAY
J. Lennon/P. McCartney

7. DEVOTED TO YOU
B. Bryant

Side 2

1. ALLEY OOP
D. Frazier

2. THERE'S NO OTHER (LIKE MY BABY)
P. Spector/L. Bates

3. MEDLEY: I GET AROUND, LITTLE DEUCE COUPE
B. Wilson/M. Love/R. Christian

4. THE TIMES THEY ARE A-CHANGIN'
B. Dylan

5. BARBARA ANN
F. Fassert

The Beach Boys had scored their first #1 album at Christmas of 1964. Not with their Christmas album (that made #6), but with *Beach Boys Concert*, a live recording made in December 1963 and polished in the studio by Brian in August 1964. A year later and just four months after the release of *Summer Days* came this. Ostensibly a "live" album, it was recorded in a studio and not on stage in front of an audience. The conceit was to produce a family sing-a-long just like the ones that used to make Wilson and Love family gatherings so much fun back in the '50s. Wives and friends were invited along. It was suggested that they record at Brian's home, but he was spending more time in the studio than in Beverly Hills, and arguably Western Recorders was his home at the time. The songs have only acoustic guitar and bongo accompaniment, with lots of shrieks, laughs, and yells overdubbed later. Everyone goofs around, most notably on the only Beach Boys originals, a medley of "I Get Around" and "Little Deuce Coupe" in which lyrics are changed and the songs generally mocked. It's a forcible statement that the car songs are behind them. As if to make the point even more forcefully, they're followed on the disc by Al's rendition of "The Times They Are a-Changin'," for which the credit reads "(Al—man with a message)." Nothing was ever done quickly by Brian at this time, but the whole of *Party!* took five days to record, dub, and mix. Among songs recorded but not included were "Ticket to Ride," "(I Can't Get No) Satisfaction," and "Blowin' in the Wind."

4

PET SOUNDS & GOOD VIBES

1966

**S**peaking decades after the events of early 1966, Mike Love said, "there was a natural progression with Brian." He was explaining why the process of making a record was "different" back then. "Recording techniques evolved which allowed us to stretch out even more in terms of sound textures. Brian took advantage of that and pioneered his way through. He blended symphonic arrangements with rock music on *Pet Sounds*."

Ten years after the album was released, Brian was completely open about what recording technique he was using when he told an interviewer, "I felt that the production was a masterpiece. *Pet Sounds* was an offshoot of the Phil Spector production technique. I'm proud of it for that reason, in that we were able to produce tracks that had a monumental sound to them. It had that Wall of Sound touch to it. My contribution was adding the harmonies, learning to incorporate harmonies and certain vocal techniques to that Spector production concept that I learned." Mike wasn't present for the majority of the recording sessions, generally only appearing along with Brian's brothers and Al to lay down the vocal tracks, but he—along with the rest of the world who heard the album—was aware that it was different from the Beach Boys' long players that had come before. For one thing it didn't have many "natural" singles on it, and that mattered to Mike (and the rest of the band).

As 1965 wound down Brian was painfully aware that it had belonged, once again, to the Beatles. They had held the #1 slot on the album chart for a total of 24 weeks, with three different releases (*Beatles 65,*

Previous page: Bruce Johnston, bottom left, standing in for Brian.
Left: Brian in the control booth at Western Recorders Studio, 1966.

Beatles VI, Help!), while his three albums of the year had made #4, #2, and #6. Although, actually the only other album by a rock and roll band to have topped the charts that year had been for three weeks and by another British band: the Rolling Stones' *Out of Our Heads*. The rest of 1965 had seen the *Mary Poppins* soundtrack top the chart for 14 weeks, the *Sound of Music* soundtrack

top it for two weeks, the *Goldfinger* soundtrack for three, and an Elvis Presley soundtrack (*Roustabout*) for the first week of the year. It must have stung a little when Herb Alpert and the Tijuana Brass's *Whipped Cream and Other Delights* closed out the year for the final five

Right: Mike Love and Brian, 1966.

SLOOP JOHN B.

CAPITOL, MARCH 1966

B-side	"You're So Good to Me"
Writers	Trad. arr.; B. Wilson; B. Wilson/M. Love
Producer	B. Wilson
Recorded	7/12/65, 12/29/65
U.S. Chart	#3 *Billboard*

The Boys' first single of 1966 was largey Al's idea. He really liked the Kingston Trio's "Wreck of the John B" (a hit for the Trio in 1958). He'd persuaded Brian that it would work done in the Beach Boys style in 1965, as he explained in the *Pet Sounds Sessions* booklet. He played the song as the Trio had done it, but essentially put in some minor chord changes to add the blues element of sadness that appealed to Brian. As Al tells the story, he played it for a while and then left it. The next day in the studio Brian had arranged it for five voices and it was ready to be recorded. The musical backing was finished in July and the vocals at the end

of December 1965. With Capitol demanding a single release and "Sloop" being the closest thing to a classic Beach Boys–sounding track that was finished, it was a natural choice. The choice of a track from *Summer Days (And Summer Nights!!)* for the B-side gave the listening public no real idea of what new direction Brian was attempting for the upcoming album. "Sloop's" inclusion on *Pet Sounds* somewhat contradicts the (much later) interpretation of the long player as a "concept" album, that concept being one boy's search for everlasting love. Not all of the songs on the new record would be about one man/boy and love trouble, just the majority.

weeks—it was exactly the kind of thing that Murry loved.

However, when in December Brian had heard *Rubber Soul* by the Beatles (see p. 94), it changed the way he approached the making of an album. For the first time,

he said, he thought of the long player as being a whole object that could be constructed using songs that worked together, instead of an album being a collection of tracks that were A-side single releases, their B-side accompanying tracks and assorted other "filler" tracks there to make each side last for more than 15 minutes (if even that). However, while many fans and critics of *Pet Sounds* are convinced that it's in some way a "concept album," perhaps thinking so because of the uniformity

The summit: Brian, left, looking nervous as Phil Spector (front) passes by. Mike Love (2nd from right) checks Phil's shoes, while Righteous Brother Bobby Hatfield (right) check's Brian's hat.

of the production, it wasn't meant to be a "concept" in narrative terms, but more in the way that it sounded. As Brian would later say, "*Pet Sounds* wasn't really conceived as a concept album. It was really a production concept album. It wasn't really a song concept album or lyrically a concept album." Brian thought in terms of harmonies, melodies, and musical arrangements, he always left the writing of words to other people, who could write what he was feeling. He was, as previously stated, looking for someone to do that with his post–*Rubber Soul* work.

During the making of *Pet Sounds,* Brian said he was "obsessed with explaining, musically, how I felt inside." He needed someone who could put his obsession into words. He turned to an advertising copywriter named Tony Asher. The two met at Western Recorders one morning at the water cooler, according to an interview Asher gave to rockcellarmagazine.com's Ken Sharp in 2013. Asher was often there overseeing jingle recordings for which he'd written the tunes and lyrics. With the studio being full of rock acts in the evening and overnight, the daylight sessions were taken up by commercial makers and movie-business work, but not all of the studios were booked during the day. Brian, said Asher, would arrive in the mornings without a booking,

but knowing he'd be able to record and work on some ideas he'd just had in a vacant room somewhere.

Brian had decided that he wanted to write songs with someone different on his new album as much because he thought that he'd finished with surfing and hot-rod songs (so Gary Usher and Roger Christian were out), as because there was no one in his immediate circle around at the time to work with. So to begin with, Asher and Brian worked out roughs at Brian's house, and then went to the studio, where various members of the Wrecking Crew would gather and Brian could make acetates of new stuff to take home and play.

The Beach Boys had flown to Japan on January 4 for what would be a 15-gig tour lasting until January 24. Carl and Dennis kept in touch with their big brother via telephone calls, during which Brian would sometimes play them the acetate recordings of what he, Asher, and the Wrecking Crew had been doing.

While his band was out there, Brian sent an acetate to Japan for them to listen to. Possibly because he wanted them to think that he was doing the usual Beach Boys thing, the acetate contained his version of the old sea shanty that they'd sung together as kids, "Sloop John B.," and for which they'd laid down backing tracks the previous year. Asher had heard it at the beginning of

"I felt that the production was a masterpiece. Pet Sounds had that 'wall of sound' touch to it."

BRIAN *Wilson*

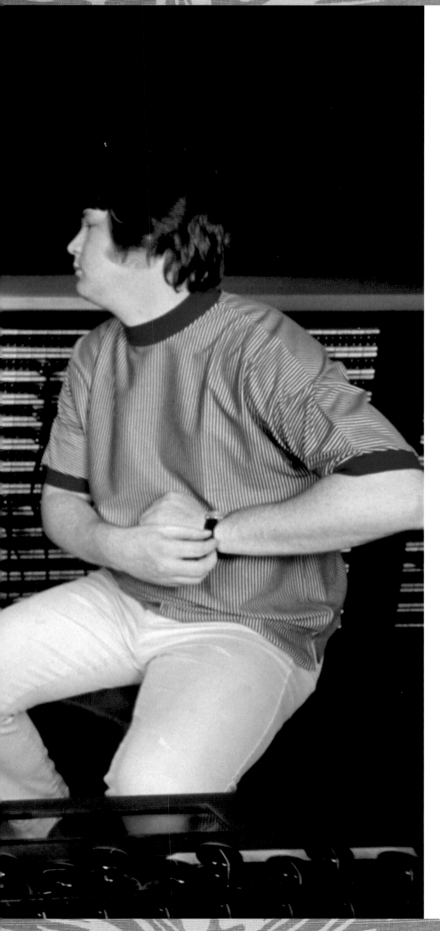

L-R: Bruce Johnston, Terry Melcher, Tony Asher, Brian Wilson
in Western Recorders, working on songs for *Pet Sounds*.

their working relationship, before they'd put anything together for the other *Pet Sounds* songs, and it sounded like the Beach Boys to him—in the sense that there were layered harmonies that carried the song. It wasn't "typical" Beach Boys though, because it was a West Indian folk song, and while the vocal harmonies are perfectly suited to the Beach Boys, the subject matter wasn't typical of them. "Sloop" stands out on the *Pet Sounds* album because the lyrics tell a story, in the way that traditional folk stories often do, which is not about teenage alienation or a search for true love, as the rest of the album's lyric songs are.

"Sloop" is told in the first-person singular, though, a narrative perspective that Brian's songs had increasingly been using over the past months. Once Beach Boys songs had told stories about "us," and invited the world to join them. Now they were mostly about an "I" and usually sung to a girl whom he loved. "I Just Wasn't Made for These Times" isn't a love song though, but is melancholic and solipsistic, while "I Know There's an Answer" is full of teenage, vaguely druggy, angst and anger.

The subject matter of the songs wasn't the only thing that Brian was changing at the time, according to Keith Badman, in *The Beach Boys Definitive Diary* (Backbeat, 2004). Usually Brian sat with each session player at sessions and either played their part to them or hummed it, as they picked up his drift. On January 18, though, he handed out written chord patterns and melody lines to everyone for the first time ever, and they worked up the backing for "Let's Go Away for a While." It sounds like a Burt Bacharach orchestration, particularly "I Just Don't Know What to Do with Myself" (Dusty Springfield, 1964), with slurred horn lines and strings, and an introductory few bars that foreshadow what follows without showing it in full. It could almost be a movie prelude piece.

PET SOUNDS

CAPITOL, MAY 1966

Producer	Brian Wilson
Engineer	Chuck Britz, Bruce Botnick, H. Bowen David, Larry Levine
Recorded	7/12/65–4/13/66, United Western Recorders, Gold Star, CBS Columbia, Sunset Sound Recorders, Hollywood, Los Angeles, CA
U.S. Chart	#10 *Billboard*
Singles	"Sloop John B.," "God Only Knows," "Wouldn't It Be Nice"

Side 1

1. WOULDN'T IT BE NICE
B. Wilson/T. Asher/M. Love

2. YOU STILL BELIEVE IN ME
B. Wilson/T. Asher

3. THAT'S NOT ME
B. Wilson/T. Asher

4. DON'T TALK (PUT YOUR HEAD ON MY SHOULDER)
B. Wilson/T. Asher

5. I'M WAITING FOR THE DAY
B. Wilson/M. Love

6. LET'S GO AWAY FOR A WHILE
B. Wilson

7. SLOOP JOHN B.
Trad. arr.; B. Wilson

Side 2

1. GOD ONLY KNOWS
B. Wilson/T. Asher

2. I KNOW THERE'S AN ANSWER
B. Wilson/T. Sachen/M. Love

3. HERE TODAY
B. Wilson/T. Asher

4. I JUST WASN'T MADE FOR THESE TIMES
B. Wilson/T. Asher

5. PET SOUNDS
B. Wilson

6. CAROLINE, NO
B. Wilson/T. Asher

Perhaps more than any other pop long-playing record, *Pet Sounds* has been reevaluated by music critics time and again since its original release, and almost invariably everyone comes to the same conclusion: "genius." The process of reevaluation was hinted at in interviews with the band in the late 1960s and early '70s, but in 1976 the reappraisal of the album's worth began in earnest with *New Musical Express*. The noted music paper's Christmas edition took several pages to look at the "Best Albums of the Year 1966." The cover was dominated by Dylan's *Blonde on Blonde*, but it also showed the Stones' *Aftermath*, the Beatles' *Revolver*, this, and *Otis Blue/Otis Redding Sings Soul*. Inside, almost half a page is given to a new review in which Bob Edmonds begins pertinently by stating that "The illness and subsequent recovery of Brian Wilson have added a painful poignancy to his old

songs, making it impossible to hear them again in their original context, unblemished by the taint of tragedy." Subsequent reappraisals have not mentioned the tragedy but are undoubtedly affected by it. How could they not feel for the tortured artist? David Leaf wrote in 1988 that "its bone-honest musical expression of an artist's soul, combined with the revelational sense of the lyrics (by Tony Asher et al.), give *Pet Sounds* its profound and timeless nature" (*Musician*). And that's been the dominant opinion of it ever since. In 1966, Norman Jopling wrote in *Record Mirror*, "It will probably make their present fans like them even more, but it's doubtful whether it will make them any new ones." Jopling, of course, didn't have knowledge of Brian's tragedy to draw upon, but he was correct back then: sales were low. Twenty years later though, the album attained platinum sales status.

WOULDN'T IT BE NICE

CAPITOL, JULY 1966

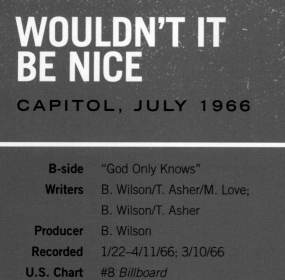

B-side	"God Only Knows"
Writers	B. Wilson/T. Asher/M. Love;
	B. Wilson/T. Asher
Producer	B. Wilson
Recorded	1/22–4/11/66; 3/10/66
U.S. Chart	#8 *Billboard*

The first track on the new album and the first truly new recording from it, "Wouldn't It Be Nice" was another Spector-like teenage symphony. The naïve lyrics are given a heartfelt honesty by Brian's voice and obvious sincerity in performance. The Beach Boys never did metaphor, allegory, or irony, and "Wouldn't It Be Nice" was no different in its intention than earlier Beach Boys recordings. What made it unusual, though, was the density and apparent sophistication of the orchestration and recording production. What was being said in words was mundane, average, and derivative, but the setting in which they are sung made them almost unique. Mixed down to mono, as all Brian's productions were, the density of sounds on "Wouldn't It Be Nice" are increased, with the result that it's imposible to tell at first what instruments are being played, unlike on the records by the Beatles, the Monkees, the Byrds, and other white, male, guitar-led bands. The B-side, which Brian worried about because of the inclusion of the word "God" in the title, is a simple and hugely effective love song. With the briefest of lyrics, the repeated title refrain leaves no doubt about the secular nature of the meaning in the song.

"Let's Go Away for a While" is an instrumental number. It was, Brian later revealed, supposed to have a vocal line, but, "I decided to leave it alone. It stands up well alone." He also called it "The most satisfying piece of music I have ever made," and notably, like the album's title track (which had formerly been a Bond-style theme tune titled "Run Johnny Run"), it wasn't a collaboration. The two instrumental numbers represent the ideal expression of what Brian was feeling.

Meanwhile, in the Far East the Beach Boys were playing pretty much the same set that made up the *Beach Boys Concert* album (including the hokey "Monster Mash"). It was as if the band playing gigs were the old version of the Beach Boys, sent out to satisfy the demands of fans who'd bought into that representation of Brian's music, while back in L.A. Brian and Tony Asher had plenty of time to work on songs together without interruption or direction from the others and were creating the new, post–surf and hot-rod Beach Boys.

Asher took paid leave from his advertising work at Carson-Roberts, where he had been employed making up jingles for Mattel toys, and spent mornings at Brian's

BEACH BOYS

BRIAN WILSON: WHY I STAY AT HOME!

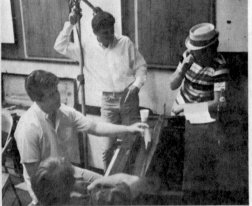

With the "Phantom" standing by, Brian runs through a song.

Brian listening to a playback of a new B-Boys record with Dennis and Al.

Six months ago Brian Wilson stopped traveling with The Beach Boys. I asked him how it was and why.

"It's worked very well and it's changed my life completely," he said. "It's a wonderful development and I, believe everyone accepts it in the right way for the right reasons. I really gave up touring to improve the musical content of the group's sound and, therefore, it was in the best interest of the group. The fan attitude has become very much healthier now. They accept traveling and my absence from tours and other realities in a very straight-forward way.

"Six months ago I bought a new house up in Beverly Hills—a beautiful place, huge with a great view. I was ready and I decided to leave the road and stay at home to get down to all the things I hadn't been able to do.

"I arranged the house so I had a big room full of music and atmosphere and I started to plan the new direction of the group. We'd been successful up to then but I wanted to move ahead in sounds and melodies and moods and for months I plotted and planned.

"For a month or two I sat either at a huge Spanish table looking out over the hills, just thinking, or at the piano playing 'feels.'"

"Feels" he explained were "musical ideas, riffs, bridges, fragments of themes. A phrase here and there." The tiny seeds which, deftly and accurately, will burst into bright, brilliant cultivated rooted plants. And after the thinking and the feels, came a further two months of nursing until more than a dozen songs were in full bloom.

One song he played me. It was obviously a very special one. It had the tight, bright clarity of the Beach Boys, the soaring harmonies, but it had something extra. It had several moods.

"I wanted to write a song containing more than one level. Eventually I would like to see longer singles—much longer than at present. I believe the public is ready for them—not just for the sake of writing longer songs but so that the song can be more meaningful. There isn't nearly enough time in two minutes to do a complete job. A song can, for instance, have movements, in the same way as a classical concerto only capsuled."

Brian Wilson is clearly excited about the new plateau. And so are the other Beach Boys. Though he admits they don't always see alike. "We're often into different things," he said. "In a way, we're disorganized. Our publicity arrangements haven't been properly coordinated and therefore our exposure hasn't been what it might be. Though because of this we've been able to preserve something of ourselves. And we're getting round to publicity now."

When the present album is completed, the Beach Boys are off on tour again. Brian's place will be taken, as usual, by Bruce Johnston, handsome 22-year-old who also sings with Terry Melcher as Bruce and Terry.

And Brian will stay at home overlooking Beverly Hills, in a house soon to be fitted with a complete recording studio.

42

BLOW-OUT!

BRUCE JOHNSTON: I'm The "Phantom!"

The Beach Boys without Brian: Mike, Carl, Bruce, and Al. Dennis was not feeling well when this was taken just before a recent concert.

At least Bruce is reading the RIGHT pop publication!

Bruce Johnston doesn't have to work at all . . . but he works harder than most pop people.

He's half of Bruce and Terry (the Terry being Doris Day's son, Terry Melcher), a bright new singing team.

He's all of Bruce Johnston, a bright new singer about to record a song produced by Terry and written by boss Beach Boy Brian Wilson.

And he's the "phantom" part of The Beach Boys, traveling with them in place of Brian, who, as you discovered on the page facing this one, has stopped touring.

If that sounds breathlessly confusing, imagine how busy Bruce feels!

The reason Bruce wouldn't have to work if he didn't want to is that his Dad is the vice-president of Rexall Drugs, one of the country's largest drug chains. The reason Bruce wants to work is because he has decided to make a solid contribution to pop music.

A short, athletic, 22-year-old with dark hair and blue eyes, Bruce still recalls the day he joined The Beach Boys. "It was last spring," he says, "and I had just driven across country from New York to Los Angeles when Mike called to ask me to fill in for Brian, who wasn't feeling well. I hadn't planned to join a group . . . but it's been a year now. A great year."

He's used to his role as the surprise Beach Boy, unexpectedly performing for fans who might have expected Brian. But, once the reason Brian stays home is explained, Bruce is as warmly accepted as any one of the "real" Beach Boys.

He also is looking forward to being accepted on his own. And Bruce promises that you'll be hearing from him alone . . . soon!

For Their ACTION ADDRESS Flip To Page 62!

Flip teen magazine interviews Brian Wilson and Bruce Johnston, 1966.

house waiting for him to awaken. Although called to be there at 10 a.m., and with a working man's habit of appearing at his "office" on time, Asher would inevitably find Brian still in bed when he arrived, and so the lyricist would wait, drink coffee, and chat with whoever was around (usually Marilyn).

After Brian had risen and eaten and was ready to get in the sandbox, he'd play snatches of piano, hum a melody, and start talking. The conversations they had were to form the basis of Asher's lyrics for the new album. Usually, Asher would later recount, the topics of conversation were girls (never women), relationships, and breaking up (to make up). Asher would recount the experiences he'd had during his adolescence (he was 26 in 1965). That was when he'd felt similarly to how, it seemed, Brian was feeling now (at the age of 23).

Asher has always been very open about the fact that while he might have put the words on paper for the songs on *Pet Sounds*, all he'd done was "interpret" Brian's ideas for him. Once written out, Brian would edit to fit as he sang them along to his melody.

The first number that they worked on, as Asher explained in his 2013 interview with Ken Sharp, would become known as "You Believe in Me." "He already had

impersonal, and full of signs and wonder. Its author, Gene Clark, claimed that the song was about a trip to London, but whatever the source of inspiration, it's most certainly not a teenage love affair.

At the same time, the Beatles' "Nowhere Man" was almost Kafkaesque with its depersonalized third-person narrative. The nation's #1 single in January 1966, Simon and Garfunkel's "Sound of Silence" was a hymn to alienation, and it swapped places at #1 with the Beatles' "We Can Work It Out," Lennon and McCartney's pragmatic reconciliation treatise that dared to tell the world that "life is very short" in a three-minute pop song. It was all very far from surf, sun, hot rods, girlfriends, and crushes.

The one number on *Pet Sounds* that deviates from the path of adolescent love in its lyrics, "I Know There's an Answer," was originally written by Brian with Beach Boys road manager Terry Sachen after an acid trip. When first recorded, it was called "Hang on to Your Ego," but that line was substituted by Mike with the title lyric. The song uses the word "trip" and is sung from

Brian would often take walks in the mddle of the night in Hollywood, usually with friends and hangers on. Sometimes drugs had been taken...why else walk over the top of a car?

a removed first-person perspective, addressed to people who don't live in their heads (a "head" was then a slang term for recreational drug users) to find an "answer"— to the meaning of life, perhaps? This was written well before Mike would become immersed in Transcendental Meditation, but it suggests a spiritual, searching side to the Beach Boys that hadn't been heard before.

Compared to that track, "Wouldn't It Be Nice," with its echoes of "Puppy Love" and "Not Too Young to Get Married," is a child's nursery rhyme. By the way, listen to the 1965 recording by Manfred Mann of Burt Bacharach's "My Little Red Book" in comparison with "Wouldn't It Be Nice" and there is a clear relation between them musically—almost as much as there is with "Be My Baby" by the Ronettes (1963). Compare also though, the way that an adult lyricist, Hal David,

"We were a surfing group when we left the country...."

AL *Jardine*

treats the subject of a broken relationship (or marriage) in his and Bacharach's "A House Is Not a Home" (Dionne Warwick, 1964) with "That's Not Me." Both are ostensibly about the same subject, but Asher's lyrics mention parents (or rather, "my folks"), a pad, and splitting for the city. David's read like a passage from a John Updike novel and manages to conjure a sense of abject loneliness out of an empty chair. Brian's affecting voice and soaring music make his songs unique, but the innocence of the lyrics combined with their idiosyncratic setting have made them almost impossible for other artists to cover.

"A House Is Not a Home" has drawn fantastic performances from an array of artists from Dionne Warwick and Dusty Springfield, to Barbara Streisand, Aretha Franklin, and Luther Vandross. Of all the tracks on *Pet Sounds*, only "God Only Knows" has been covered by a range of different artists, beginning with Andy Williams in 1967 (a very odd version with discordant piano and vast depths of reverb) through to Taylor Swift in 2011, taking in Olivia Newton John (1974), Neil Diamond (1977), David Bowie (1984), Elvis Costello (1993), Mandy Moore with Michael Stipe (2004), and the BBC Music (all-star version, 2014). Perhaps that's because, as Brian said of "God Only Knows," "You can hear the melody and the chords. It's not a great Beach Boys record. But it's still a great song." The simple sentiment is universally understood and the chorus an easily understood statement of undying love.

And as much as Brian may have later rambled on about "God" in a spiritual and nonsecular sense, it has no religious meaning at all. Rather, as he also said, "it just goes to show feelings." Not that he didn't worry about the use of the word "God" in the title; pop songs hadn't done that before, in any context. Brian worried that radio wouldn't play it, and Marilyn worried too: "I thought it was almost too religious," she'd later say. "Too square. At that time." In March 1966, John Lennon would state that, "we're more popular than Jesus right now" in a UK newspaper interview, riling some Christians in America into building bonfires with Beatles records. Brian's ditty didn't come close to starting any bonfires, but that matter of being seen as too square would continue to niggle away at him for a time to come.

There's no doubt that Brian wanted desperately to be considered as "hip," but as Terry Melcher (who was called into the studio by Brian to sing on *Pet Sounds*) would tell *Rolling Stone* in 1971, Brian "isn't fashionable. He's definitely not fashionable in any sense of the word as it might apply to anything." Perhaps Jules Siegal, writing in the debut issue of *Cheetah* magazine in 1967, explained it best and most simply: "Brian Wilson and the Beach Boys were still too square. It would take more than "Good Vibrations" and *Pet Sounds* to erase three and a half years of "Little Deuce Coupe"—a lot more if you counted in those...custom tailored, kandy striped sport shirts they insisted on wearing on stage."

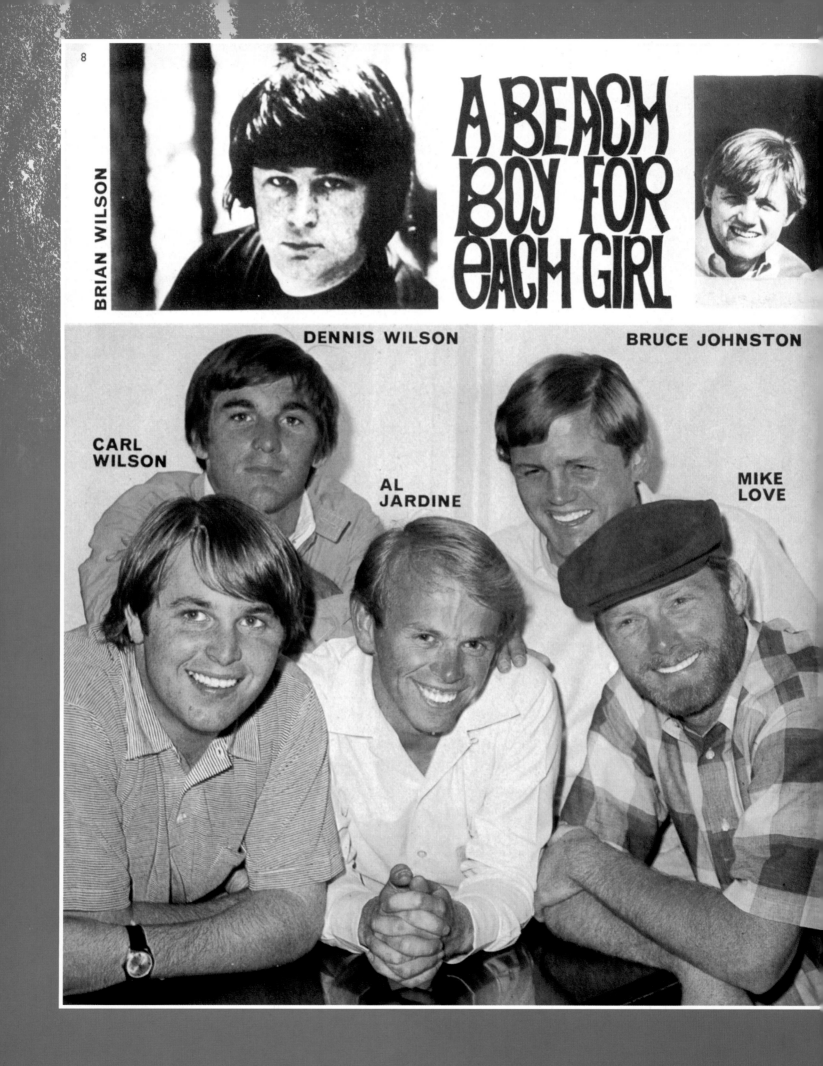

8

BRIAN WILSON

A BEACH BOY FOR EACH GIRL

DENNIS WILSON

BRUCE JOHNSTON

CARL WILSON

AL JARDINE

MIKE LOVE

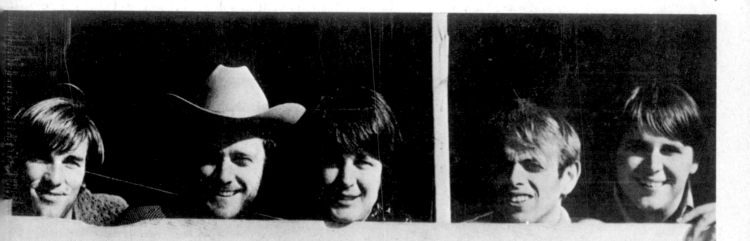

No matter which Beachboy is *your* favourite, you'll love this exclusive story on Brian Wilson by RAVE's Stateside raver Jackie Harlow...

■ Brian Wilson, founder of the Beach Boys, and the one whose talent has contributed most towards their terrific success these past five years, sat meditating in his New York hotel room.

He doesn't come to New York often, since most of his activity is now directed away from the group appearance-wise, so when he does, it could be said that the bells ring out in welcome. In fact, it's several months now since Brian was able to take an active interest in the Beach Boys' travels. But while he knows he's missing out on some of the kicks, he's happier in the knowledge that while Carl and Dennis Wilson, Al Jardine, Mike Love and Bruce Johnston are barnstorming their way across the world, he's home in Hollywood working on their next single, album or whatever's to be after that.

And there lies the key to their success, because in five years they've sold something like twenty million discs, and are the biggest home grown box office draw in the country, not to mention the highest-selling American name on Capitol Records. Besides having all this to their credit, the Beach Boys are nice, regular guys who never get into trouble and don't have any musical hang ups.

Guaranteed Sellout

A lot of American acts blow dates. The Beach Boys don't, and not only do they always show up on time, and are a pre-guaranteed sellout, but they're terribly well organised with a kind of round the clock mechanism.

For instance, when they come to New York for a date, they have a string of appointments, interviews, photo sessions and, very occasionally, some kind of press reception.

However they spend their days (nights are reserved for concerts), they're always very busy, and a five minute lapse can blow a whole schedule. So no matter how tired, and how late they've been out the night before, when the Beach Boys leave instructions for an early morning wake up, they get up and make no bones about it. They leave all arrangements in the hands of Roy Hatfield, their travelling publicist friend, and road manager Dick Duryea, son of movie actor, Dan Duryea, who take care of everything most admirably.

When here, there is always a limousine service on hand twenty-four hours a day, and since they are up for about twenty hours of it, it comes in pretty handy!

Own Interests

When a concert is finished and the Beach Boys are back in the city, the fun begins. Naturally all have their own interests, and so invariably they split up at night. On their last trip to New York, evenings found most of them out clubbing, or sometimes just having friends over to their hotel for a meal, some drinks and lots of talk.

There's a loose saying in pop that the people who start a trend are always the ones to sustain themselves. This is why the Beach Boys have been continually successful in the field of records and personal appearances.

The Beach Boys created the original surf movement and the West Coast sound. The expression has now passed into everyday music, but the sound has not.

Brian Wilson said, "I remember one day when my brother Dennis came home from school and told me that a bunch of his friends wanted me to write a surfing song. I took a crack at it and called it 'Surfin'.' That was in the early autumn of 1961. My dad, Murry Wilson, took it to Capitol, and they released it as our first single—only they called it 'Surfin' Surfari'. Anyway it was a smash, and I guess that's how the West Coast sound came about."

Brian says the group has advanced a lot since then, and after about three and a half years, decided to get some kind of East Coast influence into its music..."I saw a chance to broaden the appeal without really changing the style at all. I started writing different types of lyrics with the same musical sound."

So, after a string of surfing hits, the Beach Boys came up with songs like "When I Grow Up To Be A Man", "The Little Girl I Once Knew", "Barbara Ann", and just recently, "Wouldn't It Be Nice". All these were far enough away from the West Coast to be just plain, darn good material and tremendous hits.

Brian's decision to leave the group on active dates came as no surprise to those who knew him. Touring, writing and producing records was far too much for him, and since he felt it was more important to go on writing hits, the rest of the group substituted Bruce Johnston, a performer of some repute.

By Bruce going out on the road with the group, this meant Brian had all the time in the world to sit in his office and evolve new sounds and ideas. He said, "It's sometimes better to stay behind and work, otherwise the Beach Boys might not be where they are today.

"Sure I miss being out on the road, but it's kind of a nice feeling to see all your records go up the Charts. When the rest of the guys are away I start preparing new material for us to record on their return. I think they prefer it this way too—the worry is off their shoulders.

"I would like to expand our style and versatility. We're doing it, slowly. Often, I find that just watching what's happening in the Charts helps a lot."

Whatever they're doing, the Beach Boys most certainly don't have to worry about losing their lead in the popularity stakes.

Enormous Act

As an attraction, the reason they make it so big is contact with their audiences, who can easily identify themselves with the five boys on stage. There's no message in what they're playing and, believe it or not, a lot of people like it that way. They've been an enormous record act since "Surfin' Safari", but it took a couple of years longer than that to build their status as the top college act in the country. It might not have taken so long if, in the event of their original success, they'd have gone out on tour more often. But it's only in the latter years of their success, that they have hit the road.

The present, most enviable success of the Beach Boys is founded on good old fashioned hard work and a great sound. And it's paying the finest rewards possible.

Naturally, with contemporaries and newly formed, Beatle-haircut bands singing about drugs (and soon civil unrest, Vietnam, and anti-establishment sentiment, too), Brian's songs would be examined in a different context than the one in which he felt he was working. His 17-year-old wife wanted to hear her husband being romantic and singing of love in a way that he had heard it when he was 17. It was just that he was five years (at least) out of date. As much as he loved the Beatles, Brian worshipped Phil Spector and Elvis Presley, both of whom were old-style pop geniuses. Later in 1966, when Elvis was recording near Brian's studio, Brian couldn't bring himself to go and meet him, stating, "I've worshipped that man for ten years and I can't just walk into his studio and say hello." Perhaps too in awe of the past, Brian couldn't really understand the confusing "now" in which he was working and competing.

In all of the many long and varied and candid interviews Brian did, he never mentioned Dylan, either as a songwriter, performer, or competitor. If Dylan had scored more hit singles, then perhaps Brian would have paid more attention—Dylan had managed only three Top 10 hits in five years, and none at #1. Even Johnny Rivers had scored a #1 (and five Top 10 hits) in that time (Rivers is mentioned by Brian in that argument with Murry in the studio, captured on tape while trying to make "Help Me, Rhonda").

The other lyric written by Asher for *Pet Sounds* that isn't about a boy-girl thing is "I Guess I Just Wasn't Made for These Times" (he said it was the most difficult to write). Rather, it's an adolescent poem about not being able to fit in. It's an appeal to a higher power or authority figure who can direct the singer as to where to turn and what to do when "fair weather friends cop out." It's also possibly quite close to expressing the sense of nostalgic longing that Brian had for earlier, simpler days, when the word of Murry was final and no one messed with it. In 1966, Brian was the man with the responsibility for

keeping things together and keeping the family in food, cars, and houses, not Murry. He would eventually spend around $70,000 on creating *Pet Sounds,* too.

When the rest of the Beach Boys turned up at Western Recorders in mid-February to begin their work on the album, there was a little unease about whether they'd be able to afford to buy another car or house. What they heard that day didn't sound right to them, as Asher recalled. "They were saying, 'What is this? This is not Beach Boys music.'" Mike, the oldest band member and de facto leader when they were touring, is reported to have snapped, "Don't fuck with the formula," when he heard "Hang on to Your Ego."

The tapes of the recording session that day (for "Ego") reveal a lot of noise from Mike as Al attempts his vocal lines. At one point Mike says the song is "hilarious." To Mike the whole of what he'd heard was "ego music," and because he and the rest of the Boys were being used solely as the singers, and as backing singers mostly to Brian, the project was not what he—or what Capitol Records, either—thought was actually a Beach Boys album.

"I probably said, 'this is a bullshit statement,'" Mike would later say. "'You guys are just fucked up on drugs,' and I probably didn't sing it. The thing about the ego was you take acid and get rid of your ego, and I wasn't interested in taking acid or getting rid of my ego."

Having been used to getting three albums a year with at least two singles on each, Capitol was still waiting for the first releases of 1966 from Brian in February, so he presented them with "Caroline, No." There were no other Boys to be heard on the tape, and it didn't sound like a hit. The decision was made that, in lieu of anything else, it would be released as a single in March, but under the name of Brian Wilson and not the Beach Boys.

Before then, in mid-February, Brian had reached back to his teens again and hired Paul Tanner, a lecturer on the history of jazz at UCLA, to play his bespoke electro-theremin on "I Just Wasn't Made for These Times."

L-R: Al, Brian, covering Mike's view, at the shore, 1966.

Tanner had made something of a fad out of the electro-theremin in the late 1950s with an album of space-styled instrumentals (*Music for Heavenly Bodies*, 1958) and in 1963 used it to good effect on the theme tune to *My Favorite Martian* TV series.

A smaller version of the wand-conducted theremin, the electro worked via a fader, with the resulting sounds being not too dissimilar to that of a trombone—which was unsurpising, since Tanner was an excellent trombone player and had been a member of the original Glenn Miller Orchestra. Apparently he'd been called to the studio with no knowledge at all of who Brian was and never having heard the Beach Boys before. Doubtless Murry knew all too well who Tanner was, though, since the professor had been at the forefront of developing and playing the kind of space age sounds and adult cocktail jazz that he aspired to—which means Brian probably knew about him, too. He certainly knew he wanted that sci-fi movie soundtrack noise from the electro-theremin.

Tanner was used on "Times," and later "Good Vibrations" and "Wild Honey." In 1966, the sound of

his bespoke sliding, ethereal instrument (or somehting like it) was common on recordings by exotica orchestras who were then experimenting with early electronic instruments and the very new Moog synthesizer (electronic composer Wendy Carlos was then building her own in New York). But it was only after Brian's use on *Pet Sounds* that rock and pop bands began using it, too.

The *Pet Sounds* cover shoot was done at the San Diego petting zoo, with photos by George Jerman in mid-February (it was the shoot that inspired the name, and not the other way around). That was followed by the only session on which the Beach Boys played instruments ("That's Not Me"). The end of February saw the beginning of a very long process of recording what Brian said was "going to be better than 'You've Lost That Loving Feeling'" (a Spector production, of course,

for the Righteous Brothers). That may have been on his mind following a visit to Gold Star and a meeting with Spector and the Brothers, for which Brian wore a less-than-fetching white cap and matching suit, which made him look even more uncomfortable than he clearly was.

"Good Vibrations" had five days given over to its recording and was then put aside in order to finish the album (it wasn't going to be included). The band went out on tour in mid-March, by which time it was clear that "Caroline, No" wasn't going to be a hit, and so less than two weeks later "Sloop John B." was released as a single.

It had been three months since the last Beach Boys single, which at the time was an age, and given how the scene had changed since then—the Byrds and the Rolling Stones had had two #1 singles, Barry McGuire's "Eve of Destruction" and Simon and Garfunkel's "Sound of

Left: Al and Mike in the sound room at Western Recorders.
Above: Dennis looking dapper, undisturbed by background noise.

Silence" had also both topped the charts—Capitol and Brian were naturally nervous about how "Sloop" would fare. It made it to #3, which at least gave them hope for the success of *Pet Sounds*.

Meanwhile, Brian was still working on "Good Vibrations," but not with Tony Asher. The ad man had made a few appearances at recording sessions when the rest of the Boys were working with his lyrics, but didn't feel too welcome. He had nothing to do with the writing of "Good Vibrations," and so his involvement with Brian was at an end.

As was often the way, Brian had begun hanging out in the studio and at home with a new bunch of people and picking up on their vibrations since the beginning of the year. Among them was a 23-year-old composer, songwriter, and musician named Van Dyke Parks. They'd met

through Terry Melcher at one of his parties in February, and hit it off. A former classical music student and child actor with connections in the movie business, Parks wrote the arrangement for "Bare Necessities" in Disney's *Jungle Book*, but the movie business didn't open up for him in the manner in which he hoped, so he moved into the L.A. music scene. He soon became involved with some of the new psychedelic bands that were appearing at Hollywood clubs. Among them was the Byrds, hence his connection to Melcher (Parks played organ on *Fifth Dimension*).

Following the mastering of *Pet Sounds* in April, Brian took an acetate home and played it to Marilyn as they lay in bed—and cried. "This was his soul in there," she told *Rolling Stone* in 1976. "He was so proud of it." Unfortunately the people at Capitol Records responsible for making Beach Boys records a hit were not impressed. There was talk of not releasing it at all, but in the wake of the success of "Sloop John B.," they relented and issued ads to the music press announcing the May release of *Pet Sounds*. But as a backup plan they also decided to compile a first Beach Boys "greatest hits" album.

Brian began writing songs with Van Dyke Parks in between trying to finish "Good Vibrations." Because he saw the studio as a place to be sociable, there were often friends and acquaintences in the control booth while recording was going on. With Parks there, some of his friends also started to appear, among them David Anderle, an A&R man who'd signed Frank Zappa to the Verve label. Brian recalled that the "Good Vibrations" sessions had almost got out of hand. "We ran wild with drugs, were being very creative on drugs," and that was affecting his ability to decide what he wanted from the song. Anderle recalls hearing an R&B version of "Vibrations" that Brian was going to give to another label for one of their R&B acts to cover. Mike recalled that "it sounded like Wilson Pickett should be recording it."

It didn't happen. Brian had another idea (the sixth or seventh to date) on how to finish the song, including adding cellos (a Van Dyke Parks idea), although it would still take more than a dozen further sessions over the course of three months for it to be finalized.

While Brian contemplated "Good Vibrations," he and Parks began working together on songs for a new album, one that would be even better than *Pet Sounds* or *Revolver*. It would have different parts, movements, and ideas that no one had tried before on a pop record. It was going to be called *Dumb Angel*, he said. The first song for it was titled "Heroes and Villains," and its lyrics were an impressionistic and imaginative depiction of a Wild West town that suited the era far more perfectly than the lovelorn numbers on *Pet Sounds*.

However, opposed as he was to what Brian had done with *Sounds*, Mike Love was spitting fury at the words

to the new song. "He [Parks] was over acid-ized," Mike fumed. "I always thought if you're going to write something it ought to make some sort of sense." Apparently, when confronted by Mike in the studio while recording "Heroes and Villains" with the question of what lines "meant," Parks simply shrugged, told him work it out, and left the room, infuriating Mike even more.

Mike was possibly much happier when Capitol released *The Best of the Beach Boys* in July. *Pet Sounds* had peaked at #10 on the charts and was beginning its descent. The track listing of the compilation was still pretty much what they were performing live on stage, and they hadn't considered recreating tracks from *Pet Sounds* live on stage yet.

Van Dyke Parks (in hat) at Western Recorders with session pianist Don Randl, working on "Good Vibrations."

The Beach Boys who toured the world playing their *Best Of* collection in 1966: L-R: Mike, Bruce, Al, Carl, Dennis.

BEST OF THE BEACH BOYS

CAPITOL, MARCH 1966

Producer	Brian Wilson, Murry Wilson, Nick Venet
Engineer	Chuck Britz
Recorded	4/19/62–4/11/66, United Western Recorders, Gold Star, CBS Columbia, Hollywood
U.S. Chart	#8 *Billboard*
Singles	"Help Me, Rhonda," "I Get Around"

Side 1

1. SURFIN' SAFARI
B. Wilson/M. Love

2. SURFIN' USA
B. Wilson/M. Love

3. LITTLE DEUCE COUPE
B. Wilson/M. Love

4. FUN, FUN, FUN
B. Wilson/M. Love

5. I GET AROUND
B. Wilson/M. Love

6. ALL SUMMER LONG
B. Wilson/M. Love

7. IN MY ROOM
B. Wilson/G. Usher

Side 2

1. DO YOU WANNA DANCE?
B. Freeman

2. HELP ME, RHONDA
B. Wilson/M. Love

3. CALIFORNIA GIRLS
B. Wilson/M. Love

4. BARBARA ANN
F. Fassert

5. YOU'RE SO GOOD TO ME
B. Wilson/M. Love

6. SLOOP JOHN B
trad. arr. B. Wilson

7. GOD ONLY KNOWS
B. Wilson/T. Asher

The UK release of the first Beach Boy's greatest hits collection has two tracks more than on the U.S. version, and doesn't include seven songs that are on the U.S. release. In America, *The Best Of* comprised singles and B-sides, and includes "Catch a Wave," "Surfer Girl," "Little Honda," "The Warmth of the Sun," "Louie, Louie," "Kiss Me Baby," and "Wendy," none of which are on the UK disc. While "Help Me, Rhonda" and "Do You Wanna Dance?" weren't included on the U.S. release, Capitol reissued them as singles in the States. In the United Kingdom the album sold incredibly well, making it to #2 on the album charts, but the U.S. version only made it to two places higher than *Pet Sounds* had. Brian felt that its release cut into potential sales of *Pet Sounds* and that Capitol put time and money into promoting the collection that would have been better spent on the new record. As Murry and Mike had warned him, by messing with the formula on *Pet Sounds*, Brian had not only alienated Beach Boys fans but also executives at Capitol. What nobody could yet understand was that the Beach Boys were considered to be a nostalgia act by their original fans—those kids who'd bought into the surf culture five years earlier were now young adults with different concerns, and while Brian was still singing about adolescent love on *Pet Sounds*, the music that surrounded it was too complicated for adolescents to get. And given the choice, the by-now older teenagers and early twentysomething original fans would rather buy a *Best Of* album to play at parties and sing along to than immerse themselves in the complicated and dense layers of *Pet Sounds*. They wanted to dance, not sit in the dark listening to bicycle bells and dog barks.

GOOD VIBRATIONS

CAPITOL, OCTOBER 1966

B-side	"Lets Go Away for a While"
Writers	B. Wilson/M. Love; B. Wilson
Producer	B. Wilson
Recorded	2/17–9/21/66
U.S. Chart	#1 *Billboard*

Mike Love told a reporter in 1976 that when "Good Vibrations" was released, "The number one disc jockey in New York, Cousin Brucie, said to me that it scared him. He said he hated it—he hated "Good Vibrations" because it's so different." Cousin Brucie was right to be worried, because for the first time in more than two years, for the 3 minutes 35 seconds that this song lasts, the Beach Boys were relevant again, and dangerous. There was a new vibe alive among the youth of America that was revolutionary, drug-infused, and determined to break down old ways of doing everything, exclaiming "Make love, not war!" The emerging hippie movement of San Francisco, which was rolled across the country by Ken Kesey's Pranksters in the summer of 1964, dispensing free LSD, holding love-ins, and opening minds, had finally seen the "good vibrations" they'd emitted taking hold among the wider populace. Brian didn't mean any direct reference to psychedelia with the song, of course, although he'd taken a few trips. To him, the inspiration was his mother and the "vibrations" that are all around, the lyrics an attempt to chant into being only the good, banishing the bad. The B-side (an instrumental) was inspired by Burt Bacharach, its title representing a growing desire Brian felt to "escape" from everything.

The Best of the Beach Boys outsold *Pet Sounds* pretty quickly. With "Good Vibrations" still not finished, in mid-August, Capitol released "Wouldn't It Be Nice" b/w "God Only Knows" as a single. Its success (#8 on the U.S. chart) can only have made Brian confident in what he was attempting to do in the studio with new songs and sounds. His confidence was further bolstered by newly appointed publicity officer Derek Taylor (the long-time Beatles associate) starting a campaign that declaimed "Brian Wilson is a genius." "It came about," Taylor would remember, "because Brian told me that he thought he was better than most other people believed him to be." So, Taylor had musical peers and contemporaries exclaim Brian to be a "genius" in interviews. Having the critical approval of his peers may have offset some of the disappointment felt at the low sales numbers for *Pet Sounds*.

After sessions throughout the summer with the intention of creating the new album by the end of the year, in early September Brian retitled *Dumb Angel* as *Smile*. Things had changed in the U.S. music industry, Brian had noticed. "We used a more cheery title," he explained in an interview that year while talking up *Smile*, adding that "the whole album is going to be a far-out trip through

The Beach Boys on their second trip to London, with
Bruce (far left) in place of Brian, November 1966.

the old West, real Americana but with lots of interesting
humor." The emphasis on cheerfulness may well have
been on account of the American public having taken
the Monkees to their hearts. Coincidentally, Van Dyke
Parks had auditioned for a role in the TV series that
helped make Davy, Micky, Michael, and Peter household
names across the country (and then the world).

The Monkees television series began in September
1966 and swiftly became a hit. Inspired by the movie *A
Hard Day's Night*, the ad-libbed, loosely plotted *Monkees*
TV show broke new ground in filming technique and
production, while making its cast enormous pop stars.

The Monkees' musical output owed something to the
Beatles, but was all-American in form and content, most
of their songs were written by successful Brill Building
writers Tommy Boyce and Bobby Hart, with a couple
by Gerry Goffin and Carole King. The songs had classic
hooks and choruses; the arrangements were guitar-led
and slightly psychedelic-sounding. But humor was a big
part of the songs, as it was the show. The final song of
their debut LP, "Gonna Buy Me a Dog," like *Pet Sounds*,
closed the album with barking sounds.

Their debut single, "Last Train to Clarksville,"
released in August, made #1 in November 1966. "I'm a
Believer," released in November, was #1 on December
31 (for seven weeks). More incredibly, the eponymous
debut album was released October 10, 1966, and made
#1 on the U.S. album charts on November 12. It stayed
there until February 10, 1967.

With those kind of numbers, anyone would smile.

5

SMILE!
SURF'S
UP

1967·1970

I n 2006, Brian Wilson gave an interview to *Ability* magazine, a Time Warner publication dedicated to health and disability issues. He was interviewed by the editor-in-chief, Chet Cooper, and senior health editor Gillian Friedman, MD. In the course of the talk Brian revealed that he heard "voices" in his head: "For the past 40 years I've had auditory hallucinations in my head, all day every day, and I can't get them out. Every few minutes the voices say something derogatory to me, which discourages me a little bit, but I have to be strong enough to say to them, 'Hey, would you quit stalking me? F*** off!'" He goes on to say that the voices appeared after "I'd taken some psychedelic drugs, and then about a week after that I started hearing voices, and they've never stopped." Which puts the beginning of his psychotic episodes around late 1965, or early the following year.

Throughout 1966, Brian was smoking cannabis and taking LSD, both of which may have masked his illness. They certainly will have contributed to the auditory hallucinations that he suffered and that he apparently tried to drown out with music. In that 2006 interview, when Friedman remarks how he was already a successful musician when they started, Brian replies, "Right. I believe they started picking on me because they are jealous. The voices in my head are jealous of me." He doesn't say if the voice was Murry's.

As usual Brian's work schedule was grueling—"Good Vibrations" had taken more than 94 hours of recording time in four different locations across 22 different sessions (as Badman reports) that year, and they had been conducted in between creating *Pet Sounds* and *Smile*. There were promotional duties, writing with Parks, and late night/early morning walks around L.A. with friends like David Anderle and Michael Vosse.

In October 1966, Brian told a camera crew and a journalist visiting his home that he was writing "a teenage symphony to God," using a term Tom Wolfe had chosen to describe Phil Spector's recordings in his *Kandy-Koloured Tangerine-Flake Streamline Baby* collection (1965). Brian was attempting to create a symphonic structure with different movements and parts in the style of his great favorite, "A Rhapsody in Blue," by George Gershwin. The problem was, he couldn't concentrate on just one movement or piece and finish it before another part occurred to him and he had to get something recorded for that. "They're all vignettes," Mike Love would later explain. "You see, that's Brian Wilson's greatest work—not the sustained riffs of a blues

"Musically speaking, we used to be totally reliant on Brian, but now we're branching out."

MIKE *Love*

band, but the little musical vignettes—ten or twenty seconds of a verse, a chorus, a shot here or there and then out. Sometimes things fit together and sometimes they were dropped. There's no way it could be made sensible and logical." Brian agreed with Mike about that.

All of the vignettes and the way that Brian worked impressed people around him, though, dazzling them with his invention and drive. The noted documentary maker David Oppenheim interviewed Brian during the filming of his 1967 documentary *Inside Pop: The Rock Revolution* (presented and written by venerable conductor and composer Leonard Bernstein). Oppenheim

Previous page: Brian at the end of the 1960s.

Above: L-R: Brian Wilson, Bruce Johnston, Carl Wilson, Al Jardine, Mike Love.

said, "I would beg Brian not to change a piece of music because it was too fantastic, but when Brian did change it, I have to admit it was equally beautiful."

Oppenheim shot film of Brian playing a sublime version of a song titled "Surf's Up" on piano, but it was the only footage of Brian to be included in the documentary—there was no interview with him screened.

Over the following nine months, many backing tracks Brian wrote and conducted or played, intended for *Smile*, were lost, abandoned, or appeared on future Beach Boys albums ("Surf's Up" became, in a different form, the title track to the 1971 album). But for a long time the band and Capitol believed that *Smile* would be the next Beach Boys album to follow *Pet Sounds*; they encouraged Brian in its making. Brian's continued insistence of his new work being happy and humorous helped to persuade the record company to indulge him. With the Monkees indomitable presence on the album chart in 1967 (see page 127), it could be said that they

HEROES & VILLAINS

CAPITOL, JULY 1967

B-side	"You're Welcome"
Writers	B. Wilson/V. D. Parks; B. Wilson
Producer	B. Wilson
Recorded	10/20/66–6/4/67
U.S. Chart	#12 *Billboard*

This was the closest that Brian Wilson came to realizing his teenage symphony concept. "Heroes and Villains" took longer than "Good Vibrations" to complete, and even then it wasn't finished as far as Brian was concerned. But, desperate for a release from the Beach Boys, this was the first newly recorded music that Capitol felt that they could release by the band, and it was the first in in over nine months. The lyrics by Van Dyke Parks are almost impenetrable, impressionistic, and representative of the LSD- and cannabis-soaked days and nights spent trying to create *Smile*. Parks said that he intended it to be a "historically reflective" ballad about the Spanish and Indian past of America. Brian's winsome, sad rendition of the lyrics lend them a sense of meaning that isn't easily found, though. As with almost everything Brian was recording at the time, "Heroes" manages to sound like a lament, even as it roars along. Later, Brian would reveal that he, Parks, and various other band members and musicians, friends, and hangers-on would spend hours in the studio, in the dark, on the floor, taping voices and noises. The B-side sounds like one of those sessions, albeit with a slight structure and only the title as lyric. It's one of the slightest things they ever released, inspired Brian claimed, by Al asking if he could try some LSD.

had replaced the Beach Boys as the leading American band of the day. On a visit to London in February, members of the Monkees were photographed visiting Paul McCartney, and Mike Nesmith was invited to Abbey Road studios, where the Beatles were working on what

Below: All at sea and lacking Brian. L-R: Mike Love, Bruce Johnston, Dennis Wilson, Al Jardine, Carl Wilson, 1967.

Phil Spector (left) with Ike and Tina Turner at Gold Star
Studio, recording "River Deep-Mountain High," 1966.

would become *Sgt. Pepper's Lonely Hearts Club Band.*
The Liverpudlians may have preferred to show off to
Brian, but he wasn't leaving his L.A. studios.

In the previous summer, Brian had been invited to
a mixing session for the latest album by another British
band, but in L.A. at the RCA recording studios. Rolling
Stones manager Andrew Loog Oldham, co-owner

of Immediate Records Music Publishing, the UK
distributor of Brian's sheet music, was a fan of *Pet Sounds.*
He played *Between the Buttons* for Brian. The Stones'
fifth album, released in February 1967, would make
#2 on the U.S. chart, far outselling *Pet Sounds.* It must
have sounded like a bad dream to Brian, with its deliberately unharmonic backing vocals that seemed to mock
the perfect pitch of the Beach Boys. With references to
death, displaying a wholly cynical view of the world, and
suggesting "Let's Spend the Night Together," where

"Acid showed me a combination of sounds–how to combine different instruments."

BRIAN *Wilson*

Brian would dare only long for marriage and innocent contact, it's almost the anti-*Pet Sounds*. The mix is dirty, and the reverb serves to space out rather than solidify and layer instruments. The cover image, taken by Gered Mankowitz at 5:30 a.m. with a camera smeared in vaseline, shows a dissolute and clearly drug-addled bunch of misfits. You sense that if a goat had been present for the shoot the Stones would have slaughtered it and smeared blood over their faces.

Also, early in 1967, a new L.A. band released their debut album, the eponymously titled *The Doors*. As with the Stones, their music, outlook, and public image was the antithesis of the smiling, healthy, surfing sunshine and simple romance of the Beach Boys. When the Doors' original version of "Light My Fire" hit the #1 spot in late July (for 3 weeks) it kept the Beatles' "All You Need Is Love" out, limiting it to only a week at #1. The hip world was changing, becoming darker and more adult, asking difficult questions of listeners, replacing old certainties about love, romance, religion, and politics. Brian's world was disintegrating all around him—Phil Spector had apparently retired from making records following the failure of Ike and Tina Turner's "River Deep–Mountain High" to become a huge hit. The final Ronettes single, "I Can Hear Music," only made #100 in the charts the same year (but the song would go on to become a bigger hit for the Beach Boys in 1969).

Perhaps if the Boys' leader had accompanied them on their tour of the United Kingdom at the end of 1966, his faith in the power of his music may have been reinforced. The Boys sold out the tour and had huge crowds of mostly female fans swamping their every move, screaming at every utterance. Instead, attempting to create a "movement" of his teenage symphony about the elements, in late November he'd given musicians at Gold Star studio a toy fireman's helmet to wear, lit a small fire in a bucket ("so we could smell smoke," Brian told a reporter), and created a glorious noise, titled "Fire." According to some reports from the studio, seasoned session musicians who were aghast at the hats and smoking bucket were equally amazed when they heard the playback of what Brian had been conducting them to record.

Legend has it, however, that when days later Brian heard that a building a few blocks away had burned down around the time of his recording (and discovered that there had been a high reporting of fires in L.A. in general), he threw away the session tapes, thinking that his music had somehow caused the conflagrations. It was the beginning of the end of *Smile*, even if it wasn't obvious at that time.

In anticipation of the delivery of the *Smile* master tapes—and because Brian had promised them the new album—Capitol had half a million sleeves printed for *Smile* and delivered early in 1967. Actually, Brian hadn't even finished the promised single, "Heroes and Villains," let alone the album. Then, Van Dyke Parks was offered a solo recording contract by Warner Brothers records, and so he became a less than regular presence at recordings in January. The pair parted company in April.

The Wilson brothers had become all too aware of their elder brother's increasingly erratic behavior, so Carl and Dennis began work in the studio without Brian,

but using the same musicians. They intended to create music for Brother Records, which had come into being in late 1966, and was an attempt on their part to take more control over what they recorded and released, albeit via Capitol as distributors. However, it wasn't clear that the move worked, and according to a 1967 *NME* interview with Mike, when Brian failed to give Capitol the masters to "Heroes and Villains," their UK subsidiary released "Then I Kissed Her" without consulting them.

The label said they did it to promote the May 1967 tour of the UK, but the Boys can only have been surprised there'd been no consultation with them on it.

The release of *Smile* was officially cancelled in June 1967, following which the band assembled at Hollywood Sound Recorders to record a new album. They undertook an unusual way of working. "We'd just make up stuff," Carl later recalled. The tape was kept running and some pieces of *Smile* were revisited, changed, and included, not least "Vega-Tables" and, of course, "Heroes and Villains." At the same time, America was delighting in the Beatles' *Sgt. Pepper's* album, which had been inspired at least in part by *Pet Sounds*.

Just as Brian was giving up on his magnum opus, his father was beginning the process of recording his:

Capitol Records had handed Murry Wilson a deal to record an album for them.

Exactly why they did so isn't clear, but perhaps there was still a feeling at the company that Murry might have some control over his oldest son and be able to put him back on the right pop road. Murry was still involved in his sons' business affairs, insofar as he still administered the publishing rights for all the Wilsons' songs.

Opposite: Brian attempts a swim in the ocean to promote the release of the *Smiley Smile* album.

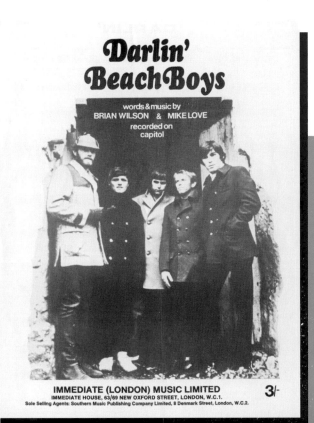

DARLIN'

CAPITOL, DECEMBER 1967

B-side	"Here Today"
Writers	B. Wilson/M. Love; B. Wilson/T. Asher
Producer	B. Wilson
Recorded	10/11–27/67; 3/11–25/66
U.S. Chart	#19 *Billboard*

After the obscure lyrics and almost baroque, overcomplicated music of "Heroes and Villains," this R&B-influenced pop song signaled a change of direction for the Beach Boys. Brian's touching falsetto was gone, replaced with a more earthbound, slightly harsh vocal by Carl. With soulful horns (and even a mention of "soul" in the lyrics), "Darlin'" sounds like a fortaste of what bands such as Blood, Sweat, and Tears and Chicago would soon turn out, albeit in funkier, louder forms. "Darlin'" was begun as a song for a band called Redwood, lead by a friend and frequent visitor to Brian's house, Danny Hutton. Brian wrote and produced a couple of songs for Redwood, who soon after changed their name to Three Dog Night and scored a big hit with Nilsson's "One" in 1968. But Mike's insistence that he concentrate on Beach Boys business prompted Brian to produce this (with added lyrics by Mike) for the Boys instead. Although a radio hit, it failed to sell as well as the past two releases, beginning a downward sales projectory for Beach Boys singles that would persist over the next nine years. The B-side was lifted from *Pet Sounds* and features a Bach-inspired middle-eight section. The B-side's production sounds very different when compared to that of the A-side.

Brian Wilson in humorous mood, 1966.

SMILEY SMILE

CAPITOL, SEPTEMBER 1967

Producer	The Beach Boys
Engineer	Chuck Britz, Jim Lockert
Recorded	2/17/66–7/14/67, United Western Recorders, Sunset Sound, CBS Columbia Square, Wally Heider Studios, Brian Wilson's home, Hollywood
U.S. Chart	#41 *Billboard*
Singles	"Good Vibrations," "Heroes and Villains"

Side 1

1. HEROES AND VILLAINS
B. Wilson/V. D. Parks

2. VEGA-TABLES
B. Wilson/V. D. Parks

3. FALL BREAKS AND BACK TO WINTER
(W WOODPECKER SYMPHONY)
B. Wilson

4. SHE'S GOIN' BALD
B. Wilson/M. Love/V. D. Parks

5. LITTLE PAD
B. Wilson

Side 2

1. GOOD VIBRATIONS
B. Wilson/M. Love

2. WITH ME TONIGHT
B. Wilson

3. WIND CHIMES
B. Wilson

4. GETTIN' HUNGRY
B. Wilson/M. Love

5. WONDERFUL
B. Wilson/ V. D. Parks

6. WHISTLE IN
B. Wilson

This became the Beach Boys' least successful album. One reviewer at the time called it "undoubtedly the worst album ever released by the Beach Boys." The problem was that it wasn't *Smile*, the often- and long-promised "teenage symphony" that Brian and the others had been talking up almost from the moment that *Pet Sounds* came out. Instead of a lavish, complicated, interlinked series of movements that constituted what would be "the greatest pop album ever" (as Brian had suggested) came this slight collection of pseudo-psychedelic ramblings and sub-Monkees comedy songs. It's much improved by the inclusion of "Good Vibrations" and "Heroes and Villains," but after the fantastic opening track the stark and silly "Vega-Tables" doesn't sound whimsical and vaudevillian like a Monkees track such as "Your Auntie Grizelda"; it just sounds like filler. The "Woody Woodpecker Symphony" may sound more interesting at a distance of several decades, but in 1967, it would have sounded just like the soundtrack to a cartoon (the staple of Saturday morning kids' TV). "She's Goin' Bald" and "Little Pad" are crying out for Davy Jones's Mancunian accent to carry them. None of it even matches "Zilch" from the Monkees' *Headquarters* though, and that's because the TV combo's interweaving voices intoning nonsense is the only track of its kind on the album and doesn't distract from the great pop songs ("You Told Me," "For Pete's Sake," "Shades of Gray"). "Good Vibrations" kicks off side 2 strongly but is never matched by any of the following tracks. It was not warmly received by many (if any) critics, and reviews were overwhelmingly awful.

Murry certainly had a conversation with Brian about LSD around that time. As he recalled to *Rolling Stone*, they were in a car and Murry asked Brian, "Do you think you're strong enough in your brain that you can experiment with a chemical that might drive you crazy later?" Naturally, in Murry's telling of the story, he had the last word: "And he agreed that he'd never do it again." With sales of Beach Boys records falling, Murry was going to show Brian how to make a record "properly." Working with arranger and conductor Don Ralke—possibly most famous for producing *But You've Never Heard Gershwin with Bongos* (1960)— Murry worked up a few of his tunes, a couple by a plumber he'd met named Eerik Kynor who came to fit a bathroom for him, a song by Al Jardine, and (according to the sleeve notes) "Murry's favorite of all his son's compositions," "The Warmth of the Sun." At a time when Herb Alpert and the Tijuana Brass were selling millions of largely instrumental albums, the time was ripe for a Wilson-fronted instrumental LP to make big waves in the business. Sadly, the string-laden, leaden-paced album, pumped by an organ sound that was outdated in 1952, failed to even make it into pop music's shallows. *The Many Moods of Murry Wilson* were doubtless dark after it flopped in October 1967.

Before then Brian and Marilyn moved house. He had a studio built in their new home, but began to spend more time—just as Murry would and had done—not getting out of bed for days in a row. The Beach Boys moved the recording of what would become *Smiley Smile* into Brian's studio, hoping to draw him downstairs at times with a tune he liked.

That summer, despite being asked to be part of the organizing committee for the Monterey International Pop Festival and scheduled to appear as the headline act on the Saturday, the Beach Boys withdrew at the last moment, with little explanation except that Carl, who was fighting the draft as a conscientious objector and making regular court appearances, wasn't up to it. Of course Brian wasn't at all up to it, but that wasn't a reason the Beach Boys wanted or could afford to admit in public. One of the festival organizers, John Phillips of the Mamas and the Papas, thought that Brian was scared that the hippies in the crowd would laugh at the Boys' striped shirts, and so cancelled.

Their failure to appear at Monterey, combined with the desire to continue to succeed as a singles chart pop band, meant that the Beach Boys would spend the next four years being largely ignored or ridiculed in the fast-growing alternative (once undergound) music press, where reputations and hipness were judged, decided, and proclaimed.

When "Heroes and Villains" was released in July 1967, it had been nine months since "Good Vibrations" had been a hit, and it failed to make the U.S. Top 10 (peaking at #12). In its wake, Capitol released another best of collection (*Volume 2*), which crawled to only #50 on the charts. There was a real worry that the Beach Boys were irrelevant and past it as a recording act. The release of *Smiley Smile* (peak position #41) in September and the single "Wild Honey" (peak #31) in October did little to change that opinion. But the *Wild Honey* album did slightly better, making #24—the same position the single from it, "Darlin'" had made in December.

At the end of 1967, the Beach Boys were still a major draw on the live performance circuit, though, and they were supported by hip new acts like Buffalo Springfield, Strawberry Alarm Clock, and Soul Survivors. As the headline act, their set list comprised only hit singles, although with fewer early surf and hot-rod numbers.

In February 1968, Mike Love became the most visible member of the band when he appeared in newspapers around the world in the company of the Beatles, in India. He and the rest of the Beach Boys (minus Brian) had met the Maharishi while in Paris in December 1967.

Mike Love (left) ties Al Jardine in microphone cable during work on the humorous *Smile* project, 1967.

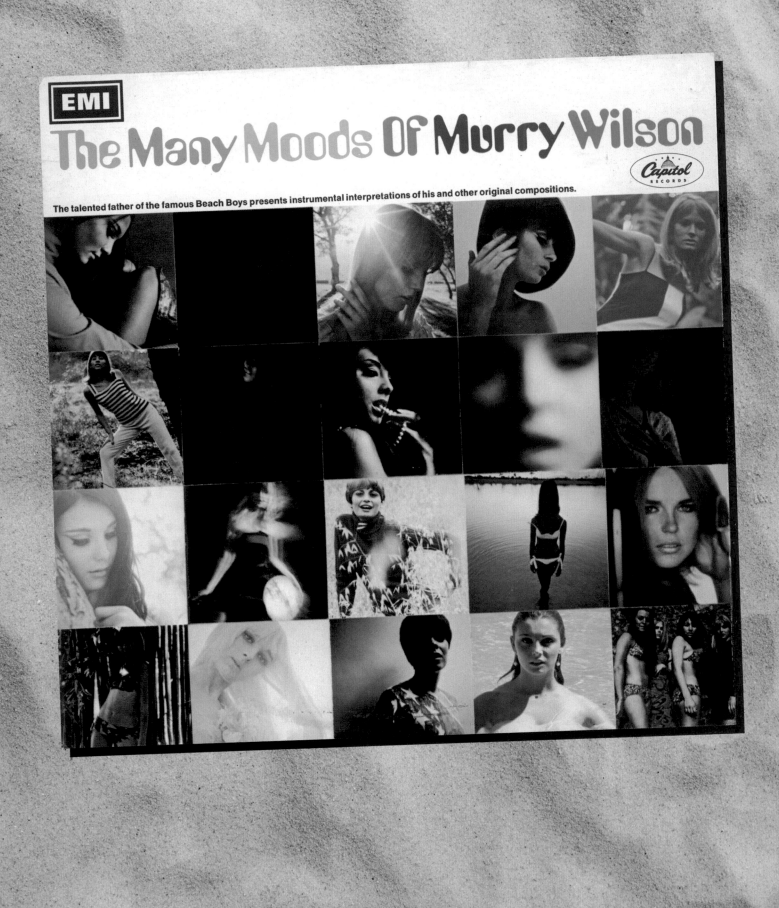

THE MANY MOODS OF MURRY WILSON

CAPITOL, OCTOBER 1967

Producers	Murry Wilson, Brian Wilson
Engineers	Stan Ross, Chuck Britz
Recorded	6–7/67, United Western Recorders, Gold Star Studios, Hollywood
U.S. Chart	N/A
Singles	"Leaves"

Side 1

1. LOVE WON'T WAIT

M. Wilson

2. THE HAPPY SONG

E. Kynor

3. THE WARMTH OF THE SUN

B. Wilson/M. Love

4. BROKEN HEART

G. Kazanis

5. LEAVES

M. Wilson

6. THE PLUMBER'S SONG

E. Kynor

Side 2

1. PAINTING WITH TEARDROPS

M. Wilson

2. ISLANDS IN THE SKY

R. Henn

3. JUST 'ROUND THE RIVER BEND

D. Ralke/D. Patrick

4. ITALIA

A. Jardine

5. HEARTBREAK LANE

M. Wilson

6. BETTY'S WALTZ

M. Wilson/A. Wilson

The title can only have brought a smirk to the faces of the Wilson brothers. The level of irony at play is perhaps in relation to the hubris shown by Murry in choosing his "favorite" of Brian's songs ("Warmth of the Sun") on which to demonstrate to the kid how it should be done—in a string-soaked, cocktail jazz arrangement that was all the rage in 1957. Exactly why Capitol agreed to release the album is unclear. It's trumpeted on the cover as being by the "talented father of the famous Beach Boys," and the liner notes set out the credentials of "Murry Wilson—songwriter!" using more exclamation marks (five in the first 12 lines) than should ever be necessary—but in truth it's an old-fashioned sounding, expensive vanity project. Perhaps Capitol believed that given how the Beach Boys had succeeded, that anyone else Murry found for them would, too. The LP serves up music by three of Murry's recent musical "discoveries": Rick Henn of the Sun Rays (managed and produced by Murry along Beach Boys lines); Erik Kynor, a plumber who impressed him while installing a new bathroom at Murry's home; and George Kizanis, an old pal. Keeping it in the family, Murry contributes two numbers and shares the credit on "Betty's Waltz" with Audree. There's also a track by Al Jardine, which was produced by Brian, albeit uncredited. But, as Murry's sleeve notes point out, "The music business has been good to the entire Wilson family," and, he continues, "this album, which has been mixed as emotionally as possible, retaining color, shading and warmth, is humbly offered to the public." Sadly for him, the public didn't accept the offer.

'Who's a good guru?" asked Lennon. L-R: Patti Harrison, John Lennon, Mike Love (in hat), Maharishi, George Harrison, Mia Farrow, Donovan, Paul McCartney, Jane Asher, Cynthia Lennon

After a day spent learning about Transcendental Meditation, Mike was hooked. "It was the most relaxed I'd ever felt in my life," he'd later recall. He was the only Beach Boy to make the trek to Rishikesh, though, where he spent two weeks in competitive meditation with John Lennon, George Harrison, Jane Asher, Mia Farrow (in the middle of a divorce from Frank Sinatra), Donovan (his "Mellow Yellow" had made #2 on the U.S. charts just before Christmas), and various hangers-on. Because of the presence of the Beatles, the sparsely furnished ashram was besieged by the world's media; photos and news footage of the celebrity meditators made regular appearances around the world. Mike was often spotted in the company of a Beatle and may have had an influence on the writing of Lennon and McCartney's "Back in the USSR," with it's reference to "Ukraine girls" that ironizes Mike's "California girls."

The day of Mike's twenty-seventh birthday (March 15) and also his final day in India, the Beatles and others hosted a party for him, and they sang songs specially composed for the event that were smartly captured by Mike's cassette recorder. McCartney and Jane Asher left two weeks later; Lennon and Harrison remained until mid-April, when they left after accusing the Maharishi's motives of being less than purely spiritual. Although Harrison's fascination with Indian spirituality would grow, the Beatles' interest in, and cooperation with, the guru came to an immediate end. Mike didn't share their reservations, though, and he would go on to involve the Beach Boys further with the giggling guru.

For the first three months of 1968, Brian, Dennis, Carl, and Al worked on a new album, both at Brian's house and at Western Recorders. On April 1, the Boys began another tour, but on the fourth, the assassination

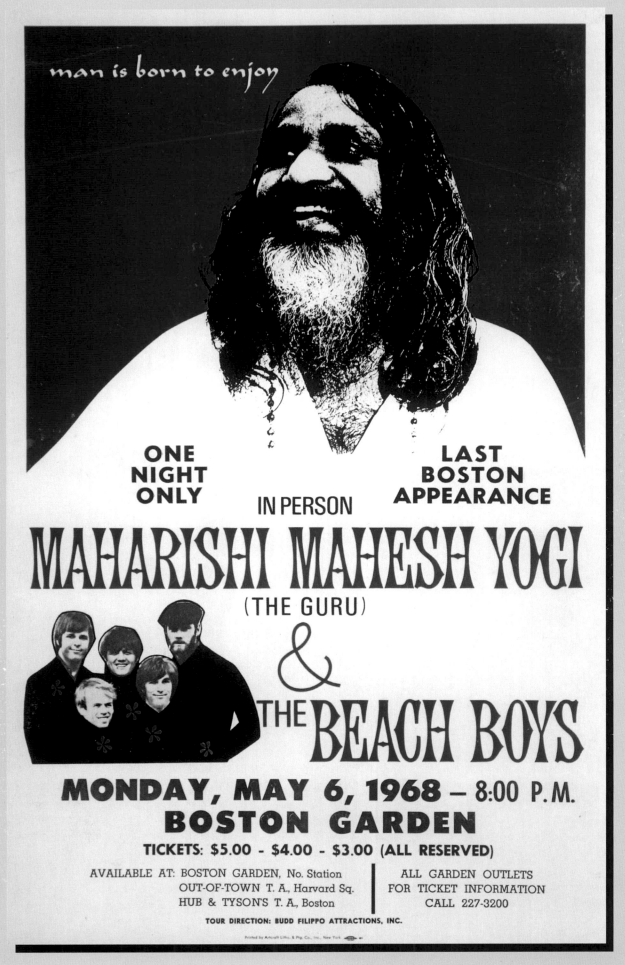

146

Poster advertising a date on the 'joint headline' tour of 1968.

of Martin Luther King Jr. in Memphis forced the cancellation of several dates as America erupted into chaos and civil unrest.

As a consequence of Dennis having time off, and in keeping with his increasingly erratic and drug-fueled lifestyle, he made the acquaintance of a young girl, who in turn led him to a meeting with an aspiring songwriter, drifter, and self-styled cult leader named Charles Manson.

Dennis picked up a couple of girls in Malibu, took them to his home (once belonging to cowboy movie star Will Rogers), and left them there while he went to the studio. On his return, Manson was at Dennis's house, along with many more young (teenage) girls. Dennis extended a welcome to them all, took to calling Manson "The Wizard," and partied with them all. Soon Dennis was writing songs with him. At one point, Dennis introduced Audree to Manson and the girls—despite her being worried about Murry discovering that she'd been to Dennis's house, which had a reputation among the family and friends as being in a constant state of orgy (Dennis once boasted that he'd paid for $1000 worth of VD treatments for the girls, Manson, and himself). Manson looked, Audree later told *Rolling Stone*, "like an older man" in his white robe, surrounded by "darling young girls, I thought. But leeches."

Not long after Dennis's personal guru moved in with him, the Beach Boys went off on tour with Mike's international guru, the Maharishi, as a co-headline act. The plan was for the Boys to play a live set in the first half of a show, and in the second for the Maharishi to talk to the audience and attempt to get them all meditating. The Boys' previous tour had seen very good attendance (especially at venues where Davy Jones of the Monkees appeared as "MC"). The screaming fans from the previous tour were not inspired to attend the Beach Boys/Maharishi gigs, though, and venues were rarely even a third full. The tour was cancelled after seven of the 20 dates played. A single released to help promote the tour ("Friends," b/w "Little Bird") barely scraped into the top 50.

For the first time in four years, Brian wasn't recording or even writing songs while the band toured. At the end of May, the Boys recorded versions of Bacharach and David's "Walk on By" (a Top 10 hit for Dionne Warwick in 1964), "Old Folks at Home (Swanee River)" (the 1851 minstrel number), and "Ol' Man River" from *Showboat* (by Oscar Hammerstein II and Jerome Kern).

They also recorded a song by Mike inspired by a recent surf trip, titled "Do It Again" (released as a single in July, b/w "Wake the World,"); it reached #20.

"Brian Wilson is The Beach Boys. He is all of it. Period. We're nothing. He is everything."

DENNIS *Wilson*

WILD HONEY

CAPITOL, DECEMBER 1967

Producer The Beach Boys
Engineers Jim Lockert, Bill Halverson
Recorded 9/26–11/15/67, Wally Heider Studio, Brian Wilson's home, Hollywood
U.S. Chart #24 *Billboard*
Singles "Wild Honey," "Darlin'"

Side 1

1.WILD HONEY
B. Wilson/M. Love

2. AREN'T YOU GLAD
B. Wilson/M. Love

3. I WAS MADE TO LOVE HER
S. Wonder/L. M. Hardaway/H. Cosby/S. Moy

4. COUNTRY AIR
B. Wilson/M. Love

5. A THING OR TWO
B. Wilson/M. Love

Side 2

1. DARLIN'
B. Wilson/M. Love

2. I'D LOVE JUST ONCE TO SEE YOU
B. Wilson/M. Love

3. HERE COMES THE NIGHT
B. Wilson/M. Love

4. LET THE WIND BLOW
B. Wilson/M. Love

5. HOW SHE BOOGALOOED IT
M. Love/A. Jardine/B. Johnston/C. Wilson

6. MAMA SAYS
B. Wilson/M. Love

In late 1967, Brian was taking longer bed breaks from the studio. He lay above the sound room or paced the floor upstairs, listening through the walls and ceiling as people came and went, making noises, playing music and records. Sometimes Brian appeared in his studio to work with Danny Hutton, soon to be the lead voice in Three Dog Night, on material for Redwood. Other times, though, when trying to put together a new Beach Boys album, Carl (and Dennis) were to be heard playing some Motown records (only the Supremes had matched the Monkees in terms of chart success in the previous year) and other hits of the day—like the Young Rascals' "Groovin'," which had taken aspects of Brian's production techniques, married them to soul music and hippie jargon, and scored a worldwide hit. The Boys were clearly getting into more soulful sounds at the time, and they recorded a version of another soul-influenced #1 hit of 1967 during sessions for this album, "The Letter" by the Box Tops. So it's little surprise that soulful, R&B-influenced pop should be the Beach Boys' "new direction" when this album appeared. They always tried to stay relevant and current with the trends of the day, so the cover art, a detail from a stained glass window in Brian's house, suggests a psychedelic influence (they'd recently toured with the Strawberry Alarm Clock, so knew about the psychedelic graphics that were in vogue). The title is a play on the elixir of bees, a staple of Brian's kitchen and symbol of the emerging health-food fad—Brian would later open a health-food store, the Radiant Radish, in Los Angeles. It was also slang for young girls. The only cover version on the LP is of Stevie Wonder's "I Was Made to Love Her." There are four lead vocals by Carl and two by Brian, with the rest shared. The production sounds much simpler and the results more listenable than *Smiley Smile*. It proved more successful in sales terms, too, and suggested that there might be life left in the band, after all.

Carl shared the production desk with Brian as the recording took shape—at a much faster rate than had been the case in the past two years. "Do It Again" sounded as if it could have been recorded pre-1964 and was a thowback in sound and lyrics, but it was a hit, and it came between two flops.

The album *20/20* was recorded in June, mostly at Brian's home. The same month *Friends*, a largely TM-influenced and very brief album (half of the 12 tracks are less than two minutes long, only two are in excess of three minutes), was released and failed to chart.

In July, Charles Manson appeared at Brian's studio to record his songs, with Brian and Carl producing. Dennis helped out. Various of Manson's girls made themselves available for whatever was asked of them. It was later estimated by the band's business manager at the time, Nick Grillo, that more than 100 hours of tapes were recorded with Manson. Not all were songs, though, and there were plenty of "sessions" during which Manson, Dennis, and the girls took LSD and taped their "happening."

The material was not good enough for anyone connected to Brother Records to want to release it (plus, Brian didn't like him). Neither did Terry Melcher want to produce or promote Manson to anyone, despite Dennis introducing the pair with that intention. Melcher's rejection of Manson would later have terrible consequences.

One Manson song though, "Cease to Exist," was rewritten by Dennis and given a less bluesy melody and the alternate title of "Never Learn Not to Love." It was released as a B-side to the flop single "Bluebirds over the Mountain" in December 1968. Recorded in September, "Never Learn" was credited solely to Dennis, and when Manson discovered his lack of credit he reportedly attacked Dennis in his home, stole or ruined all of his clothes, and wrecked the house.

After the attack, Dennis ordered the Family to move out, and also left. When the Family departed they took one of Dennis's cars with them to Spahn's Movie Ranch

Above: Charles Manson, convicted thief and murderer, in 1968, a potential artist for the Beach Boys' Brother Records label.
Opposite: Film director Roman Polanski sits outside the front door of 10050 Cielo Drive, Hollywood where his wife Sharon Tate, their unborn child, and four others were murdered.

in Topanga Canyon, without asking his permission.

From there they moved to a couple of ranches in Death Valley, and at one (Barker's) Manson "paid" the owner for their rent with a Beach Boys gold record award given to him, or stolen from, Dennis. After writing an album's worth of material, Manson reached out to Melcher to come and hear his new concept album. The concept, based on the Beatles' "Helter Skelter" track (from *The Beatles*) predicted a worldwide war between blacks and whites in which only Manson and his family would survive. Melcher accepted the invitation to hear the demos and have dinner at the Family residence, but failed to show up.

Manson went looking for Melcher at the last address he had for him: 10050 Cielo Drive. Melcher wasn't there, but the occupants, including pregnant actor Sharon Tate, were spooked enough to let Melcher know. The producer agreed again to visit Manson at Spahn's and listen to his songs, which he did in May 1969. Soon after, Manson decided that Helter Skelter was coming and that he and the Family had to strike first. In July they killed two drug dealers, and on August 8, he sent Family members to 10050 Cielo Drive with instructions to kill everyone there. Among the six victims was the unborn child of Tate and film director Roman Polanski, who was in Europe. The following night the Family killed Leno and Rosemary LaBianca.

Manson was arrested in connection with one of the drug dealer deaths in October 1969, but it wasn't until December that he and other Family members were officially charged with all of their crimes.

FRIENDS

CAPITOL, JUNE 1968

Producer	The Beach Boys
Engineer	Jimmy Lockert
Recorded	2/29/68–4/13/68, Brian Wilson's home, Hollywood
U.S. Chart	#126 *Billboard*
Singles	"Friends"

Side 1

1. MEANT FOR YOU
B. Wilson/M. Love

2. FRIENDS
B. Wilson/C. Wilson/D. Wilson/A. Jardine

3. WAKE THE WORLD
B. Wilson/A. Jardine

4. BE HERE IN THE MORNIN'
B. Wilson/C. Wilson/D. Wilson/M. Love/A. Jardine

5. WHEN A MAN NEEDS A WOMAN
B. Wilson/D. Wilson/A. Jardine/S. Korthof/J. Parks

6. PASSING BY
B. Wilson

Side 2

1. ANNA LEE, THE HEALER
B. Wilson/M. Love

2. LITTLE BIRD
D. Wilson/S. Kalinich

3. BE STILL
D. Wilson/S. Kalinich

4. BUSY DOIN' NOTHIN'
B. Wilson

5. DIAMOND HEAD
A. Verasco/L. Ritz/J. Ackley/B. Wilson

6. TRANSCENDENTAL MEDITATION
B. Wilson/M. Love/A. Jardine

The year of 1968 was confusing for everyone in America, but must have seemed particularly baffling to Brian. His brothers and cousin had wholly embraced a guru (the Maharishi) so that his band could be the standard bearers for bringing Transcendental Meditiation to America. Yet the world needed love, according to the Beatles, whose "soundtrack" album *Magical Mystery Tour* topped the charts for the first two months of the year. Meanwhile The Monkees had lost their appeal, and Simon and Garfunkel had taken over as the preeminent music makers of America. Theirs was a stripped-down, sweet, two-part harmony with acoustic guitars and songs that had a personal-political as well as a purely political edge. With students protesting against Vietnam, for legalization of drugs, and for peace not war, the "message" was becoming a central element of pop music (the Boys had just toured with Buffalo Springfield). The problem for the Beach Boys was that America wasn't interested in a guru already denounced by the Beatles, and the only messages to be found on this record concerned loving babies ("When a Man Needs a Woman"; Brian's daughter Carnie was about to be born), welcoming the new day ("Wake the World"), or driving to Brian's place ("Busy Doin' Nothin'"). While the psychedelic cover (art by David McMacken) was perfectly contemporary, at least, the Boys' music wasn't. Oddly, the soul music–influenced promise shown on *Wild Honey* is missing here. It's almost as if, having lost their identity as a truly original musical outfit with the collapse of *Smile*, they'd run out of other musical styles to try. Sadly, it seems, their TM experiences hadn't offered much inspiration, either. The album leaves the listener wondering, where to next?

I CAN HEAR MUSIC

CAPITOL, APRIL 1969

B-side	"All I Want To Do"
Writers	J. Barry/E. Greenwich/P. Spector
	D. Wilson/S. Kalnich
Producers	C. Wilson; D. Wilson
Recorded	10/1/68; 11/21/68
U.S. Chart	#24 Billboard

There's a terrible irony in the fact that the Beach Boys' cover of a Ronettes original record should be a hit on pop charts around the world, and yet Brian Wilson have nothing to do with it. But that was the case with the last song that Mrs. Ronnie Spector and her girl group released, in 1966. As with everything that Phil Spector was turning out at the time, the Ronettes's version of Jeff Barry, Ellie Greenwich, and Spector's great pop song failed to make any impression on a chart that had changed enormously from those that he had topped for so long. Spector famously gave up producing pop songs after the failure of the world to appreciate the masterful creation that was Ike & Tina Turner's "River Deep-Mountain High" in 1966, which was roughly around the same time that Brian gave up trying to make anything that wasn't as good as Spector's "Be My Baby." In truth this isn't as good as the original, even though it was a bigger hit. Carl both produced and sang lead vocals on the A-side, and at least its success gave him confidence to continue producing records for the Beach Boys, since Brian wasn't. The B-side is co-written, produced, and sung by the other Wilson brother. Dennis's number is a fat rock-and-roll riffed, driving number over which he strains his larynx with feeling.

By then the L.A. artistic and movie-making communities had begun to realize the precariousness of their lifestyles and the hippie ideal was beginning to lose some of its appeal. For some time, runaway kids in San Francisco had been declared a public menace. Biker gangs that had been supposedly subsumed into the love and peace movement were proving incapable of curbing the violent tendencies of their members: crowd violence at a free Rolling Stones gig in Hyde Park in July (to partly commemorate the death of founder member Brian Jones) had begun with the Hells Angels, who were acting as "security." Later in 1969, the same band would compound their misguided and foolish trust in the Angels by employing Sonny Barger's Angels as "security" at a free gig held at Altamont Speedway circuit in northern California, on December 6. Film cameras captured the attack and fatal knifing of an audience member waving a gun, by various Angels. As the Stones, unaware of the stabbing, attempted to continue to perform, Meredith Hunter died of his wounds.

As the great hippie ideal began to wither, it seemed that the Beach Boys' career was doing likewise. Following the failure of 20/20 to sell (although it was a hit in the United Kingdom) they had a taste of single success with

Above: The Whiskey a Go Go, Sunset Strip, November 1970. L-R: Al Jardine, his wife Lynda Sperry, Diane Rovell, unknown, Brian Wilson and Marilyn Wilson.

their cover of the Ronettes's 1966 single "I Can Hear Music." Their career seemed so moribund that when Murry approached his eldest son, offering to help write a song, Brian accepted with alacrity.

The result was "Break Away," inspired in part by watching *The Joey Bishop Show* together on TV, partly by the Monkees, but mostly by Murry's overreaching ambition to write a great song with Brian. Oddly though,

he chose to be credited as Reggie Dunbar on the label. Asked why, Brian could only reply, "He was nutty."

Fittingly, the single was to be the final release of any new Beach Boys record through Capitol Records, with the contract between the two parties having reached an end. It was also to be the last recording solely credited to Brian as a producer for more than four years.

Distressingly for Brian, Sea of Tunes ceased to be a wholly Wilson-owned company when Murry sold the family's publishing business (supposedly for $700,000) to the publishing division of Herb Alpert and Jerry Moss's A&M Records (founded in 1962).

The photo used on the cover of *20/20*.

20/20

CAPITOL, FEBRUARY 1969

Producer	The Beach Boys
Engineer	Steve Desper
Recorded	9/29/67, 6/68–11/68, United Western Recorders, Brian Wilson's home, Hollywood
U.S. Chart	#68 *Billboard*
Singles	"Do It Again," "Bluebirds over the Mountain," "I Can Hear Music"

Side 1

1. DO IT AGAIN
B. Wilson/M. Love

2. I CAN HEAR MUSIC
J. Barry/E. Greenwich/P. Spector

3. BLUEBIRDS OVER THE MOUNTAIN
E. Hickey

4. BE WITH ME
D. Wilson

5. ALL I WANT TO DO
D. Wilson/S. Kalinich

6. THE NEAREST FARAWAY PLACE
B. Johnston

Side 2

1. COTTON FIELDS (THE COTTON SONG)
H. Ledbetter

2. I WENT TO SLEEP
B. Wilson/C. Wilson

3. TIME TO GET ALONE
B. Wilson

4. NEVER LEARN NOT TO LOVE
D. Wilson

5. OUR PRAYER
B. Wilson

6. CABINESSENCE
B. Wilson/V. D. Parks

After the abject failure of the all-new *Friends*, and in order to fulfill the final contractual obligation to Capitol Records (with whom the band and their management were in legal dispute over royalties), the Beach Boys looked backward to go forward. Pretty much without Brian's involvement, Carl and the band searched out various tapes of material recorded by their erstwhile leader—who was suffering a particularly debilitating episode of mental ill health in the late summer of 1968—and worked many of them into song shape. So this album ends with what sounds very much like a track that should and could have been included on *Pet Sounds* ("Cabinessence"). It had been mostly constructed in the fall of 1966. The first track, though, was new and had been written and recorded in the summer of 1968, in between sessions with Charles Manson at Brian's house (track 4, side 2 is based on one of Manson's compositions). Originated by Mike after a day's swimming, and titled "Rendezvous" to start with, it reaches back to the Boys' surfing heyday in sound and style—and it made #20 on the U.S. singles charts when released in July 1968, the highest position they'd manage for the next six years, as it turned out. The follow-up single ("Bluebirds Over the Mountain," a cover of rockabilly artist Ersel Hickey's 1958 song) flopped, but "I Can Hear Music," the Ronettes' cover, made it to #24. When *20/20* is most successful the band sounds like the Beach Boys and not anyone else. The old-time numbers (especially Lead Belly's "Cottonfields") are suited to the multipart harmonies and mostly up-tempo beats. Although the cover is missing Brian—he's on the inner gatefold—the music is filled with his presence, and successfully so.

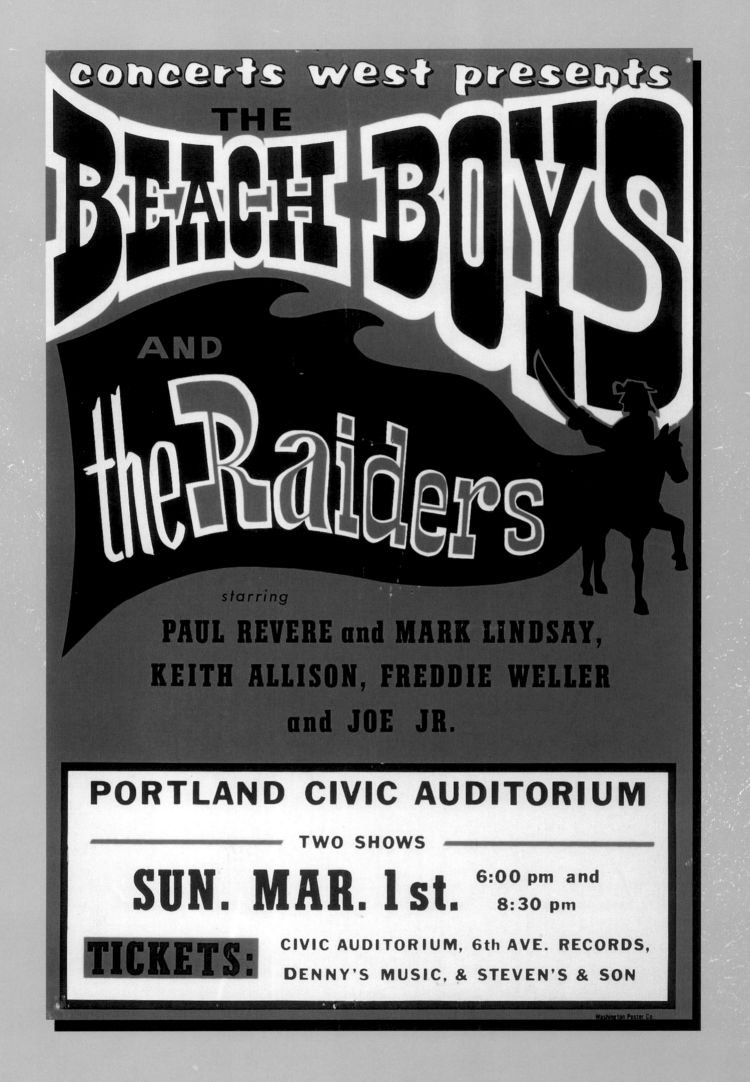

Left: Poster for a performance in 1970 for which Mike was missing, because he was recovering from stress-related illness.

Murry thought he'd made a great deal but had shown a complete lack of faith in his son's ability to write successful, popular new music. He also obviously saw no future value in the Boys' catalogue.

In April 1969, the Beach Boys issued proceedings against Capitol to reclaim $2 million of supposed unpaid royalties (it was later settled) and at the same time announced several investment projects that they owned, including a real estate syndicate and cardiovascular clinic in Florida (and Brian's Radiant Radish health-food store in Hollywood). They also planned to build a state-of-the-art 16-track studio in a building they'd bought in L.A., plus sign new acts to their Brother Records label. In May, however, Brian called a press conference and told the world that his band was bankrupt, just as they were beginning a tour of Europe, and that the band's future depended upon the tour going well. From France, Bruce issued a statement that read in part, "While we all admire Brian immensely for what he does for the group, it's a fact that creative people are funny and don't know much about business." The Radiant Radish lasted until summer 1970.

In June, the Beach Boys became the first Western pop music act to perform in the Eastern bloc when they played three gigs in Czechoslovakia (less than a year after the Russians had crushed an anti-Soviet protest movement). It was the highlight of a very successful European tour, but at the end of which the band returned to America and life with no recording contract. They had begun and continued to record a new album, however, at Brian's house and Gold Star Studio. Despite the new recordings, between July and mid-October the Boys and their managers Nick Grillo and Fred Vail were rejected by a raft of record companies. They had a reputation for being unreliable, with too many egos in the band, and they'd not had enough sales in the past two years for anyone to take a chance that they'd ever be as successful as they once had been.

However, in October, the band announced a deal with the Reprise arm of Warner Brothers Records that would pay them a $250,000 advance per album and release them under the Brother imprint. Van Dyke Parks, then head of audio visual services at Warner Bros., told journalist Scot Keller that he was responsible for getting the company's boss, Mo Ostin, to sign the Beach Boys: "I personally begged him to sign them." In the wake of Murry's sale of Sea of Tunes and the fallout from the Manson Family murders (Dennis was asked to testify and refused), signing the deal was the best news the band would get all year.

The new year (1970) didn't get off to a flying start, though. Brian was called into live action with the band for the first time in several months when Mike was hospitalized. Having fasted too hard and meditated for too long, he'd suffered a physical and psychological collapse. Brian enjoyed the shows, calling the experience "the best three days of my life, I guess," in an interview. He wasn't getting out of his house much prior to those dates in Canada, Oregon, and Washington state.

The first Reprise-release single, "Add Some Music To Your Day," only reached #64 on the U.S. charts in April. Later the same month Capitol released "Cotton Fields" b/w "The Nearest Faraway Place," and it became the first Beach Boys single to not chart at all. The band was in New Zealand at the time.

In May 1970, the Boys handed what they thought was their debut long player to Reprise, only to have it rejected. It carried the working title *Add Some Music to Your Day*, which was one reason for the rejection, since the single had flopped. The release and failure of "Slip on Through" b/w "This Whole World" as a single intended to promote the new album didn't help. So the

band returned to recording new material. At the end
of July, Canadian Terry Jacks attempted to produce the
recording of "Seasons in the Sun" (lead vocal by Carl)
in Brian's studio, but with no success. Jacks would go
on to have a huge hit with his version of the song in
1974, though.

In August, Dennis began filming a lead role in an
independent movie titled *Two-Lane Blacktop*, co-starring
James Taylor, Laurie Bird, and Warren Oates, and directed by Monte Hellman, a graduate of Roger Corman's
rapid-production studio. Dennis had few lines but
looked great, as does the movie, which became a cult
classic after it flunked at the box office. Much the same
could be said of the first Reprise-release Beach Boys
album. Finally titled *Sunflower* and released at the end
of summer, it didn't sell, but *Rolling Stone*—ever since
the Monterey no-show among the harshest critics of the
Boys—gave it a very good review, calling it "finally an
album that can stand with *Pet Sounds*."

In November, Brian attended Beach Boys gigs at
L.A.'s Whiskey a Go Go. They sold out four nights, with
people eager to see Brian on stage in the city for the
first time since 1966. Not all the reviews were stellar,
but there were mentions of the older surf songs revving
up the crowd.

That was something that the Boys would hear more
of on the European tour that closed out the year. It was
something they would increasingly hear. People liked
those oldies but goodies.

**Right: Carl Wilson (seated) in control of the mixing
desk, in London, with a BBC engineer, 1970.**

SUNFLOWER

BROTHER/REPRISE, AUGUST 1970

Producer	The Beach Boys
Engineer	Stephen Desper
Recorded	7/9,14/69, 10/6–11/18/69, 1/2–2/2/70, 7/7–21/7/70 Gold Star Studio, Brian Wilson's home, Hollywood
U.S. Chart	#151 *Billboard*
Singles	"Add Some Music to Your Day," "Slip on Through," "Tears in the Morning," "Forever"

Side 1

1. SLIP ON THROUGH
D. Wilson

2. THIS WHOLE WORLD
B. Wilson

3. ADD SOME MUSIC TO YOUR DAY
B. Wilson/J. Knott/M. Love

4. GOT TO KNOW THE WOMAN
D. Wilson

5. DEIRDRE
B. Johnston/B. Wilson

6. IT'S ABOUT TIME
D. Wilson/B. Burchman/A. Jardine

Side 2

1. TEARS IN THE MORNING
B. Johnston

2. ALL I WANNA DO
B. Wilson/M. Love

3. FOREVER
D. Wilson/G. Jakobson

4. OUR SWEET LOVE
B. Wilson/C. Wilson/A. Jardine

5. AT MY WINDOW
B. Wilson/A. Jardine

6. COOL, COOL WATER
B. Wilson/M. Love

"*Sunflower* is the truest group experience we've ever had," Carl Wilson claimed in a British music paper interview following its release. Brian, talking to *Rolling Stone*, said, "Overall the record is good but it doesn't please me as much as I wish…given some good airplay, the record should do very well." As we know, it didn't do well at all. The first long player release on a new label (part of Warner Bros.), the record had a complicated gestation period, and after being delivered in one form with a different title (*Add Some Music to Your Day*) it was rejected as not good enough. The label boss who signed them, Mo Ostin, demanded better, and actually, although the public disagreed, the first Reprise-era Beach Boys LP is pretty good. It's not as well constructed as *Pet Sounds* nor as coherent in style as *Wild Honey*, but the mixture of styles, perfect harmonies, and crystal-clear sound add to a collection of solid songs. As usual there are a lot of influences on show, from Leon Russell–style piano rolls and swooping, cooing female backing singers (on Dennis's "Got to Know the Woman") to Bruce's Bacharach-like "Deirdre" and the "heaviest" sound they'd made so far on "It's About Time" with Carl singing lead (and a very Temptations-light middle break; think "I'm Losing You"). Bruce Johnston's "Tears in the Morning" deserved to be a hit; with its background accordion and strings it bears comparison with "Where Do You Go to My Lovely," a smash hit in 1969 by Peter Sarstedt. Brian appears on the cover, in a photograph taken by Ricci Martin showing how all the Boys were now fathers. At some point in 1969, Brian had seriously suggested they rename the band simply the Beach, because they'd grown up. No one agreed with him on that, but they had grown up; here's the proof.

A *Sunflower*-era photoshoot without Brian.

6

ENDLESS SUMMER

1971·1980

SURF'S UP

BROTHER/REPRISE, AUGUST 1971

Producer The Beach Boyst
Engineer Stephen Desper
Recorded 11–12/66, 1//70, 3–7/71 Sunset Sound Recorders, Columbia Studio, Brian Wilson's home, Hollywood
U.S. Chart #29 *Billboard*
Singles "Long Promised Road," "Surf's Up"

Side 1

1. DON'T GO NEAR THE WATER
M. Love/A. Jardine

2. LONG PROMISED ROAD
C. Wilson/J. Rieley

3. TAKE A LOAD OFF YOUR FEET
A. Jardine/B. Wilson/G. Winfrey

4. DISNEY GIRLS (1957)
B. Johnston

5. STUDENT DEMONSTRATION TIME
J. Leiber/M. Stoller/M. Love

Side 2

1. FEEL FLOWS
C. Wilson/J. Rieley

2. LOOKIN' AT TOMOROW (A WELFARE SONG)
A. Jardine/G. Winfrey

3. A DAY IN THE LIFE OF A TREE
B. Wilson/J. Rieley

4. TIL I DIE
B. Wilson

5. SURF'S UP
B. Wilson/V. D. Parks

Having impressed Brian Wilson after interviewing him for local radio, DJ Jack Rieley quickly sought to impress Carl Wilson, too, and did so by writing a mission statement (not that it was called that in 1970) in which he pointed out what was needed to get the Beach Boys back at the forefront of American popular music. Simply put, they had to write songs like the successful acts of the day, not the acts of a decade earlier, as Brian was still inclined to do. Rieley suggested that Carl take over from Brian as musical director and that the band produce the new album themselves. In order to emphasize their move away from the surf culture that was pushing them in to the nostalgia market, they'd call it *Landlocked*. Rieley and Carl wrote a couple of songs that took inspiration from Robert Frost ("Long Promised Road") and Dylanesque alliterative wordplay ("Feel Flows"), while Mike and Al took the issues of the day—the death of Mother Earth, civil unrest, establishment fascism—and made like rioting was that year's surfing ("Student Demonstration Time," "Don't Go Near the Water"). Even Bruce was allowed in on the songwriting and contributed the rather lovely ballad "Disney Girls (1957)," in the style of Bobby Goldsboro's "Honey." To top it all off, Rieley got Brian to co-write a pro-conservation song ("A Day in the Life of a Tree") with him, and to contribute what Brian called "the most personal song I ever wrote for the Beach Boys," titled "Til I Die." While it has a gorgeous tune, its lyrics are inane nonsense but, nonetheless, they're now regarded as being "artful." Finally, and as proof of Rieley's supreme influence on him, Brian allowed him to search out "Surf's Up" from the morass of *Smile* tapes and make that the title track. It made it the best Beach Boys album in five years.

Band decisions were made about everything from set lists to real estate purchases in the democratic fashion. For a long time Mike, Al, and Bruce held sway over Carl, with Brian often absent for meetings due to ill health, and Dennis missing because that's what he was wont to do. As Rieley tells it, he straightened them out and rebalanced the power in the voting system, holding sway against Mike and Al's desire to keep the surf and hot-rod nostalgia act going and helping Carl, Brian, and Dennis to become a fully functioning rock act, writing and playing new material on record and on stage.

Early in 1971, the Beach Boys began recording new songs for inclusion on an abum with the working title *Landlocked*. Taking Rieley's advice, Mike and Al had written a couple of numbers for the album that were designed to appeal to a generation of kids for whom protesting was what surfing had been a decade earlier. "Student Demonstration Time" by Mike took the tune and intention of Lieber and Stoller's song for Elvis's *Jailhouse Rock* (1957), "Riot in Cell Block #9." A kind of "Rioting USA" ("if everybody had a campus, across the USA"), the song names Berkeley, Isla Vista, Jackson State prison, and the May 4, 1970, killing of four students by the National Guard at Ohio State University. It was a long way from Neil Young's "Ohio," though.

"Don't Go Near the Water" by both Al and Mike exploited the newly emerging environmental movement, playing on worries about the pollution of the sea. Rieley and Brian co-wrote "A Day in the Life of a Tree," inspired by their fears at how the planet was dying. It uses a single tree to represent the whole world. The finished song is sung by Rieley, who in the 1996 correspondence on the fan forum claimed he was tricked into doing it by Brian asking him to sing a "guide" vocal, which became the finished article. But in 1974, Rieley had told *Rolling Stone* that he was the last person to record the vocals after everyone else had tried and failed, before Brian asked him to sing it. It was, Rieley said, "the last thing I

expected I'd have to do," but he did it, and then "Brian went on and on about how much he loved it. It was perfect and just what he wanted all along." Rieley was delivering a lot of what Brian wanted at the time.

In what must have seemed an odd move, the Beach Boys were booked into New York's Carnegie Hall in February 1971, where they tried out their first two-hour-long set. The sellout crowd gave them a rapturous reception. Then, at the end of April they made a surprise appearance in the middle of a Grateful Dead gig at the Fillmore East in New York. At first the Dead and the Boys jammed together, then the Boys were given the stage to themselves (to play "Good Vibrations" and "I Get Around") before the Dead returned to the stage and jammed with them some more.

While the Carnegie Hall concert went down well, the Dead gig had a mixed response from the crowd—but it did put them in the same orbit as the Dead, and that was all that mattered to Rieley, who believed the Boys belonged among the rock hierarchy. All they needed to do now was release an album that won critical acclaim.

Smartly, Brian was persuaded to allow Rieley and Carl to extract enough of the song "Surf's Up" from the numerous *Smile* tapes that he'd hidden at home and include it on *Landlocked*, which was then retitled *Surf's Up* and released at the end of August 1971. The use of the already almost legendary "lost" song was enough to guarantee critics would review the LP favorably—in part, at least. *Time* magazine liked the record, calling it "one of the most imaginatively produced LPs since last fall's *All Things Must Pass* by George Harrison and Phil Spector." Brian must have loved that.

Other reviews were mostly positive. Many of the writers applauded the "return" of Brian to the Beach Boys fold, especially as a creative force. In actuality however, Brian had little to do with the recording of the album (and he would later describe his own vocal on the title track as being "a piece of shit"). Bruce Johnston

took to publicly stating as much. He then compounded what was considered by some as a mistake in talking about such things by damning Rieley for making the album a "hyped-up lie." *Surf's Up* sold better than their previous three releases had, though, eventually reaching #29 on the *Billboard* album chart.

In September 1971, the Beach Boys, with Ricky Fataar playing drums and Dennis playing keyboards and singing, performed at the Carnegie Hall (two shows) as part of a tour that would run until the end of the year. The tour showed how clearly splits had developed within the band, with Carl, Ricky, and Dennis on the bus while Mike and Al traveled separately, often cruising a TM plane as their earthly vehicle ate up the miles between gigs. In December, Nick Grillo was fired and Jack Rieley became the sole administrative player and overseer of the Beach Boys' career direction.

With Carl's endorsement, Ricky Fataar and Blondie

Opposite: Dennis in Amsterdam, 1972.

Left: Mike Love on stage in Hilversum,

Netherlands, November 1972.

The cost of the operation—the building and breaking down of the "new" studio, the logistics of flying it all to Holland and then reassembling it—was enormous and time-consuming. Moffit was given until June 1, 1972, to make it all work.

Meanwhile the band recorded a new album at Brian's home studio, Village Recorders, and Sunset Sound (with Moffitt engineering). *Carl and the Passions: So Tough* included two songs written by Fataar and Chaplin, and only three co-written by Brian Wilson. The album has no songs with a Brian Wilson lead vocal, nor does it include any songs written or performed by Bruce Johnston. Released in May 1972, it made #50 on the album chart.

In April 1972, Bruce Johnston left the Beach Boys. The official line on the matter was that the split was mutual. Speaking to the *NME* not long after, Bruce said that he left because there was an "uncomfortable feeling around in the band." He went on to say that he was surprised every member of the Boys hadn't quit, and that it was clear to him that Brian "was not coming back to the band." After leaving the meeting at which he quit, Bruce said, he went home and wrote a song. It was called "I Write the Songs," and three years later it became one of the biggest hit singles of the year for Barry Manilow (becoming his signature tune in the process).

When Bruce went home to his Hollywood house, the Beach Boys (minus Brian, for the time being) packed their families into airplanes and moved to the Netherlands, where they'd greatly enjoyed previous tours. By the time *Carl and the Passions* was released, the Beach Boys were on a month-long European tour. While they toured, Jack Rieley plotted and planned to get Brian out of his house and onto an intercontinental flight.

Chaplin became a part of the Beach Boys for both touring and recording. They didn't get to do either with the band until March 1972, though, due to the Boys taking time out, which was spent in Holland. They found the experience so relaxing that, with Rieley's encouragement, they decided to record their next album in the Dutch capital.

Unfortunately, they couldn't book studio time because there were no studios available that could meet their needs. The solution to their problem was to ask one of the engineers who ran their Santa Monica recording complex, Stephen Moffitt, to first build and then transplant a mixing console and studio to Holland for them.

The ad campaign for *Carl & The Passions* used the band's name as large as possible in contrast to the LP sleeve.

CARL & THE PASSIONS—SO TOUGH

BROTHER/REPRISE, MAY 1972

Producers	B. Wilson, D. Wilson, C. Wilson, M. Love, A. Jardine, R. Fataar, B. Chaplin
Engineer	Stephen Moffitt
Recorded	12/4/71–4/13/72, Brian Wilson's home, Hollywood
U.S. Chart	#50 *Billboard*
Singles	"You Need a Mess of Help to Stand Alone," "Marcella"

Side 1

1. YOU NEED A MESS OF HELP TO STAND ALONE
B. Wilson/J. Rieley

2. HERE SHE COMES
R. Fataar/B. Chaplin

3. HE COME DOWN
A. Jardine/B. Wilson/M. Love

4. MARCELLA
B. Wilson/T. Almer/J. Rieley

Side 2

1. HOLD ON DEAR BROTHER
R. Fataar/B. Chaplin

2. MAKE IT GOOD
D. Wilson/D. Dragon

3. ALL THIS IS THAT
A. Jardine/C. Wilson/M. Love

4. CUDDLE UP
D. Wilson/D. Dragon

Carl and the Passions was, of course, the name that Brian gave the teenage band that he asked Carl to join, renaming it in his youngest brother's honor. As the production credits on the sleeve note, while all band members—including the two recent recruits, South Africans Ricky Fataar (drums) and Blondie Chaplin (guitar)—produced the record, credit goes to "especially Carl." Since Brian's withdrawal from the recording studio, it had been Carl who took control of the faders in the studio. It was he who brought in the ex-members of the Flame—the first (and only) band to sign to Brother Records other than the Beach Boys—to the band. Carl produced *The Flame* album in 1971, and it sounds curiously old-fashioned, whereas this record sounds much more contemporary. While the Flame were notable for being a good late-Beatles pastiche, there are only the occasional sounds of the former Fab Four to be heard here (a guitar solo on "Marcella" could be by George Harrison, although it's Chaplin, for instance). The album is generally unlike any other Beach Boys release, and it contains more contemporary rock music influences than old; "Hold On Dear Brother," with its pedal steel, ponderous drums, and langorous vocals could be an outtake from recent releases by the Band. Lead vocalist Blondie Chaplin has a more country-tinged sound than anyone else in the Beach Boys, although on his and Fataar's "Here She Comes" he sounds more as if he's been listening to Steely Dan. Sadly, the non-secular theme of "He Come Down" isn't an ironic take on Brian's infrequent descent from his bedroom to the studio below, but a T.M. gospel number. The standout and only truly unique tracks are by Dennis, though—"Make It Good" is a minimalist ballad on which his cracked and creaking voice conveys real emotion. "Cuddle Up" is a haunting ballad that sounds like a desperate cry for a parent or sibling's love. Only Harry Nilsson was making such affecting music at the time.

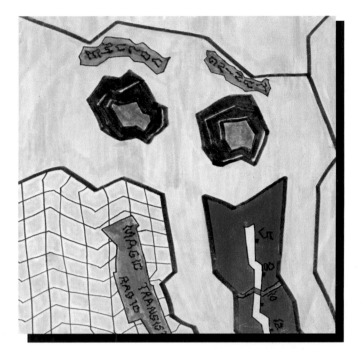

Above: The sleeve for *Mount Vernon and Fairway*, the seven-inch single given away with early copies of *Holland*.
Opposite: Poster for a gig six months after Ricky Fataar (fourth left) and Blondie Chaplin (second right) had joined.

In the early years of the 1970s Brian Wilson suffered from mental illness that was exacerbated by an increasing intake of drugs. The use of opiates masked the symptoms of his illness and offered his family and colleagues reasons to explain his odd behavior, such as the one Rieley recalled (in 1996): he was called to Brian's house by a distraught Marilyn, and found her husband digging a grave in their garden. Brian glowered at Rieley after complaining that Marilyn wouldn't cover him with the earth when he got into the hole. Then he broke into gales of laughter. Rieley didn't know if it was an elaborate prank or "serious."

Getting Brian out of L.A. and away from bad influences became imperative. Even Dennis, who often sided with his brother in arguments with the band, agreed. It was suggested that a "holiday" would do a great deal of good. Rieley had to book two flights for Brian to Europe before he made it, but when he did he spent the first weeks not leaving his rented house. Over the seven-month stay, though, Brian began to get out, even occasionally cycling to the studio in a converted barn on a farm just outside Amsterdam. The majority of *Holland* was made with minimal input from Brian. The nighttime sessions that he did undertake (alone) resulted in the spoken-word *Mount Vernon and Fairway (a Fairytale)*, narrated by Jack Rieley and included on a separate seven-inch disc given away with the album.

The Dutch studio was wound up, boxed, and shipped back to L.A. in September 1972. *Holland* was mixed and finished in California and released in January 1973, although it was initially delayed by Reprise requesting an extra song that could be released as a single.

Fortuitously, Van Dyke Parks visited with Brian in the fall and reminded him of another song they'd begun for *Smile*, titled "Sail On, Sailor." It was reworked, recorded, and added to the track listing (co-credited to three additional people, among them Rieley). Its release as a single in February 1973 did little to help sales of the album

(only making #79 on the singles chart), but *Holland* sold better than *Carl and the Passions* had, making #36 on the U.S. LP chart. Its release marked the end of Rieley's involvement with the band. He wanted to stay in Holland and did so, making a couple of visits to L.A. on Beach Boys business for a while, though, because the band asked him to remain in his administrative position until they could find a replacement.

During an American tour in April, Brian appeared on stage at the first big L.A. gig (at the Palladium). He didn't perform, but walked on stage a few times at what was described by reviewers as a triumphant return to California. Tellingly, with no Jack Rieley around to say otherwise, the band played old Beach Boys songs mid-set and for the encore; they'd not done so for over two years.

In June 1973, Murry Wilson died from a heart attack. He'd suffered an earlier arrest and was at home, recuperating and being looked after by Audree, when it happened. Immediately after it Brian flew to New York and Dennis to Europe. Neither attended the funeral. On his return to Los Angeles, Brian went into his bedroom and stayed there. Mourning his father's death, suffering mental illness, and consuming vast quantities of cocaine, cannabis, and prescription drugs, Brian added food to his ever-growing list of addictions.

XAVIER UNIVERSITY
PRESENTS
in concert
THE BEACH BOYS

they've changed even more than you

NOVEMBER 10, 1972 8:30 P.M.
AT
XAVIER UNIVERSITY FIELDHOUSE

TICKETS AVAILABLE AT:

$4.50 ADVANCE
$5.00 AT DOOR

XAVIER U.
U. OF CINCINNATI
ALL TICKETRON OUTLETS
NEW YORK TIMES
SIGHT & SOUND
GLOBE RECORDS
THE UNIVERSITY SHOP

you vote - we win in '72
AN AMERICAN CONCERTS PRODUCTION

HOLLAND

BROTHER/REPRISE, JANUARY 1973

Producer	The Beach Boys
Engineers	Stephen Moffitt, Rob Fabroni
Recorded	6/3–9/4/72, Baambrugge, Netherlands 9/15–10/4/72, Village Recorders Studio, Hollywood
U.S. Chart	#36 *Billboard*
Singles	"Sail On, Sailor," "California Saga/California"

Side 1

1. SAIL ON, SAILOR

B. Wilson/V. D. Parks/T. Aylmer/R. Kennedy/J. Rieley

2. STEAMBOAT

D. Wilson/J. Rieley

3. CALIFORNIA SAGA/BIG SUR

M. Love

4. CALIFORNIA SAGA/THE BEAKS OF EAGLES

R. Jeffers/A. Jardine/L. Jardine

5. CALIFORNIA SAGA/CALIFORNIA

A. Jardine

Side 2

1. THE TRADER

C. Wilson/J. Rieley

2. LEAVING THIS TOWN

R. Fataar/B. Chaplin/C. Wilson/M. Love

3. ONLY WITH YOU

D. Wilson/M. Love

4. FUNKY PRETTY

D. Wilson/M. Love/J. Rieley

When Jack Rieley, the radio DJ recently installed by the band to take care of "career direction," suggested getting Brian away from L.A. and that the band record in a totally different environment, naturally Holland was their first choice of destination. In a move that was extravagant, even by 1970s too-rich rock stars standards, not only did the band move their families to another continent in order to make a new record, but they also transported a whole recording studio to do so. In the early 1970s, electronic recording equipment was enormously heavy, big, and complex to build and operate. The album deserves to stand as a monument not to the assorted musicians who wrote and played on it, but to Stephen Moffitt, the engineer who constructed (twice!) the studio that allowed them to produce what is largely a bunch of intriguing songs that at times sound as if they're by other groups, like the Band or Little Feat. "Sail On, Sailor," "The Trader," and "Funky Pretty" are the picks. There was also a fey extra EP that came in a seven-inch single format with the LP. It's the EP that later became of most interest, being a musical "fairy story" that Brian had planned on making the foundation of the whole album. Concept albums were all the rage in the early 1970s, of course, but Brian's *Mount Vernon and Fairway (A Fairy Story)* was semi-autobiographical, and the title refers to the intersection where the Love family lived. It's the story of how the magical power of music heard via a transistor radio can change a life, and was possibly inspired by the brilliant *The Point* (1971) by Nilsson. Jack Rieley narrates the story like a dad telling a bedtime story. *Rolling Stone* made *Holland* one of their albums of the year, even though Brian contributed very little to the record. "Sail On, Sailor" was added after the album was initially delivered, on the order of Reprise. It had begun in 1966, as a collaboration between Brian and Van Dyke Parks, but was added to by former Association singer Tandyn Almer, Jack Rieley, and Philadephia soul singer Ray Kennedy.

"I was taking some drugs and I experimented myself right out of action," Brian would later say. "I was hiding away from everyone and everything....Added to that I was very depressed with the Beach Boys. I couldn't talk to them and nobody in the band would relate to me."

That didn't mean that the Beach Boys ended, though. In October 1973, *The Beach Boys in Concert* was released. Recorded mostly in 1972 but with recent additions, the double album was the most successful record release they'd had in more than five years, outselling *Surf's Up*. Almost simultaneously, they chose to replace Rieley with Mike's brother, Stephen Love. He chose to take the job description of "manager," leaving the "career direction" to his brother—although he did contribute to Blondie Chaplin's depature, after a fight between the pair following a gig at New York's Madison Square Garden, in December 1973.

With Blondie gone and Stephen Love taking care of business, the Boys had a couple of vacancies in their setup. They filled both with the employment of James

Guercio, the original producer, manager, and sometime songwriter for Chicago. Intitially he agreed to play bass for them while on tour, but soon found himself advising on music-related aspects of the band's activities. Stephen Love knew all about accountancy, but nothing about the music industry. Guercio, in contrast, knew not only the music business but also Hollywood. He had recently produced and directed a major movie, *Electra Glide in Blue* (1973) starring Robert Blake, for United Artists. Although it had been panned by critics and flopped at the box office (like *Two-Lane Blacktop*), it would become something of a cult classic in the late 1970s.

A busy man, Guercio had built and ran Caribou Ranch recording studios in Colorado (Elton John's *Caribou* was recorded there in 1974), so he was employed by the Beach Boys in a strictly part-time capacity.

Guercio didn't have much to do for the first couple of years of his part-time employment, except keep after Carl to get the Beach Boys writing and recording a new album. Not that they needed to, especially.

The world wasn't particularly hankering after *new* Beach Boys material, and hadn't been since mid-1974, when Capitol revived the Beach Boys name and brand around the world by releasing a double-album "best of" compilation titled *Endless Summer*. Later, Mike Love would claim that he came up with the idea for the title, but it's just as likely that someone at Capitol realized the potential of using the same title that had been given to an award-winning and hugely successful documentary film about surfers made by Bruce Brown in 1966.

All of the tracks on the album date from between 1962 and 1965, and the success of the release endorsed Mike and Al's belief that people who paid to see the Beach Boys in concert wanted to hear their pre-1967 material as much, if not more, than they do later stuff. *Endless Summer* became only the second Beach Boys LP to make #1 on the U.S. album charts (surprisingly, none of their studio releases ever made it to the #1 spot). From then on, the number of old songs increased in the Beach Boys live performance set list.

By the end of 1974, Ricky Fataar had left the band and Dennis was once again playing drums in concert. On December 21, the Boys broke the attendance record at the National Exhibition Hall in Sacramento. It had been set in 1964 by the Beatles. One reporter noted at the time that "Caroline, No," "The Trader," and "Funky Pretty" (the latter two from *Holland*) had been replaced in their set by "In My Room," "Warmth of the Sun," and "I Can Hear Music." Capitol's re-releases of the Boys' albums in two-for-one double-album packages in 1974, along with *Endless Summer*, had tapped them into a generation of kids who were enjoying a rock-and-roll revival.

Chuck Berry scored his first and only #1 pop hit with "My Ding-a-Ling" in 1972, not long after Elvis Presley had made #2 with "Burning Love." A new wave of rock-and-roll revival acts were touring America with some success, not least of which were Sha Na Na, who'd wowed the Woodstock crowd in 1969 with their version of Danny and the Juniors' "At the Hop." The box office success of *American Graffiti* in 1973 (it took in more than $55 million) pushed the soundtrack album to #10 on the *Billboard* Hot 200 chart. It included two Beach Boys songs—"All Summer Long" and "Surfin' Safari"—along with 39 other oldies but goodies from 1953–64.

In April 1975, Capitol released *Spirit of America*, another double-album compilation that included the few singles releases that they hadn't crammed onto *Endless Summer*. It included "Break Away" and "Please Let Me Wonder," neither of which were hits, but the release wasn't specifically designed as a hits compilation; rather, it was presenting the Beach Boys as the only truly all-American answer to the Beatles.

The album's cover-art illustration mixed Mickey Mouse with baseball, Mount Rushmore, the Golden Gate Bridge, Native Americans, and the *Apollo* moon-landing in a cartoon celebration of everything that was great about America.

Opposite: L-R: Bruce, Mike, Alan, Carl, and Dennis in Amsterdam, Netherlands, 1974.
Below: Ad for *Holland* in the music press.

The Beach Boys 'Holland' HOLLAND

their new one-and-a-half albums!

This album includes one 12 inch & one 7 inch 33⅓ rpm disc £2.59

ENDLESS SUMMER

CAPITOL, JUNE 1974

Producers	Brian Wilson/Murry Wilson/Nick Venet
Engineer	Chuck Britz
Recorded	4/62–6/65, Capitol Studio, Western Recorders, Gold Star Studio, Hollywood
U.S. Chart	#1 *Billboard*
Singles	N/A

Side 1
1. SURFIN' SAFARI
2. SURFER GIRL
3. CATCH A WAVE
4. THE WARMTH OF THE SUN
5. SURFIN' USA

Side 2
1. BE TRUE TO YOUR SCHOOL
2. LITTLE DEUCE COUPE
3. IN MY ROOM
4. SHUT DOWN
5. FUN, FUN, FUN

Side 3
1. I GET AROUND
2. GIRLS ON THE BEACH
3. WENDY
4. LET HIM RUN WILD
5. DON'T WORRY BABY

Side 4
1. CALIFORNIA GIRLS
2. GIRL DON'T TELL ME
3. HELP ME, RHONDA
4. YOU'RE SO GOOD TO ME
5. ALL SUMMER LONG

In 1973, the Beach Boys released a live album, imaginatively titled *The Beach Boys in Concert*. Of the 20 tracks it contained (recorded in the summers of 1972 and 1973), five came from the pre–*Pet Sounds* era. The success of the release, making #25 on the album chart, prompted Capitol to issue yet another "best of" compilation, their fifth. Clearly the Beach Boys were on the up again, and as long as they included old songs in their live set—even if they were mostly reserved for the encore—then Capitol figured that there'd be a new market for the old songs to be gathered together in one package. Someone in the Capitol marketing department was smart enough to not use an old photo of the band on the cover, and also smart enough to not use the words "collection," "greatest," or "best of" in the title, either. Mike Love claimed that *Endless Summer* was his

choice of title. It may well have been, and he had possibly been inspired by the seminal surfer documentary film of the same title that had been enormously popular and influential on its release in 1966. Whatever the inspiration, the package, a double album of pre-1966 Beach Boys hits wrapped in a startling, graphic gatefold sleeve (illustrated by Keith McConnell), proved to be enormously successful. It gave the band only their second-ever #1 hit album in America (the first had been the live album of 1964) and had an enormous impact on the touring Beach Boys' repetoire. By mid-1974, the number of pre–*Pet Sounds* songs in their live set was raised to seven or eight out of 21. By including other pre-1970s songs, their set quickly became a nostalgia fest for fans old and new. At the end of the decade their setlist would include only seven or eight songs that they'd recorded post-1971.

The success of the compilations helped to reposition the Beach Boys in the history of U.S. popular culture.

The Beach Boys spent most of 1975 touring, and during the latter part of the year shared a bill with Chicago. The Boys had Chicago's James Guercio playing bass on stage and overseeing the management of the tour for both acts. They'd often ended shows jamming together on the Rolling Stones' "Jumpin' Jack Flash."

While the Beach Boys toured, Brian stayed in bed, mostly, occasionally breaking out of the house to attempt a recording session at RCA Studios for Bruce Johnston and Terry Melcher's newly launched Equinox Records

ROCK & ROLL MUSIC

BROTHER/REPRISE, MAY 1976

B-side	"T. M. Song"
Writers	C. Berry; B. Wilson
Producer	B. Wilson
Recorded	3/16/76
U.S. Chart	#5 *Billboard*

Brian's version of this 1957 Chuck Berry song made it higher up the charts than Berry's while lacking any of the menace of the original. The Western pop music scene was at the tail end of what had been a commercially successful period of rock-and-roll revival when this was released. It's wholly in keeping with the erzatz scene, which was notable mostly for the exaggerated quiffs modeled by the biggest parody of self known to music that was Elvis in Vegas. It's different to the music being played by guitar bands who issued fast and rough versions of old rock-and-roll songs (Blue Cheer's and the Who's versions of "Summertime Blues" played a big part in starting the revival), with its schmaltzy organ, faux-fuzz guitar backing and near-sneered vocals by Mike. Brian's attempt at recapturing the excitement that he and Mike had felt on first hearing Chuck (or Little Richard, Elvis, or even Bill Haley) is more middle-of-the-road cabaret than rock and roll, but it is undoubtedly sincere. Taken from *15 Big Ones*, the first album that Brian had actively taken part in producing for a decade, its success was somewhat surprising. It gave the band their biggest hit since 1966, and proved to be an auspicious omen; in style and content it served perfectly as a primer for the soon-to-be enormously successful *Grease* (1978).

Right: James William Guercio, manager and producer for Chicago, owner of Caribou Records, playing bass for the Beach Boys, who he'd go on to manage part-time.

label. At one of those sessions (on March 10, 11, or 12), Brian met Elvis Presley, who was working in a studio next door. According to Elvis's pal Jerry Schilling's autobiography (*Me and a Guy Named Elvis*, 2007), Brian burst in on Elvis, who didn't know who the big-bellied, bearded man was, but on invitation went into Brian's studio to hear some songs. When Brian asked if Elvis thought they had something he replied, "No," and left. In Brian's questionably unreliable autobiography *Wouldn't It Be Nice: My Own Story* (1991), the meeting happened in 1969 (difficult to prove, as Elvis wasn't recording at RCA that year), and Brian attempted to karate chop and kick Elvis, who, understandably, didn't like it, and left.

In an attempt to help her family, toward the end of 1975, Marilyn Wilson introduced Brian to a man who would seek and gain more control over Brian than even Murry had enjoyed. Dr. Eugene Landy, a one-time radio producer, once manager of the 10-year-old George Benson, psychologist, Peace Corps volunteer, and drug counselor, had pioneered a 24-hour all-controlling "treatment" for a number of Hollywood celebrity addicts. He would later tell *Rolling Stone* magazine, "I've treated a tremendous number of people in show business; for some reason I seem to be able to relate to them."

Marilyn happily ceded control to Landy, who put a lock on the refrigerator, limited Brian's phone usage, ensured that he was attended by either himself or an assistant all day every day, banned certain "friends" from entering the Wilson home, and had Brian follow a strict physical routine designed to get him fit. Remarkably, it worked—at least well enough that by the beginning of 1976 Brian was back in the Brother recording studio with the Beach Boys, working on a new album, with a bunch of session muscians.

After some heated debate and a misunderstanding between Beach Boys, the album that Brian thought he was making—one filled with new recordings of other people's old songs—eventually merged into the one that Carl and Dennis wanted to make.

Top-bottom: Mike, Carl, Dennis, Al and Brian promoting the
'return' of Brian to the studio and the release of *15 Big Ones*.

15 BIG ONES

BROTHER/REPRISE, JULY 1976

Producer	Brian Wilson
Engineer	Stephen Moffitt, Earle Mankey
Recorded	1/30–5/15/76, Brother Studio, Western Recorders, Brian Wilson's home, Hollywood
U.S. Chart	#8 *Billboard*
Singles	"Rock and Roll Music," "It's O.K.," "Everyone's in Love with You"

Side 1

1. ROCK AND ROLL MUSIC
C. Berry

2. IT'S O.K.
B. Wilson/M. Love

3. HAD TO PHONE YA
B. Wilson/M. Love/D. Rovell

4. CHAPEL OF LOVE
J. Barry/E. Greenwichr/P. Spector

5. EVERYONE'S IN LOVE WITH YOU
M. Love

6. TALK TO ME (MEDLEY)
J. Seneca

7. THAT SAME SONG
B. Wilson/M. Love

8. T M SONG
B. Wilson

Side 2

1. PALISADES PARK
C. Barris

2. SUSIE CINCINNATI
A. Jardine

3. A CASUAL LOOK
E. Wells

4. BLUEBERRY HILL
A. Lewis/L. Stock/V. Rose

5. BACK HOME
B. Wilson/B. Norberg

6. IN THE STILL OF THE NIGHT
F. Parris

7. JUST ONCE IN MY LIFE
G. Goffin/C. King/P. Spector

"Brian's Back!" the promotional campaign for this album release declared. The first record to bear the sole production credit "Brian Wilson" in 10 years, at least a third of the tracks were co-written by him. But the slogan also referred to the fact that, following several months under the supervision of psychologist Eugene Landy, Brian had emerged from his bedroom, stopped over-eating and taking drugs in vast quantities, and was lucid when included in conversations. He was mentally back. Brian's reemergence from self-imposed musical exile coincided with an upswing of interest in his old music (pre–*Pet Sounds*) and a revival of 1950s-era rock-and-roll music in general. Even Elvis Presley was drawing big crowds at gigs in Vegas. The title of the album is confusing, being the twentieth studio album release of the band's career; the "15" refers to the number of years that had elapsed since they'd first begun recording. Originally Brian wanted to only record other people's old songs—there are two Spector collaborations included—but Reprise demanded new Brian-penned material. The album reached #8 on the U.S. chart. It sounds more like an old Beach Boys album than the previous six had, but there's no "wall of sound" nor any layered, intricately devised harmonies. There is a very Brian-like structure to it though, in that Side 1 comprises "rockers," while Side 2 has ballads, the best of which is Dennis's take on "Just Once in My Life."

15 Big Ones proved to be a wholly new Beach Boys release. Although it was a part covers album, importantly, it included five new numbers written by Brian.

In June 1976, the Beach Boys' version of Chuck Berry's "Rock and Roll Music" was released as a single and made #5 on the charts, becoming their first Top 10 hit in a decade. Later that month, as part of the "Brian Is Back!" publicity campaign, Brian made a live performance appearance with the band. He sat at the piano for most of the gig in Anaheim, California, making little movement or noise. It didn't seem to matter to the audience, who cheered his simply being there. The Beach Boys now had a full backline of supporting musicians playing all the instruments on stage.

The album title *15 Big Ones* referred to the fact that the band was now officially 15 years old, and an NBC-TV special on them was made and broadcast in August in celebration of the fact. As part of it, a sketch featuring *Saturday Night Live*'s John Belushi and Dan Akroyd was filmed at Brian's house. After being directed to his bedroom they identify themselves as police and accuse him of never having surfed. He pleads guilty, and they take him down onto the beach and into the surf; all the while Brian's wearing his bathrobe and an expression of embarrassment and fear.

Right: "Brian's back!" screamed the promo for *15 Big Ones*. "I don't know where I've been," replied Brian when asked.

Following a few more TV and live appearances, Brian and the Beach Boys returned to the recording studio to make another album at the end of 1976, in what was to become a routine of production and release for the following few years. It was entirely reminiscent of the Beach Boys' routine of the early to mid-1960s.

The writing and recording of *The Beach Boys Love You* album was almost a Brian Wilson solo album. Or two albums, since Brian amassed so much material over the space of three months that he could have filled both. He was also back to old ways, though, and slipped away from Landy and his minders when possible to score drugs and hang out with friends old and new. (Roger McGuinn told a story in the late 1970s about how Brian drove up to his house unannounced and uninvited one day, entered, asked for speed, and spent the rest of the day and night working on a song using McGuinn's piano. Brian had never previously been to his house.)

At the end of 1977, Landy was fired by Stephen Love, who had taken full control of all aspects of the band's management, Guercio having left.

"I lost interest in writing songs. I lost the inspiration. I was too concerned with getting drugs."

BRIAN *Wilson*

Above: Preparing to go on stage in front of more than 150,000 people in New York's Central Park, September 1, 1977.

Stephen and Mike Love's other brother Stan (a former professional basketball player) was employed in Landy's place to keep Brian in check and out of trouble. He asked their cousin (and sometime songwriting collaborator with Dennis Wilson) Steve Korthof to assist, along with a former college football player and male model named Rocky Pamplin, and they became Brian's minders. However, Stephen Love's tenure proved to be almost as short-lived as Landy's, and he was fired in the spring of 1977, following the Beach Boys signing a new record deal with the Caribou label, owned and run by James Guercio, distributed and financed through CBS.

Stephen's unemployment was short-lived, though, and Mike, ably assisted by Al Jardine, reinstated him in August of the same year. Shortly after, Dennis Wilson became the first Beach Boy to release a solo album. Titled *Pacific Ocean Blue* (Caribou, 1977), it was critically well received, but barely scraped into the Top 100 album chart. In 2008, Brian claimed to Pitchfork Media that he didn't know Dennis had released an album.

In a critical move in the fall of 1977, with Brian regressing into obesity and drug addiction, and unable to fulfill his professional duties, he gave his corporate vote in matters of Beach Boys business to Mike Love. It followed a brief period (two weeks) when there was in effect no Beach Boys in existence, their having split after an argument following the Central Park gig. The critical shift in the Beach Boys' voting structure came as the band was fulfilling its contractual agreement for Reprise, by recording what became *M.I.U. Album*, released in October 1978 to almost universal apathy. At the same time they were agreeing to a new contract with Caribou.

In the summer of 1978 the decision was made to record a new Beach Boys album, for Caribou, in Florida, and to rehire Bruce Johnston. Primarily taken on as producer because Brian was indisposed, he once again became a full-time Beach Boy. By the time the album, *L.A. (Light Album)* was released in the spring of 1979, Marilyn Wilson had divorced Brian. While the second single from *L.A.*, "Good Timin," made it to #40 on the charts, the album had creaked to a highest place of #100.

Caribou released *Keepin' the Summer Alive* in 1980. It was to prove a sad coda to a big part of the Beach Boys' career.

M.I.U. ALBUM

BROTHER/REPRISE, OCTOBER 1978

Producers Al Jardine, Ron Altbach
Engineers Stephen Moffitt, Jeff Peters, Earle Mankey, John Hanlon, Bob Rose
Recorded 11/7–12/9/77, Maharishi Institute University, Fairfield, IA, Western Recorders, Brother Studio, Wally Heider Recordings, Hollywood
U.S. Chart #151 *Billboard*
Singles "Peggy Sue," "Come Go with Me"

Side 1

1. SHE'S GOT RHYTHM
B. Wilson/M. Love/R. Altbach

2. COME GO WITH ME
C. E. Quick

3. HEY LITTLE TOMBOY
B. Wilson

4. KONA COAST
A. Jardine/M. Love

5. PEGGY SUE
B. Holly/J. Allison/N. Petty

6. WONTCHA COME OUT TONIGHT
B. Wilson/M. Love

Side 2

1. SWEET SUNDAY KIND OF LOVE
B. Wilson/M. Love

2. BELLES OF PARIS
B. Wilson/M. Love/R. Altbach

3. PITTER PATTER
B. Wilson/M. Love/A. Jardine

4. MY DIANE
B. Wilson

5. MATCH POINT OF OUR LOVE
B. Wilson/M. Love

6. WINDS OF CHANGE
R. Altbach/E. Tuleja

When *Love You* flopped, Brian regressed—less because of the failure of the record, though, and more because of his illness. Although Carl had fired Eugene Landy because he thought that the good doctor was overcharging for his services, he could see that while under his care, Brian was healthier and more productive. So Landy was rehired and Brian underwent the same treatment, involving close control and limited access to any stimulus that triggered his addictions. Luckily, Landy thought that Brian should work, and so he set about a project originally titled *Adult/Child*. If released today it would be lauded as great art, being a bunch of sub-par, Sinatra-light recordings made with a big band and the same arranger (Dick Reynolds) that Brian had tried out with in the 1960s. However, it most certainly wasn't a Beach Boys album in 1977, so it wasn't released. Instead, Mike and Al took charge, booked

themselves (and Brian, there to "rest," it seems) into the Maharishi's university in Iowa, and set about making this album. Neither Carl nor Dennis appeared at the recordings, allowing Al to play producer along with Ron Altbach, formerly of King Harvest (who'd had a hit with "Dancing in the Moonlight," 1972). Together they made the kind of Beach Boys album that is best described as "Beach Boys lite." It's filled with the kind of hooks and musical touches that the Beach Boys once played with energetic zeal, but unfortunately here they are washed through an equalizer, swamped by sweet synth sounds and ARP-produced string arrangements. In that sense at least, it's a natural-sounding successor to *Love You*. It includes a cover of a Buddy Holly song and an attempt to write a new song for Barry Manilow in "Winds," but only "Catch a Wave" was subsequently played live by the Beach Boys.

L-R: Brian, Dennis, unknown, Audree Wilson, Carl promote the *L.A. (Light Album)* in Los Angeles, June 1979.

A 1979 music magazine advertisement for the album release.

L.A. (LIGHT ALBUM)

BROTHER/CARIBOU, MARCH 1979

Producers	Bruce Johnston, The Beach Boys, James William Guercio
Engineers	Curt Boecher, Chuck Britz, Bill Fletcher, Joel Moss, Earle Mankey, Tom Murphy, Chuck Leary
Recorded	8/28–9/1/78, Criteria, Miami, 1/2–24/79 Western Recorders Studio, Sounds Good, Studio 55, Hollywood
U.S. Chart	#100 *Billboard*
Singles	"Here Comes the Night," "Good Timin'," "Lady Lynda," "Sumahama"

Side 1

1. GOOD TIMIN'
B. Wilson/C. Wilson

2. LADY LYNDA
J. S. Bach arr A. Jardine/R. Altbach

3. FULL SAIL
C. Wilson/G. Cushing-Murray

4. ANGEL COME HOME
C. Wilson/G. Cushing-Murray

5. LOVE SURROUNDS ME
D. Wilson/G. Cushing-Murray

6. SUMAHAMA
M. Love

Side 2

1. HERE COMES THE NIGHT
B. Wilson/M. Love

2. BABY BLUE
D. Wilson/G. Jakonson/K. Lamm

3. GOIN' SOUTH
C. Wilson/G. Cushing-Murray

4. SHORTENIN' BREAD
Trad. arr.; B. Wilson

This was the first album of a new deal between Brother Records and Caribou, who were spending CBS money. The deal required significant input from Brian on any and all releases, but it doesn't look or sound as if he contributed too much to this. It opens well enough with a song he co-wrote with Carl, and it has some lovely and familiar Beach Boys harmonies, but after that J. S. Bach has more to do with the proceedings than Brian. Produced by returning Beach Boy Bruce Johnston, the album is an improvement on *M.I.U.*, although anything would be if it had as many layered harmonies, as most tracks here do. Al's love song for his wife, "Lady Lynda," could have been written and recorded ten years earlier. Most of the tracks on which Carl sings lead are tender, his voice the last remaining trace of what the Boys could once do so brilliantly. Dennis's voice on "Love Surrounds Me" is nearly as affecting as it had been on *Carl and the Passions*. There are a couple of odd numbers—"Sumahama" and "Shortenin' Bread"—and then there's the midlife crisis. Like many men approaching their forties and dreading the loss of sexual allure, the Beach Boys took to the disco (armed with an old song, from 1967's *Wild Honey*) to seek a renewal of vigor. To be fair, everyone at the time was trying out a disco song or two, and many rock acts did so with embarrassing results (even the Grateful Dead, on *Shakedown Street* in 1978, for instance). But few rock acts embraced the disco beat with a 10-minute synth, bongo, and vocoder-led epic in the way that the Beach Boys did with "Here Comes the Night." Unfortunately for them though, Bruce was no Tom Moulton, and while it's OK, the 12-inch mix was never going to set dance floors alight. Amazingly, it made #44 on the U.S. chart.

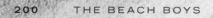

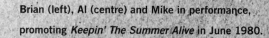

Brian (left), Al (centre) and Mike in performance, promoting *Keepin' The Summer Alive* in June 1980.

KEEPIN' THE SUMMER ALIVE

BROTHER/CARIBOU, MARCH 1980

Producer	Bruce Johnston
Engineers	Stephen Desper, Chuck Leary, Chuck Britz, Rodney Pearson
Recorded	7/23/79–2/14/80, Western Recorders, Hollywood
U.S. Chart	#75 *Billboard*
Singles	"Goin' On," "Livin' with a Heartache"

Side 1

1. KEEPIN' THE SUMMER ALIVE
C. Wilson/R. Bachman

2. OH DARLIN'
B. Wilson/M. Love

3. SOME OF YOUR LOVE
B. Wilson/M. Love

4. LIVIN' WITH A HEARTACHE
C. Wilson/R. Bachman

5. SCHOOL DAY (RING! RING! GOES THE BELL)
C. Berry

Side 2

1. GOIN' ON
B. Wilson/M. Love

2. SUNSHINE
B. Wilson/M. Love

3. WHEN THE GIRLS GET TOGETHER
B. Wilson/M. Love

4. SANTA ANA WINDS
B. Wilson/A. Jardine

5. ENDLESS HARMONY
B. Johnston

As was their way, the Beach Boys spent almost three months following the relase of *L.A.* on the road, touring America. During such a tour in the 1960s, Brian would usually be in Western Recorders (or Gold Star) working on new material but, in 1979, he was still under the guidance of Landy and restricted in his activities. He was also escaping his minders and binging whenever he could. When the band reconvened to record a new album in late July as the second Caribou release, Brian was happy to be involved—but once again, as when he began *15 Big Ones*, he was very eager to make an album of cover versions of old rock-and-roll numbers. Throughout the decade different reporters who got to meet Brian would indivdually and inevitably report how he would sit or stand in front of his home jukebox, listening time and time again to "Be My Baby" by the Ronettes. On YouTube there's footage of an interview the band conducted with *Good Morning America* in 1980, and when Brian is asked what he listens to "today," he responds "Be My Baby." The band members snort in frustration their agreement with that. Caribou rejected the idea of a covers album (although "School Days" does make it onto the album). In another nostalgic move, Brian worked with Mike on new songs. Perhaps he was hoping to recapture the magic they'd had in 1962, but they struggle to match their heyday here. Dennis was absent for the majority of the recording and was becoming increasingly distanced from the band, suffering collapses brought on by drug and alcohol abuse. Carl's two songs, co-written with Randy Bachman, lack the soul of his previous work. The majority of the album retreads familiar Beach Boys material in a way that makes the album sound not like a "new" release at all.

Preparing to take the stage at Knebworth
stately home in England, June 1980.

7

KOKOMO, MADE IN THE USA

1981·1995

On November 5, 1982, Brian Wilson was fired as an employee of Brother Records, and so was no longer a member of the Beach Boys. According to a *Rolling Stone* article from June 7, 1984, he received notice in a letter from Al, Mike, Carl, and Dennis at their lawyers' office. He was also almost bankrupt and owing back taxes, divorced from Marilyn, and living with a nurse named Carolyn Williams (plus her three children), whom he'd met when she tended to him on her night shift in the psychiatric wing of a hospital in 1979. His body weight had risen to its highest ever, and his consumption of drugs and alcohol was out of the control of even Williams. Brian would leave his house without warning, going in searching of whatever he craved, whenever he could.

The situation that Brian and the Beach Boys were in hadn't just happened, of course. Following his discovery that Marilyn and Rocky Pamplin were having an affair, in late 1978, Brian had moved out of their home and begun to eat, drink, and snort without restraint. Pamplin and Stan Love were still supposed to look after him, but Brian naturally didn't want Rocky around. Stan couldn't

Previous page: Back, L-R: Bruce, Mike; Front Carl, Brian, Al, 1985.
Right: Brian by his swimming pool, 1981.

manage Brian 24 hours a day, and anyway Brian was soon being kept company by a female fan who'd hung around his house for the past couple of years, and with whom he felt comfortable. Stan left Brian alone with her, and he was free to do as he pleased. Unfortunately, that included wandering from bar to bar playing the piano for drinks, or becoming so incapacitated by drink and drugs that the police would have to take him home, often having found him, disoriented, wandering the streets looking disheveled, dirty, and sometimes bruised.

In early 1979, Brian was hospitalized for the first time and met Carolyn Williams. On leaving the hospital he asked to be looked after by her, and soon became dependent on her in the way that he had with Marilyn. Williams moved in with him. She also took to touring with the band when Brian was able to travel and was reported (by Gaines in particular) as being present at official Beach Boys business meetings, much to the dismay of the rest of the band. Unfortunately, she was not able to keep tabs on Brian constantly, though, and

"My private life has become my career. I'm too on top of it musically to ever quit."

BRIAN *Wilson*

he was admitted to the hospital after an incident with sleeping pills in 1981. However, most of the illegal drugs that he got at that time came from his brother, Dennis.

At the end of the 1970s, Dennis seemed to be set on a course of self-destruction. He'd always been fond of wild company and couldn't resist any female who offered him sex. As he neared the end of his 30s the once handsome and fit surfer had become bloated and gray-faced, and when put in front of a microphone he was slurring his words more and more.

When former manager of the band Fred Vail said to *Rolling Stone* that, "Dennis Wilson was the essence, the spirit of the Beach Boys, we used to think of him as the Steve McQueen or James Dean of the group," he was

KOKOMO

ELEKTRA, JULY 1988

B-side	"Tutti Frutti" by Little Richard
Writers	M. Love/S. McKenzie/T. Melcher/ J. Phillips; R. Penniman/D. LaBostrie
Producer	T. Melcher
Recorded	3/22/88, 4/5,6/88
U.S. Chart	#1 *Billboard*

Written by four of the key figures of 1960s California pop, the song celebrates the Caribbean rhythm of life on an imaginary island off the Florida Keys. On *Good Morning America*, Terry Melcher credited Mike Love with being "the king of the hook" and coming up with the chorus lines that namecheck Aruba and Jamaica. It is a catchy chorus, and tied as it was to an extremely successful romantic comedy drama movie *Cocktail* (1988), starring the rising Hollywood star Tom Cruise, a lot of people got to hear the tune. It gave the Beach Boys only their third #1 single ever, and their first since "Good Vibrations." Brian Wilson is not on the recording and didn't play any part in the writing or production of the song, either. During interviews with the band (and Brian) that took place after this success, people would inevitably ask about "Kokomo," and whenever possible Mike would let the interviewer and audience know that Brian had nothing to do with it—nothing at all. Mike had good reason to feel neglected and undervalued when the success of the band that he'd help form with Brian was inevitably accredited to only the elder Wilson brother. A few years after this single's success, Mike sued Brian for non-payment of royalties for songs that a judge would decide both men had created in equal measure.

unknowingly making a more apt comparison than perhaps he knew. Steve McQueen married three times (and was dead at 50), and Dean died in an accident at 24; Dennis would not see 40, and at the time of his death he was about to be divorced for the fifth time—from Shawn, the teenage illegitimate (and at the time unacknowledged) daughter of fellow Beach Boy Mike Love.

Surprisingly, perhaps, both Dennis and Brian had been present at a gig that the Beach Boys played for newly inaugurated president Ronald Reagan at the White House in 1981. They performed and had their photograph taken with the president and first lady Nancy, and everyone stood with their arms around one another, happy to be there.

No one thought it odd that they had just played for the former governor of California who, in 1969, sent armed police into the People's Park demonstration that Mike had railed against in "Student Demonstration Time" (a student was killed and another protester blinded by police). Reagan had said back then that if it took a bloodbath to "clean up Berkeley," then so be it. Mike saw no problem with praising a president who would pass more anti-environmental preservation legislation than any other. As he said to Peter Ames Carlin, "You know, we're not politically savvy and all that, but I think we liked Reagan quite a bit."

The Beach Boys had earlier, in 1980, signaled their turn to the right when they played a benefit gig for the Republican vice-presidential candidate George H. W. Bush. It was all a part of the aging process, no doubt, and it coincided with the slew of divorces that every band member had either gone through or was approaching fast: Carl divorced Annie, his wife of 14 years in 1980; Mike ended his fourth marriage in 1982; Al divorced Lynda in 1983; Dennis, who'd been in a stormy relationship with Christine McVie of Fleetwood Mac for two years before beginning his fifth marriage, was divorcing Shawn in 1983.

Carl (left) and Dennis support one another live on stage.

The more their world changed, the more they wanted it to stay the same—which was much the same for huge swathes of America, too. It's why the band was becoming an American musical institution, part of the

entertainment establishment that projected and celeb-rated the American Dream. The place of the Beach Boys in America's ever-lasting affection became very much tied up with the rise of Ronald Reagan. Like the former B-movie actor (who had most famously played supporting roles to a chimpanzee), the Boys played on an American stereotype—their surfer dude to his cowboy lawman. Both acts reached their first career peak in the 1960s (Reagan became governor of California in 1967), and both repositioned themselves in the 1980s as essentially right-thinking, if backward-looking, public figures. And both made Washington their launch pad for their second acts.

On July 4, 1980, the Beach Boys performed in front of an estimated 500,000 people at the Washington Monument. The first dozen songs of their set were hit singles and songs from the 1960s. Only five of the 29 songs they performed that day had been written in the 1970s, and one of those was not a Beach Boys original, being Bruce's "I Write the Songs." The Beach Boys were no longer relevant as a progressive, inventive artistic entity; they existed only to mine their back catalogue. They had become—and would remain from then on—the first and best Beach Boys tribute act in the business.

It's debatable whether Brian was interested in making new music at all in the early 1980s. Dennis had certainly given up any pretense in the idea of the band being a vehicle for producing new music, and his obvious disinterest in performing cabaret show versions of their past glories manifested itself in his increasingly rare live appearances with them. When he did make it on to stage it was purely for the paycheck, and he was often so drunk or stoned, or both, that he couldn't stand or perform with any clarity.

Left: The view from the stage at the first annual July 4 Washington Monument concert, 1980; L-R: Brian, Mike, Al, Carl, Ed Carter.

Everyone in the band camp knew that Dennis was supplying Brian with drugs, sometimes as a bribe to try to get his big brother to make music with him, but often simply because Dennis knew how much it annoyed the rest of them. His "bad influence" on Brian proved too much for Stan Love and Rocky Pamplin, and, in January 1981, they took it upon themselves to warn off Dennis from getting Brian stoned. They kicked their way into Dennis's home and badly beat him up. They used a tele-phone handset to beat him, repeatedly banged his head on the floor, and threw him through a window. A year after the attack Stan was fined $750 and Rocky $250 for their home invasion.

In 1981, Carl Wilson, in an attempt to get away from L.A. and The Boys, moved to Colorado, stopped touring with the band, and concentrated on making a solo career. He released an eponymous album through Caribou in March that year, co-written with former Elvis backing singer Myrna Smith, who also sang on it. Carl then went out on tour in support of the record, but it failed to impress the public in any significant numbers. Despite that, his manager, Jerry Schilling (Myrna Smith's hus-band), kept plugging away for Carl, booking him gigs around the country.

Schilling got Carl an opening slot on a Doobie Brothers tour through June and July (he missed the second July 4 Beach Boys gig at the Washington Monument). Schilling also won a commitment from Caribou to release a second solo album by Carl. That fall he began work on it.

Also in 1981, Mike Love made several live appear-ances to promote his solo album, titled *Looking Back with Love* (Boardwalk, October 1981). It sold fewer copies than Carl's had, and was resoundingly panned by critics. Even the inclusion of "Be My Baby," produced by Brian, couldn't rescue the album from the cut-out bins. In truth the version is awful, lacking any of the original's force or majesty. Constructed solely using synthesizer backing, Mike's double-double-tracked voice fails to lift the recording beyond karaoke. The album isn't as bad as original reviews suggest, but finding it became impossible pretty quickly, as it was swiftly deleted.

Although individual Beach Boys had little success with solo releases, Caribou set about capitalizing on their collective appeal by releasing a compilation titled *Ten Years of Harmony* (the title wasn't ironic). It gathered together 29 recordings released on Brother Records between 1970 and 1980, very few of which figured in their live set, until they breached anti-apartheid sanctions by performing at the resort of Sun City in the North West province, South Africa, over Christmas and New Year 1981. They would go on to perform songs from the compilation at gigs in America, but with little success; it made only #151 on the U.S. charts.

Throughout 1982, the Beach Boys continued to tour America with Brian, although he was hospitalized in early March so that he could lose weight. The tour resumed with Carolyn in tow; on March 24, following the inspection of bags at a local airport in Florida, Carolyn was found to be in possession of cocaine. She was incarcerated, and it took almost 24 hours for Brian to pay the $300 bail required to free her, by which time the press had heard all about it and were reporting the news. Ultimately she pleaded no contest, was fined, and put on probation.

Carolyn's arrest proved to be a blip in the couple's togetherness, and she was soon back at his side and complaining that someone in the Beach Boys organization had set her up (which was unproven). The band continued to tour with Brian, and Carl made a couple of rare appearances with them in April, contradicting the rumors that he had been fired or quit. In May, Brian took an extended vacation from gigging and went into the Western Recorders Studio, reportedly to make a new recording. Many people close to him believed that it might be the very last time that they'd see him in a studio. Nothing came of the sessions.

When appearing at gigs in August and September, it became apparent that once again Brian was out of control. That was when the plan of firing him from the band and telling him that he was bankrupt was formed. The ultimate aim of doing so was to get Brian back into the care of Dr. Landy—and away from Carolyn, Los Angeles, and all of the various bad influences on him.

At a band meeting in late summer Brian had refused to entertain the idea, though, declaring that he'd never go back to Landy. But as his brothers and cousin had seen, only Landy had ever managed to straighten Brian out, and it was decided that it was the only sensible course of action open to them. When the band told Brian that he wouldn't be paid for his tour work, leaving him to believe that he had no means of

"I can tell that she (Nancy) is a California girl, what the heck!"

MIKE *Love*

financial support, Brian finally agreed to consulting with Landy. In January 1983, Brian admitted himself to the hospital for a physical examination, demanded by Landy before he was willing to take charge of the Beach Boy.

From there he was taken to Kona, Hawaii, without Carolyn Williams's knowledge. While Brian was there, Carolyn received notice to vacate the house, and soon after movers arrived to take away Brian's possessions. Williams subsequently presented a telegram to the press that she claimed was from Brian and that said he missed her and that he had been kidnapped. In response, Brian called his own press conference in Kona, at which he denied having sent the telegram and that "we" were trying to get her out of his house. Carolyn had no choice but to leave. She'd spend the next year trying in vain to meet with Brian, who returned to L.A. in March and shared a residence with housemates of Landy's choosing.

In April 1983, a press frenzy erupted over the upcoming July 4 Washington Monument concert when Secretary of the Interior James Watt "banned" rock bands from performing. He did so, he said, as they attracted "the wrong element" to their gigs. Although it was not clear whether the Beach Boys had booked the concert at the time of the "ban," they had been one of the most prominent acts at the concert in the past, and fans rallied to their support. He clearly didn't know about the "special" relationship that existed between the band and the president—Reagan promptly called Watt into his office and told him off, and then booked the Beach Boys to perform on the White House lawn on June 12—from where they went directly to Vice President George H. W. Bush's fifty-ninth birthday party.

As usual, that year the Beach Boys kept up their relentless touring schedule but did no recording. Carl's second solo album, *Youngblood*, was released but sold no better than the first. Mike teamed up with Dean Torrence to record some '60s songs for a cassette-only album titled *Rock'n'Roll City* available only

Mike Love cuddles up to First Lady Nancy Reagan, after performing on the White House lawn, June 12, 1983.

at Radio Shack stores (for $4.95), and included the Beach Boys' version of "California Dreamin'". Because of the limited release, the cassette wasn't eligible for chart placings. Mike and Dean played a tour together to promote it, though, sponsored by Budweiser, during

spring break of 1983. However, most of Mike's time was taken up with touring as a Beach Boy, although at times their lineup included only one Wilson (Carl).

Dennis had become as unreliable and unpredictable as Brian, and he missed a raft of shows that year. He showed up at the Pomona County Fairground on September 26, and played the gig, but when he returned to the same venue with the band the following night, he was too drunk to play, and the Boys banned him from getting on stage. They couldn't know it, but that was the last time that Dennis would even attempt to gig with the Beach Boys. For the following three months, Dennis

Wilson got lost in a fug of alcohol and drugs. On the afternoon of December 28, 1983, Dennis took a swim that he never returned from. He had been drinking and diving into the harbor at Marina del Rey all day from a yacht named the *Emerald*. He was searching for objects that he'd previously thrown into the sea from the deck of a yacht that he once owned and kept there, called *Harmony* and which he desperately wanted to get back. Despite being told by his companions on the boat (a girlfriend named Colleen McGovern and owner of the *Emerald*, Bill Oster) not to keep on diving, Dennis persisted in getting in and out of the water until, finally at around 4:15 p.m., he didn't get out again.

His body was pulled from the harbor by coast guard divers at 5:30 p.m. TV news cameras were reporting from the scene before everyone in the Beach Boys camp had heard from anyone else about the tragedy. Brian was told via telephone by Jerry Schilling.

Because Shawn was technically Dennis's widow—their divorce had not been finalized—she got to say what happened to Dennis in death, and she opted for a burial at sea. The president waived a federal law prohibiting the maritime ceremony, and on January 4, 1984, Dennis Wilson was laid to rest in the Pacific Ocean, about 20 miles off Santa Catalina Island.

Outside observers of the Beach Boys' career had often commented on the struggle between Dennis and the rest of the band, particularly with his cousin, Mike. As the focal point of the band in the early days, Mike had been regarded as the major attraction for teenage girls. However, handsome Dennis soon became a rival for the affection of fans. Dennis's constant insobriety grated badly with Mike's abstemious TM-inspired attitude, and there were fights between the pair, both verbal and physical. Mike's quick-witted, cutting sarcasm could hurt almost as much as one of Dennis's drunken punches.

With Dennis's death the band lost one of their formative creative members. Also, apparently, Brian lost one of his major drug and alcohol enablers. Living within the confines of what was essentially a Landy compound in Los Angeles, following his bereavement Brian struggled and fought his illness, his addictions, and his helpers. With Dennis gone, Brian didn't have easy access to the substances that sent him out of control, and under Landy's supervision he at least began to lose weight and regain a coherence to his life.

After taking the first two months of 1984 off in order to mourn, the Beach Boys went back out on tour (Brian appeared with them only three times that year, in May, July, and August). More significantly for them all, though, Brian began to work with them on a proper new Beach Boys album in June. Bruce, who'd produced the previous two albums, suggested that this time they hire a young, hot new producer named Steve Levine, who'd risen to fame as the man behind the sound of Culture Club. Bruce had first met Levine, who was then working as a studio tape operator, while in London in 1977. He had enjoyed working with the Brit, who handled the latest generation of studio equipment brilliantly, and he flew him to Los Angeles to assist on other productions at the end of the 1970s. Naturally then, Levine was delighted to hear from Bruce and the Beach Boys in 1984.

Levine's working methods—using drum tracks, Fairlight synthesizers, samples, and overdubbed instruments and voices—meant that the Boys could take their time over the work, which proved to be just as well, since they were, as he later told the author Mark Dillon for *Fifty Sides of the Beach Boys* (ECW Press, 2012), "very rusty." In fact, he revealed, Brian was so out of practice that the producer had to recommend to his employer that he take some singing lessons. Brian did so and improved markedly. The band was assisted in the studio by old friend Terry Melcher and by Stevie Wonder, who

L-R: Roger McGuinn, Brian Wilson, Michelle Phillips, John Phillips on the set of the "California Dreamin'" video shoot, 1986.

wrote a song for them and played all the instruments on it, too ("I Do Love You"). Wonder also contributed some trademark harmonica licks to other tracks.

Before recording began in earnest, the Boys appeared on the *Tonight Show* in late June, with guest host Joan Rivers. Brian appeared with the rest of the band, looking leaner (in the interview he says he lost 100 pounds) and sharper than he had in quite some time. There were some awkward moments, particularly when Mike handed off a question about groupies to Brian, who went into a speech about "Be My Baby," and then asked if Gene "my doctor, my songwriting partner, my friend" couldn't join them on the set. But generally the appearance, to publicize their forthcoming July 4 gig at the Washington Monument, went well (Brian even played at the gig).

In January 1985, the Boys played at Reagan's second inauguration ball and, minus Brian, continued their touring schedule. Improvements in Brian's health and confidence became clear when, in March, he made a solo live appearance in L.A. at the Palace Theater. A benefit gig for the city's homeless, Brian played "Da Doo Ron Ron," "Sloop John B.," and "California Girls." He repeated the same songs in concert in May at a benefit for the Malibu Emergency Room, but added two other numbers to his setlist: "Male Ego" and "I'm So Lonely," both recently recorded for a new album.

"Male Ego" was included as the B-side to "Getcha Back," the first Beach Boys single to enter the top 30 (making #26) in four years, which was released in May 1985. The album it came from, simply titled *The Beach Boys*, was released the following month, and it didn't fare so well on the charts (reaching #52). It was noticeable that the single was a deliberately nostalgic exercise in reminding the public of what the Beach Boys used to sound like (and may in part have been inspired by the enormous success of Don Henley's "The Boys of Summer" of the previous fall). The album for the most part sounded like a good, mid-1980s AOR release, and it never obviously referenced the band's past glories, except on the awful "California Calling," where it was driven home with all the finesse of a sledgehammer.

At the Beach Boys' July 4, 1985, gig they found themselves performing in front of a remarkable estimated 750,000 people. That was followed nine days later by an appearance in Philadelphia at Live Aid (to a TV audience of an estimated 1.5 billion people), during which Brian took the lead vocals on "Wouldn't It Be Nice." The rest of the year was spent touring, although without Brian.

In 1986, Eugene Landy, who had been credited as Brian's co-writer on songs for *The Beach Boys*, made contact with Gary Usher. Landy suggested to him that he and Brian work on a new album together, which Usher was happy to try. The men booked studio time from June through December, but nothing that they came up with and laid down on tape was considered suitable enough to be released at the time.

Sadly, the Beach Boys' next offering as a single release, the frankly embarrassing "Rock 'n' Roll to the Rescue," was deemed good enough by Capitol to put out in June. It was recorded in March for inclusion on yet another Capitol-released compilation (*Made in the USA*); unsurprisingly, neither was a hit. Their version of "California Dreamin'" featuring Roger McGuinn on guitar and produced by Terry Melcher (promoted by a moodily shot B&W promo video) fared slightly better, making #8 on *Billboard*'s AOR chart in September.

To celebrate their twenty-fifth anniversary that year, the Boys played a nostalgic concert on Waikiki Beach in Hawaii, with guest stars Ray Charles, the Everly Brothers, and Glen Campbell.

In 1987, Brian was offered a solo record deal by Seymour Stein, the founder and boss of Sire Records. The first release, in April, was the strained and hackneyed single "Let's Go to Heaven in My Car," a co-write with Gary Usher and Landy. It failed to chart anywhere. However, the follow-up in June, "Love and Mercy," was a much better song (credited to Brian, Landy, and his wife Alexandra Morgan), and it made #40 on the rock charts. It also sounded discernibly like the Beach Boys, and bode well for the forthcoming solo album.

The Beach Boys, having ended their recording contract with Caribou, had no label deal at the time. However, in June 1987 they enjoyed a #12 hit single as duet partners with novelty rap act the Fat Boys, on a version of the Surfari's "Wipe Out," released on Polygram's hip dance label, Urban. It was a hit mostly due to an accompanying, humorous promo video, in which Mike and Bruce are the most visible Beach Boys, with cameos by Al and Brian—Carl was absent.

BEACH BOYS

BROTHER/CARIBOU, JUNE 1985

Producer	Steve Levine
Engineers	Gordon Milne, Greg Laney, Nick Godfrey
Recorded	6/20–12/3/84, 1/85 Westlake Audio, Santa Monica; Red Bus, London
U.S. Chart	#52 *Billboard*
Singles	"Getcha Back," "It's Gettin' Late," "She Believes in Love Again"

Side 1

1. GETCHA BACK
M. Love/T. Melcher

2. IT'S GETTIN' LATE
C. Wilson/M. Smith Schilling/R. White Johnson

3. CRACK AT YOUR LOVE
B. Wilson/A. Jardine/E. Landy

4. MAYBE I DON'T KNOW
C. Wilson/M. Smith Schilling/S. Levine/J. Lindsay

5. SHE BELIEVES IN LOVE AGAIN
B. Johnston

Side 2

1. CALIFORNIA CALLING
A. Jardine/B. WIlson

2. PASSING FRIEND
G. O'Dowd/R. Hay

3. I'M SO LONELY
B. Wilson/E. Landy

4. WHERE I BELONG
C. Wilson/R. White Johnson

5. I DO LOVE YOU
S. Wonder

6. IT'S JUST A MATTER OF TIME
B. Wilson/E. Landy

The first album made after Dennis's death, this oddly titled collection—they were missing a founding and essential member, so was it an attempt to reassert their identity unchanged despite that?—bears a simple message on the back cover: "This album is dedicated to the memory of our beloved brother, cousin and friend." The dominant image above it is a color photo of the five members smiling broadly, even Brian. There is no eulogy or lament to be found on the record. Perhaps they figured it was what Dennis would want: a mostly up-tempo, contemporary AOR album. There is "Passing Friend," written by Boy George and sounding a lot like Culture Club (with whom producer Steve Levine had made his and their name), but the lyrics are obscure and Carl's lead vocal doesn't suggest it's intended to be about Dennis. Brian's contributions to the album (four songs) were all credited as co-written with Eugene Landy, whose presence in the studio made recording difficult. His need to be in control of all aspects of Brian's life couldn't be satisfied when the band and Levine had so much more knowledge of how they should work together. After a while Landy stayed away, and Brian continued happily without him. Levine recorded the basic backing tracks in London (using Fairlight synthesizers) in mid-1984, and took the Beach Boys into a Santa Monica studio in the fall of that year. Levine did a very good job, and at times his big '80s synthesized production is a very good simulacrum of a 1960s soul sound, particularly on Stevie Wonder's "I Do Love You" and "Getcha Back," which is the closest the Boys ever came to sounding like the Four Seasons. This only made #52 on the album charts, but that was better than *Keepin' the Summer Alive* had managed.

The impact of video (and to a degree, on-screen actors) would play a major part in the surprise success of the Boys' 1988 single release, "Kokomo." Having been inducted into the Rock and Roll Hall of Fame in January (with some notoriety due to a very ungracious, five-minute rant of an acceptance speech by Mike), the band interrupted a residency in Las Vegas (at Caesars Palace) to record "Kokomo" with Terry Melcher, who wanted to include it in a movie he was involved with, titled *Cocktail*, starring Tom Cruise and Elisabeth Shue.

At the time Brian was busy with his solo career, and while he and Landy were still very much in league—"Brian and I are partners in life," Landy said in 1988—the doctor's interference in the making of the *Beach Boys* album made them less than welcome guests at recording sessions. So Brian made no contribution to the writing or recording of "Kokomo."

Both the song and the movie were released in July and were big hits. "Kokomo" made #1, and *Cocktail* took in more than $72 million at the U.S. box office. Also released in July, Brian's debut solo album *Brian Wilson* received some very good reviews, but only made #54 on the *Billboard* album chart. "Kokomo" was a swan song for the Boys as far as single releases went—nothing they put out after it sold anywhere near as well.

Capitol, though, encouraged by the single's huge sales, re-signed the band to a record deal. The success of movie soundtrack singles clearly had an influence on the decision of what to include on *Still Cruisin'*, released in August 1989, and it wasn't a bad idea, either. Despite containing very little new material, and certainly none of any note, the album included recordings used on movie soundtracks, and made it to #46 in the charts, turning platinum and selling more than 750,000 copies. By this time, Brian's lack of contact with his family and business

partners in the Beach Boys was distressing to his brother and ex-wife, and once again they found themselves wanting to separate Brian from Landy, who ceased to be a practicing psychologist in 1989, when he resigned his medical license.

At the time Landy was a business partner with Brian, and together they owned a company called Brain and Genius. The B&G office contained a recording studio in which they worked on Brian's second solo album. In 1991, Sire rejected a proposed release titled *Sweet Insanity* on the basis of the lyrics (by Landy) being too awful. A risible "rap" track on it titled "Smart Girls" is the indisputable lowest point of what can probably best be described as a misguided venture. A track titled "The Spirit of Rock & Roll" is notable for having a shared vocal recorded by Bob Dylan sometime in late 1986, although it is quite unremarkable in any other way. The whole of the unreleased album (which can be found on YouTube) is an average late 1980s–era AOR album, only made distinctive by the self-conscious samples from Beach Boys tunes on several tracks.

By the time that Sire was rejecting the tapes from Landy and Brian, the eldest Wilson daughters, Carnie and Wendy, together with Chynna, their friend and daughter of John and Michelle Phillips, had become world-wide pop stars. Their debut single release "Hold On" (#1 in the U.S.) and eponymous LP *Wilson Phillips* (U.S. #2) were both released in 1990.

Brian hadn't seen a lot of Carnie or Wendy (or their mother) in the preceding years. Marilyn had been asking for help in getting Brian away from the control of Landy for a while, with little response until Stan Love, who was by then living in Oregon, became involved. Concerned enough by what he'd heard about Landy's financial and emotional control over his cousin, he took legal action in May 1990, hoping to wrest power as a legal conservator for Brian into his hands. Not that Brian was in favor of such a move, and he defended Landy in court.

The Beach Boys having just been inducted into the Rock and Roll Hall of Fame on January 21, 1988. Mike made a five-minute "acceptance" speech that upset many in the audience—which is why Carl is glaring at him. L-R: Al, Carl, Brian, Mike.

STILL CRUISIN'

CAPITOL, AUGUST 1989

Producers	Brian Wilson, Terry Melcher, Albert Cabrera, Tony Moran, Damon Wimbley, Darren Robinson
Engineers	Keith Wechsler, Mark Linett
Recorded	1964, 1965, 1966, 1987, 4/88, Capitol Studio, Western Recorders, Sound Solution, Hollywood
U.S. Chart	#46 *Billboard*
Singles	"Kokomo," "Still Cruisin'," "Somewhere Near Japan"

Side 1

1. STILL CRUISIN'
M. Love/T. Melcher

2. SOMEWHERE NEAR JAPAN
B. Johnston/M. Love/T. Melcher/J. Phillips

3. ISLAND GIRL
A. Jardine

4. IN MY CAR
B. Wilson

5. KOKOMO
M. Love/S. McKenzie/T. Melcher/J. Phillips

Side 2

1. WIPE OUT
B. Berryhill/P. Connolly/J. Fuller/R. Wilson

2. MAKE IT BIG
M. Love/B. House/T. Melcher

3. I GET AROUND
B. Wilson/M. Love

4. WOULDN'T IT BE NICE
B. Wilson/T. Asher

5. CALIFORNIA GIRLS
B. Wilson/M. Love

Don't be misled by the presence of Brian's name in the list of producers for this album; it's only there because it includes recordings that he'd made 20 years earlier, plus one more recent song, the almost self-parodying "In My Car." This is not actually a "new" Beach Boys album, but rather a collection of oldies that had recently been included on the soundtracks of different movies—"I Get Around" was featured in *Good Morning Vietnam* (1987), "California Girls" was in *Soul Man* (1986), "Wouldn't It Be Nice" was in *The Big Chill* (1983), and "Make It Big" can be heard in *Troop Beverly Hills* (1989), if you can find a Betamax tape of it. Added to them are the surprise hit duet with the Fat Boys on "Wipe Out," "Kokomo" (from *Cocktail*, 1988), and the title track, written for Chrysler (as was "In My Car") to help them sell a new Corvette. The nascent VH-1 music television

channel paid for a promotional video for "Still Cruisin'," which was then included on the *Lethal Weapon 2* (1989) soundtrack. Despite using musical reminders of "Kokomo" in "Still Cruisin'" (which even mentions Jamaica), it failed to climb any higher than #93 on the U.S. chart (although it was a hit in Austria). The second single from the album, and one of the three songs that didn't feature in a movie, "Somewhere Near Japan" was adapted from an original song by John Phillips in which he recounted his daughter's honeymoon escapade— she called him asking to be sent money and drugs to "somewhere near Japan." It's the best of the new songs but failed to achieve any chart success at all on release in 1990. The album was something of a hit, selling enough copies to be awarded a platinum disc. The power of a #1 single to help sell an album was priceless in the 1980s.

In 1991, Brian's autobiography, *Wouldn't It Be Nice*, was published. It was immediately condemned by those who knew and had grown up with Brian as being the work of Landy. Carl (along with Marilyn, Audree, Wendy, and Carnie) launched another legal action against Landy in an attempt to gain control over Brian's life.

Brian's appearances in public at the time had non-specialist commentators wondering if he'd suffered from a stroke, because he was slurring his words and one half of his mouth was permanently turned down. People who'd worked in mental health, though, recognized the symptoms of his suffering from something different. Brian's symptoms were similar to those patients who had been persistently administered large doses of psychotropic drugs over a long period. Carl's charge in court was that Landy and his assistants were keeping Brian heavily medicated, and they were acting against his will and general good. In 1992, the court ruled against Landy, and ordered that he cede all control and cease contact with Brian. The Wilson family was jubilant.

Brian wasn't through with lawsuits, though. In 1989, he had sanctioned a $100 million action in an attempt to recover the publishing rights to his songs (and Sea of Tunes) that Murry had sold in 1969. In 1992, the suit was settled reportedly for a percentage of the demanded figure. However it was followed almost immediately by a lawsuit from Mike Love—who was then leading a new musical act named the Endless Summer Beach Band. Mike was demanding recognition as co-author and back royalties be paid on more than 30 songs that he'd co-written for the Beach Boys with Brian (and others). The case would take two years to come to a settlement, and when it did, it was in Mike's favor. He won $5 million, plus an ongoing share in future royalties.

Remarkably there had been a new Beach Boys album released between the royalties case being brought and settled. Although it was credited to the Beach Boys, Brian was not on any of the tracks released as *Summer in Paradise* on Brother Entertainment (1992). Produced by

Mike and his fifth wife Jacqueline Piesen, who married in 1994, the same year that Mike won his publishing claim against Brian.

Terry Melcher, Bruce was the only band member to play any instruments on the tracks—although it was largely a synthesized affair, with programmed electronic drums, put together on an early version of ProTools on an Apple Macintosh computer. Recording took place early in 1992, in Carmel, while Brian was trying out new material of his own with Andy Paley producing at Oceanway Studio (which used to be Western Recorders).

In truth, technological innovation was the only thing about *Summer in Paradise* worth mentioning. Few of the tracks rewarded repeated listening, and that included the first song on which someone other than a Beach Boy takes a lead vocal. "Forever" was sung by actor John Stamos, the star of sitcom *Full House* (ABC, 1987–95). Stamos had invited the Beach Boys to appear in an episode in 1990, and had performed with the band as a drummer or guitarist at the occasional gig since 1989. *Summer in Paradise* was deleted within months of release (and remained out of print well into the twenty-first century).

It can only have left their fans wondering if there'd ever be another new Beach Boys album.

The lineup who recorded *Summer In Paradise*. L-R: Mike, Carl (it would be his last Beach Boys album), Al, Bruce.

SUMMER IN PARADISE

BROTHER ENTERTAINMENT, AUGUST 1992

Producer	Terry Melcher
Engineer	Keith Wechsler
Recorded	3/92, Surfman Location, Carmel, California
U.S. Chart	N/A
Singles	"Hot Fun in the Summertime," "Summer of Love"

Side 1

1. HOT FUN IN THE SUMMERTIME
S. Stewart

2. SURFIN'
B. Wilson/M. Love

3. SUMMER OF LOVE
M. Love/T. Melcher

4. ISLAND FEVER
M. Love/T. Melcher

5. STILL SURFIN'
M. Love/T. Melcher

6. SLOW SUMMER DANCIN' (ONE SUMMER NIGHT)
B. Johnston/D. Webb

Side 2

7. STRANGE THINGS HAPPEN
M. Love/T. Melcher

8. REMEMBER (WALKING IN THE SAND)
G. Morton

9. LAHAINA ALOHA
M. Love/T. Melcher

10. UNDER THE BOARDWALK
A. Resnick/K. Young/M. Love

11. SUMMER IN PARADISE
M. Love/T. Melcher /C. Fall

12. FOREVER
D. Wilson/G. Jakobson

It was not clear whether *Still Crusin'* was a new Beach Boys album, but this one certainly was. Although Brian Wilson is present only in the form of co-writer of an odd cover version of "Surfin'." But only Bruce Johnston actually plays any instruments on the album. Mike Love performs nine of the 12 songs' lead vocals (sharing five with Carl), and a complete outsider sings lead on one of Dennis Wilson's finest songs—actor John Stamos's version of "Forever" offered up here struggles to match the beauty of the original, though. The cover versions are all, without exception, thin. The opening track, Sly Stone's "Hot Fun in the Summertime," replaces Sly's original jaunty, stone-skipping beat with a more prosaic sequenced drum machine. The vocal is over-equalized and as a result sounds somewhat distant. Carl's lead vocal on the great Shadow Morton's "Remember (Walking in the Sand)" is low-key, and possibly slowed down in the final mix, which also renders the voice too far back in the mix. Melcher's production includes trebly, echoing horns, a child's organ, and over-imposing synth snare. "Under the Boardwalk" (a 1964 hit for the Drifters, written by Artie Resnick and Kenny Young) is slightly over-syncopated, and over-riffed. There's a new recording of "Surfin'" here, which oddly sounds unlike the Beach Boys—perhaps because there is nothing of the Four Freshmen to be found in it. The album's title track offers a smart referencing of the Beach Boys' heritage, too, particularly in the way that it mentions them in the third person, while musical riffs remind the listener about familiar Beach Boys hits. It demonstrates again an astute level of understanding about what Beach Boys fans want, and expect to hear from "America's Band"; fun, fun, fun in the endless summer.

8

I JUST WASN'T MADE FOR THESE TIMES

1996·2015

n August 1995, the Disney Channel broadcast a documentary titled *I Just Wasn't Made for These Times*, directed by Don Was. It was a celebration of Brian Wilson's career and included many famous people from the music industry paying tribute to Brian's songwriting genius. There are contributions from Brian and members of the Beach Boys, too. One of the most touching moments in the film is provided by Carl Wilson and Audree. Brian plays the piano, seated next to his mother, while Carl stands and sings "God Only Knows." It was the first time that all three had sat together and played music in three decades.

The film traced the making of a new album of old songs produced by Was and released under the same title. In 1993, Was had produced an album by Willie Nelson (*Across the Borderline*) that went a long way toward extending the reach of the Texan country singer into the contemporary rock market; Was was known for producing Bob Dylan, Bonnie Raitt, the Rolling Stones, Bob Seger, Elton John, and scores of other "legacy" acts, as they were becoming known. His productions were usually clean and clear and paid subtle homage to the past successes of the older acts he worked with. *I Just Wasn't Made for These Times* is no exception. Beach Boys–style harmonies lift songs that are backed by instruments that remind the listener of the over-pumped organ, brash cymbals, tinkling wind chimes, and doubled reverb of Wilson's mid-1960s recordings without creating a parody or pastiche of them.

As good as the album was, though, it failed to make any impression on Beach Boys fans (or anyone else). Perhaps they were buying Capitol Records' *The Beach Boys 20 Good Vibrations: The Greatest Hits* (April 1995), instead. It appeared that people didn't want to hear subtle, inventive reworkings of Brian's (and Mike's) classic songs; they wanted to hear the originals. Not that Brian minded, and he made two appearances in concert

Previous page: Brian performing as a supporting act for Paul Simon in Mountain View, California, 2001.
Right: "A Tribute to the Beach Boys Featuring" (L-R): Dean Torrence, Bruce Johnston, Mike Love at Super Bowl XXXII.
Following page: Willie Nelson performing with the Beach Boys at Farm Aid, 1996.

with the band at the end of April 1995, in Vegas. He didn't join them for the Big Red Boat cruise the following month, though. Ever willing to find new ways of entertaining their public, the Boys sailed the Bahamas, meeting and greeting fans before playing a gig on the docks in Nassau.

The lineup of the Beach Boys was becoming somewhat fluid by this time. Mike Love and Bruce Johnston were ever present, Al and Carl were missing shows, and David Marks had made a few guest appearances to ensure that there were at least three "original" Beach Boys on stage. Since they rarely (if ever) played songs written after 1970—excepting "Kokomo," naturally—the frontmen and backing band were always spot on with their versions of what had become a fixed set. Pretty much every gig from 1985 to 1999 began with "California Girls," and when the stage was big enough, it could be invaded by female dancers dressed in costumes befitting the stereotype assigned to the region they hail from according to the song.

Toward the end of 1995, with his name on two less-than-successful solo album releases, Brian was persuaded to join with the Beach Boys on a new recording. It wasn't a typical Beach Boys album, though. Since the surprising and overwhelming success of Garth Brooks in the early 1990s, the American music scene had warmly embraced all things country. In a way that was reminiscent of the disco and rap phenomenons, by the mid-1990s musicians of all styles were working with country music artists or recording country songs.

STARS AND STRIPES VOL. 1

RIVER NORTH, AUGUST 1996

Producers	Mike Love (Executive), Brian Wilson, Joe Thomas
Engineers	Rick Fritz, Larry Greenhill, Roger Nichols, Peter Doell
Recorded	10/95–6/96, River North Studios, Chicago, IL; Pedernales, Austin, TX; Mastertonics, Nashville, TN
U.S. Chart	#101 *Billboard Hot 200*, #12 *Billboard* Top Country
Singles	"I Can Hear Music," "Don't Worry Baby," "Little Deuce Coupe," "Long Tall Texan"

Side 1

1. DON'T WORRY BABY Lorrie Morgan
B. Wilson/R. Christian

2. LITTLE DEUCE COUPE James House
B. Wilson/R. Christian

3. 409 Junior Brown
B. Wilson/G. Usher/M. Love

4. LONG TALL TEXAN Doug Supernaw
H. Strzelecki

5. I GET AROUND Sawyer Brown
B. Wilson/M. Love

6. BE TRUE TO YOUR SCHOOL Toby Keith
B. Wilson/M. Love

Side 2

7. FUN, FUN, FUN Ricky Van Shelton
B. WIlson/M. Love

8. HELP ME, RHONDA T Graham Brown
B. Wilson/M. Love

9. THE WARMTH OF THE SUN Willie Nelson
B. Wilson/M. Love

10. SLOOP JOHN B. Colin Raye
Trad. arr.; B. Wilson

11. I CAN HEAR MUSIC Kathy Troccoli
J. Barry/E. Greenwich/P. Spector

12. CAROLINE, NO Timothy B Schmidt
B. Wilson/T. Asher

Mike Love is prominently listed on the artwork for this album as executive producer, and it's clear that he made the selection of songs chosen to be converted into country beach anthems (they include six co-authored by him). The inclusion of "Long Tall Texan" is a reminder of early Beach Boys live performances when they'd giddy up to the Western sing-along that was first a hit in 1959, for Henry Stzelecki's band of brothers, the Four Flickers, and again in 1963, for the Kingsmen. Country music was the hottest genre on the U.S. charts in the mid-1990s, and being a distinctly American music it made some kind of sense to take the beach to Nashville (Chicago and Austin, too) and have country artists add twang to Beach Boys songs. It's a musical mashup that works well, especially since none of the artists who sing lead are bigger than the Beach Boys were at the time. There are no real A-list

Nashville cats mewling about cars, girls, and the California way here, excepting Willie, whose contribution is by far the best. Presumably Garth Brooks, Alan Jackson, Vince Gill, Reba McEntire, and Trisha Yearwood were too busy or uninterested in taking part in the Beach Boys' country project. Also presumably the use of the "Vol. 1" in the title was intended to signal the beginning of a slew of such releases (this remained the only one after 20 years). In truth, this is a peculiar Beach Boys album in that while it contains songs that are part of their never-ending touring set list, the Boys only supply backing harmonies, which were laid down later in L.A. At least it was produced by Brian (with his newly acquired collaborator, Joe Thomas). Tellingly, beachboys.com, an unofficial online resource that lists and reviews all of the band's ouptut, includes this release in their "tribute album" section.

234

Always eager to be a part of the latest fad in music, in October 1995, Brian and the Boys entered Willie Nelson's studio in Pedernales Country Club, Austin, Texas, to begin work with Willie on an album to be titled *Stars and Stripes Vol 1.*

Every track on the album featured the talents of a country music artist, among them Lorrie Morgan, Toby Keith, and Sawyer Brown. The first public airing of the Beach Boys' new direction came in June 1996, at Nashville's Fan Fair, when after performing five songs of their usual set the Boys (including Brian) invited each country star on stage to perform with them. The album was released in August 1996, and made #101 on the *Billboard* album charts, which was much better than the unfortunate *Summer in Paradise* had managed, but not as good as the last greatest hits album had done.

A happy, healthy Brian Wilson with second wife Melinda Ledbetter in December, 1995.

Still, Brian was proving to be productive in the early to mid-1990s, largely because his health had improved significantly after his split with Gene Landy. Subsequent diagnosis of his condition led to a change of medication, to which Brian responded well. He had also married Melinda Ledbetter, whom he first met in 1986, when she demonstrated a car for him as a salesperson. Landy was still in charge of Brian's affairs at that time and encouraged the pair's initial dating. However, after a while Landy changed his mind about Melinda and prevented them from meeting. Following the dissolution of Brian and Landy's partnership, Brian made contact, and the romance developed. They married in February 1995, and went on to adopt five children together. Melinda also encouraged Brian to repair his relationships with his family, especially with his children and Carl.

Daughters Carnie and Wendy, having enjoyed pop stardom, were eager to work with Brian, to perform with him on stage and in the studio. Carnie and Brian had recorded a song for bassist Rob Wasserman's solo album *Trios* in 1994, ("Fantasy Is Reality/Bells of Madness"), which had been produced by Don Was. The father-daughter pairing was big enough news for *Entertainment Tonight* to film a short piece at Brian's house and in the recording studio, showing them working together for the first time. It was undoubtedly the most publicity Wasserman ever got for one of his esoteric albums (that one included contributions from Marc Ribot, Branford Marsalis, and Edie Brickell, among others). The finished track features lead vocals by Carnie accompanied on piano by Brian, who contributes mostly backing harmonies, chorus lines, and a repeated mantra fade out.

Both Carnie and Wendy appeared in *I Just Wasn't Made for These Times*, singing backing vocals on a live version of "Do It Again." In the documentary the performance is intercut with home-movie footage of Brian playing with his daughters when they were babies and toddlers (some of which had been shown on *Entertainment Tonight*). Brian's performance is markedly improved from his 1994 appearance with Wasserman and Carnie.

Following Brian's commitments to the Beach Boys and *Stars and Stripes*, he agreed to record new songs with Carnie and Wendy (as the Wilsons, since Wilson Phillips disbanded in 1993). The resulting album (*The Wilsons*, 1997), included four numbers on which Brian made a significant contribution, including, surprisingly, a new version of "Til I Die," which is oddly upbeat. The album failed to replicate the success of previous Wilson Phillips albums, though, and there was no follow-up release. Still, it stands as a tribute to a hugely improved relationship between father and daughters.

In November 1997, Capitol released a four-CD boxed set titled *The Pet Sound Sessions*, which had caused family and inter–Beach Boys disagreements for more than a year. The package included the mono album, a stereo remix, a CD of alternative versions and other unreleased recordings, plus a CD of a capella versions. Mike was concerned that promotion of the album would once more invoke the idea that it represented the pinnacle of the Beach Boys' career and reignite the idea that Brian was a genius, the rest of the band his vocalists. The sleeve notes, written by David Leaf, author of a pro-Brian, Beach Boys book titled *The Beach Boys and the*

"I like The Beach Boys and I like recording with them. But as people we don't get along."

BRIAN *Wilson*

California Myth (Grosset and Dunlap) in 1978, were not to Mike's liking, and so production was held up while he wrote a separate introduction to the booklet.

Someone had suggested that the Beach Boys tour to promote the release of the boxed set and play the whole album, in sequence. Carl, doubting the band and particularly Brian's capability to do that, refused.

Carl also had other, far more serious, things concerning him than a reissued album at that time. His solo career had stalled following two albums that sold poorly, but in the early 1990s, he began recording with old friends Gerry Beckley (of America), who had toured as part of the Beach Boys, and Robert Lamm of Chicago, the Beach Boys' co-headliners on tour in 1989. Their music was perfectly suited to the AOR, FM-radio market. Sessions began in 1992, but a full-scale album project wasn't finished by the time, in late 1996, that Carl was diagnosed as suffering from lung cancer with secondary traces in his brain. (*Like a Brother*, featuring five songs with Carl singing lead, was released in 2000.)

No public announcement was made about Carl's illness until 1997, by which time he was about to undertake a course of chemotherapy. In August, Carl made his final appearance as part of the Beach Boys on the fourth night of a six-date residency in Atlantic City. An eyewitness at a gig earlier that month wrote on a fan forum in 2007, that Carl looked terrible and took part only in the opening number ("California Girls"), and "God Only Knows." A report on a performance three days before the final show (in New Jersey) listed on the *Endless Summer Quarterly* website esquarterly.com by Gregory J. Mazzeo, states that Carl took lead vocals on "Sail On, Sailor" more than halfway through the set, and two songs later Mike commented with feeling on Carl's fight against illness as he introduced "God Only Knows."

The survival rate of lung cancer patients was (and remains) not good, with around 30 percent of sufferers making it to a year after diagnosis, and less than 8 percent to five years, but Carl—with the support of his second wife, Gina, his children, Jonah and Justyn and their mother, Annie, among others—hoped to beat the disease. Naturally Carl had the support of all his family, but Audree, then in her 80th year, was in poor health and she died in December, 1997.

Both of her remaining sons attended the funeral (making it one more than had appeared at Murry's), where it was remarked that Carl looked surprisingly well—which can only have been because he was undergoing a brief period of remission. Following a family gathering at Carl's house in January 1998, to watch Super Bowl XXXII, Melinda was reported as saying that Brian didn't think that he'd see Carl again. He didn't.

Carl Wilson died on February 6, 1998, and was buried at Westwood Memorial Park, Los Angeles four days later. Brian was distraught and clinging to Melinda; he cried openly and loudly. Eulogies were delivered by the Movement of Spiritual Inner Awareness founder John-Roger (Carl had been a member of his church), Jerry Schilling, Gerry Beckley, and Jonah and Justyn Wilson.

In an interview conducted a few months after the funeral (to promote the release of his solo album *Imagination,* 1998), Brian commented that he and Carl hadn't "really" spoken to one another for 25 years. "We couldn't deal with each other, so we didn't talk to one another." A common theme of all the interviews with Brian in late 1998, was that of loss and loneliness—he was the sole remaining member of the Wilson family who'd resided at, fought, sung, and eventually outgrown 3701 West 119th Street, Hawthorne, California. "I'm the last of the Wilsons," he proclaimed. He wasn't, of course, the last of the Beach Boys, though, and perhaps wasn't even any longer a Beach Boy at all.

The *Pet Sounds Sessions* box set was released a year later than intended, which was to celebrate the band's

thirty-fifth anniversary. As a consequence in 1998, Brian found himself being asked about *Smile*, and during interviews to promote *Imagination* he had to steer conversation away from material that he'd abandoned thirty years earlier. But if it was frustrating for Brian to have to keep dealing with questions about *Pet Sounds* and *Smile*, imagine how it must have been for his cousin.

Arguably, Mike was the only original founding member to have understood that the appeal of the Beach Boys lay in their past and first successes. While *Pet Sounds* figured among them, he had seen and proven that songs recorded earlier were more popular, more requested, and more financially rewarding for all of them.

He was also inclined to exploit recent successes where

Carl Wilson at one of his final Beach Boys appearances, 1996, sharing a joke with Bruce Johnston and Al Jardine.

possible. The Beach Boys' biggest hit single of the post–*Pet Sounds* era had been written and recorded without any input from Brian, and "Kokomo" was the musical calling card of the contemporary Beach Boys at the end of the twentieth century.

In the emerging Internet age, "legacy" acts were being repackaged in new formats and developed as brands that could be licensed to areas of commerce that, on the surface, had little if anything to do with rock-and-roll music. Rock and pop songs had been licensed to television and radio advertisements to help sell a range of goods.

SMILE

CAPITOL, NOVEMBER 2011

Producer	Brian Wilson
Engineers	Mark Linett, Alan Boyd
Recorded	10/15/65–6/19/71, Western Recorders, Gold Star, Capitol Studio, Brian Wilson's home, Hollywood
U.S. Chart	#27 *Billboard*
Singles	"Cabin Essence"

LP1/Side 1/Movement 1

All songs by B. Wilson/V. D. Parks unless stated

1. OUR PRAYER

B. Wilson

2. GEE

W. Davis/M. Levy

3. HEROES AND VILLAINS

4. DO YOU LIKE WORMS (ROLL PLYMOUTH ROCK)

5. I'M IN GREAT SHAPE

6. BARNYARD

7. MY ONLY SUNSHINE (THE OLD MASTER PAINTER/ YOU ARE MY SUNSHINE

H. Gillespie/J. Davis/C. Mitchell

8. CABIN ESSENCE

Side 2/Movement 2

1. WONDERFUL

2. LOOK (SONG FOR CHILDREN)

B. Wilson

3. CHILD IS FATHER OF THE MAN

4. SURF'S UP

LP2/Side 1/Movement 3

1. I WANNA BE AROUND/WORKSHOP

J. Mercer/B. Wilson

2. VEGA-TABLES

3. HOLIDAYS

B. Wilson

4. WIND CHIMES

B. Wilson

5. THE ELEMENTS: FIRE (MRS. O'LEARY'S COW)

B. Wilson

6. LOVE TO SAY DADA

B. Wilson

7. GOOD VIBRATIONS

B. Wilson/M. Love

Side 2/LP Exclusive content

1. YOU'RE WELCOME (Stereo)

2. VEGA-TABLES (Stereo)

3. WIND CHIMES (Stereo)

4. CABIN ESSENCE (Session excerpt and stereo backing)

5. SURF'S UP (Session excerpt, stereo)

Better late than never, *Smile* was released 44 years after first being slated to appear, and with its original cover (commissioned from artist Frank J. Holmes). The wait was, according to reviews, worth it, if only to lay to rest some of the multitude of rumors that abounded about the recording. Fittingly, given the nature of the album's creation story, Capitol produced a varied package of versions. In October 2011, *Smile* first appeared as a download, via Apple's iTunes. A month later not only one physical version of the album appeared, but three. The single CD (and vinyl) presented the album as it would (probably, possibly) have appeared in 1967. The double-disc version included extra stereo mixes, unfinished pieces, and outtakes, but the five-CD boxed set contains everything (possibly, probably) that the true Beach Boys fan could want and that could be rescued from the hundreds of hours of tapes that Brian Wilson abandoned in 1967. The boxed set was, as Al Jardine put it, "the Holy Grail for Beach Boys fans," and presumably those hunters for the Grail were satisfied. Although, apparently there are still some tapes…

Mike Love with his Beach Boys in 2015, when
Club Kokomo VIP tickets were sold at gigs.

Everything from makeup to motorbikes, perfume to dishwashing liquid has used pop music to sell it since Elvis joined the army. However, as the 1990s came to a conclusion, enterprising rock-and-roll acts (and their business managers) had begun to extend the reach and return of their heritage into other, more lucrative areas.

The Rolling Stones endorsed a Volkswagen Golf model range in 1995, in return for tour sponsorship and a royalty. In 1997, David Bowie bonds based around the future success of his pre-1990 catalogue of songs were sold for $55 million to Prudential Insurance Company of America. The following year the same bond trader (David Pullman) sold a similar bond on behalf of Holland–Dozier–Holland, the Motown songwriting trio, for $30 million. As the deal struck with Chrysler for *Still Cruisin'* had shown, the Beach Boys were an attractive brand, ripe for commercial exploitation.

However, the band name was the property of Brother Records and subject to control of all the band members. But "Kokomo" as a name was not the property of anyone. As co-writer of the song and a Beach Boy, Mike had a celebrity worth that he attempted to put into play when he registered a trademark for "Mike Love's Club Kokomo" in January 1996, intending to develop an "eater-tainment" chain of club-restaurants.

He made financial history by sending out the first CD-ROM seeking financial backing from investors. The opportunity was described as being for "Mike Love's Club Kokomo...a restaurant/club/brand developed to appeal to a family demographic, while promoting the preservation of natural habitats and the production of alternative resources. The locations are styled in a California meets the Caribbean theme and feature casual dining, live and interactive multimedia entertainment

and a brand name retail store for the entire family." It wasn't a wholly profit-making venture, as the release explained: "A percentage of the chain's profits will be donated annually to a rotating number of environmentally conscious charities." The initial location was planned to open in Las Vegas in late 1997. (It didn't.)

The CD-ROM offered, as Mike explained in the press release that announced it, "a really great presentation with our music and my voice-over walking the viewer through a conceptual location, so they can experience the concept for themselves." It failed to attract enough investment at the time, sadly, and the trademark application was abandoned in 2007. However, in 2015, "Club Kokomo" was used as the selection choice for VIP tickets to Beach Boys gigs. Included in the price (at approximately four times the standard ticket) were a pre-show VIP meet-and-greet and a photograph taken with the Beach Boys, participation in a question-and-answer session with the band, access to an exclusive VIP-only soundcheck, an autographed VIP access pass, and a complimentary drink.

Club Kokomo VIP tickets were a direct descendant of Mike's smart recognition early on of the potential for commercial branding, sponsorship, and exclusive offers on Beach Boys recordings. The success of the Radio Shack cassette-only recordings that he and Dean Torrence made in 1983 was repeated in 1997, when a deal was done with Union 76 Gas stations and NASCAR to release an album. He, Bruce, and David (billed as "From the Beach Boys") along with Torrence recorded new versions of 10 Beach Boys car songs for release on a cassette to be distributed only via Union 76 Gas stations in 1998. All of them sound so close to the originals as to almost be them.

Also that year, Mike, Bruce, David Marks (who had officially rejoined the Beach Boys at Mike's invitation in October 1997, to fill Carl's place), and Dean Torrence appeared in the pre–Super Bowl XXXII game entertainment package. Billed as "A Tribute to the Beach Boys Featuring Mike Love, Bruce Johnston, David Marks, Glen Campbell, Dean Torrence, and John Stamos," they performed as part of a history of California shows alongside the 5th Dimension and L.A.-born country singer Lee Greenwood. Watching on TV, Al Jardine was reportedly a little surprised to see his bandmates take the stage: he'd not been told about the booking. Presumably neither had Brian or Carl, who were watching their last ever Super Bowl together at Carl's house. Not that they would have cared to be there, perhaps.

It can't have been too much of a shock that Al hadn't been called about the gig, though, given that around the time David Marks rejoined the Beach Boys officially in October 1997, Al had pretty much retired from touring with them. He did remain as a board member of Brother Records, and so retained an interest in Beach Boys business—just not all of their live performances.

Even after moving his home from L.A. to Big Sur, and like the rest of the band, Al played his part in ensuring that the Beach Boys remained a family business. Mike's brothers and cousins had been employed on the business rather than the performing side of the Beach Boys, Brian's (first) wife and daughters had sung with the band, and Al's son Matt had toured with them since the late 1980s. Matt became an official backing band member (and vocalist, taking Brian's falsetto parts) in 1990, after passing an audition.

In 1998, the Jardines set up their own touring outfit, calling it Beach Boys Family and Friends. For their first gig, the inaugural Carl Wilson Walk Against Cancer and Benefit Concert on October 18, they were joined on stage by Matt's brother Adam, Al's brother-in-law Billy Hinche, Carnie and Wendy Wilson, and Cass Elliott's daughter Owen. Daryl "Captain" Dragon played piano, just as he had for the Beach Boys in the early 1970s, when his wife, Toni Tennille, sang backing vocals.

After performing at a few gigs (plus a TV chat show),

Al's Beach Boys were hit with a writ from Brother Records in April 1999, charging him with infringing the trademarked name of the Beach Boys. He had to stop using the Beach Boys in his band name.

Following Carl's death, Mike toured with the California Beach Band as well as the Beach Boys (who played an Australian tour in December). The California Beach Band appearances (sometimes unofficially listed as "America's Band") only ever guaranteed that Mike Love would be on stage, while the Beach Boys always included either and/or Bruce and David, too. The song lists played at gigs by both acts were interchangeable, as too, was the backing band, which in 1998, included regular Beach Boys player Jeff Foskett, who'd taken over the falsetto parts invented by Brian—but who toured as part of Brian's backing band in late 1999.

David Marks left the touring Beach Boys in July 1999, leaving Mike as the only founding member and Bruce the only other "official" member on stage. This actually meant that, as long as Al's Friends and Family were touring and performing some of the same songs, Beach Boys fans had twice the number of opportunities to hear their back catalogue played live by founding members. Al's set up had Carnie and Wendy singing lead, with Al and Matt backing and switching leads, while Mike and Bruce added the singing skills of John Stamos, Chris Farmer, Phil Bardowell, and Adrian Baker to their own.

To add to the confusion surrounding Beach Boys gigs at the end of the '90s, there was also the touring entity the Endless Summer Band, featuring Al Jardine—but in the early 1980s Mike Love and Dean Torrence had listed the name Endless Summer Beach Band as the backing combo on two recordings for tiny Santa Barbara–based label Hitbound Records (both were giveaways: "Da Doo

Right: Al Jardine on stage during the Beach Boys *50th Anniversary Tour*, 2012.

"It was me with the concepts and Brian with the music, and that's where the strength lay."

MIKE *Love*

Ron Ron" b/w "Baby Talk" in 1982 for Radio Shack, and "Be True to Your Bud" in 1983, for Budweiser).

At the end of the century, however, everything would become much simpler, because all licenses to use the name the Beach Boys expired on December 31, 1999. All future new licenses had to be approved by the directors of Brother Records.

Those allowed to vote on the awarding of licenses at Brother were Mike, Brian via his legal representative, the estate of Carl, Al Jardine, and Brother Records' legal representative (because the company owned Dennis's vote, acquired from his estate). In January 2000, Brother refused Al the right to a license for the use of the Beach Boys name to advertise any touring band he led. Mike, however, did acquire a license to tour as the Beach Boys.

Al retitled his band Al Jardine's Family and Friends Beach Band and issued a writ against Brother to gain access to the name of the act that he'd helped to create. (It failed.) His outfit played a few gigs that year while, as usual, Mike and Bruce fronted a Beach Boys band that toured throughout 2000, playing gigs across America.

Aptly, while Mike and Bruce were fronting the Beach Boys on tour and Al was paying his own tribute to their shared musical heritage with his Friends and Family, Brian

Wilson had undertaken his first solo tour. Beginning in Ann Arbor in March 1999, Brian, accompanied by a small orchestra of a dozen multi-instrumental musicians, performed almost 30 songs from his extensive back catalogue. Three dates in March were followed by six more in June in America, and then four in Japan in July. The year was ended with nine dates in America and a New Year's Eve performance in Redondo Beach, California, at which Brian sang "Auld Lang Syne."

The first tour's set list was filled with early Beach Boys songs, some classic *Pet Sounds*–era numbers (including the title track, "God Only Knows," "Caroline, No," and "Good Vibrations") and a few more recent numbers. In April 2000, Brian performed with the band at the Roxy in Los Angeles and recorded two nights, from which *Live at the Roxy Theater* was collated. It was released on Brian's own label (Brimel) and made exclusively available via his website for a year only, from June 2000.

In July 2000, Brian took to the stage again, in Easton, Pennsylvania, with a slightly different small orchestra. The night was divided into distinct parts, the first played by the orchestra alone, who struck up "The Wilson Suite," arranged by Van Dyke Parks and conducted by Larry Baird. It included snatches of classic Beach Boys hits and tracks from *Pet Sounds*, but no solo songs.

That was followed by Brian and the band performing a dozen numbers from the previous year's live set. The third and headline section of the two-hour-long performance came last: *Pet Sounds* was played by Brian, his band, and the orchestra in its entirety. The audience response was reportedly as awestruck as Brian had been the first time that he'd heard his performance with band and

orchestra in rehearsal. For as long as the album had been in existence Brian had doubted that he'd ever be able to perform it all live, on stage. It was only after first hearing an L.A. band called the Wondermints play some of his songs in 1995, that he'd begun to consider

Below: Elton John with Brian at Radio City Music Hall in 2000.

performing with a band other than the Beach Boys, who could make his songs sound good. Working with Darian Sahanaja, Nicky Wonder, Mike D'Amico, and Probyn Gregory of the band, along with Jeff Foskett (with whom he felt most comfortable), Brian developed a live version of *Pet Sounds* that improved with each performance.

As worldwide audiences reacted positively to each performance of *Pet Sounds* live, it gave Brian the confidence to try what had previously been completely unthinkable to him: reconstructing his *Smile*.

Tentative first steps toward *Smile*-era material being considered as suitable for live performance came at a Christmas party in 2000, when Brian took a request to play "Heroes and Villains." The party erupted into cheers and requests to play it again to an apparently delighted Brian. In March 2001, a Brian Wilson tribute night in New York's Radio City Music Hall opened with the Choir of Harlem singing "Our Prayer." Later Glen Campbell performed "Surf's Up" to rapturous applause. Later that year, when Darian Sahanaja of the Wondermints (with support from Melinda) suggested that Brian tour playing *Smile*, he surprisingly agreed.

It took three years before they got around to performing *Brian Wilson Presents Smile*, but eventually did so in London, on February 20, 2004. The show was recorded and released in album form in September (on Nonesuch). It was his second album release of the year, and followed a collection that included high-profile collaborations with Eric Clapton, Elton John, and Paul McCartney. *Gettin' in over My Head* (Rhino) is essentially a compilation, bringing together numbers recorded over the course of several years previously. *BWPS* made a remarkable #13 on the U.S. album charts, but *Gettin' in Over My Head* struggled to #100.

The following decade proved to be one of Brian's most prolific periods of work since the 1960s. After recording a Christmas album (for Arista) in 2005, he worked on a series of *Pet Sounds* fortieth anniversary concerts

Opposite: Appearing on *Good Morning America* in June 2012. L–R: Mike, David, Brian, Bruce, Al.

the following year. In 2007, he toured extensively and began work on songs that would become, in 2008, a new album. Titled *That Lucky Old Sun* (Capitol), it used a spoken-word narrative interspersed with musical interludes. Devised and co-written with Scott Bennett and Van Dyke Parks, it made #21 on the U.S. album charts.

Clearly Brian Wilson could sell albums again, as his takes on the music that he and Audree loved so much was to prove. *Brian Wilson Reimagines Gershwin* (2010, Walt Disney), a vanity project released before he'd recorded *In the Key of Disney* (2011, Disney), amazingly made #26 on release. The *Disney* album didn't fare as well, though, only reaching #83 on the U.S. chart.

Meanwhile, Mike and Bruce's Beach Boys continued to tour the band's greatest hits to no obvious decline in demand. In 2006, they joined Brian, Al, and David on top of the Capitol building to celebrate 40 years of *Pet Sounds*. In 2011, the Beach Boys released a charity single, "Don't Fight the Sea," originally recorded in 1976 with a lead by Al (it was included on his debut solo album, *A Postcard from California*, Fontana, 2010) with proceeds going to survivors of an earthquake in Japan. Later that year, and inspired by the success of *Brian Wilson Presents Smile*, the five surviving Beach Boys helped to promote Capitol's release of *The Smile Sessions*. It made #27 on the U.S. album charts and won a Grammy.

To celebrate 50 years as a touring act, the Beach Boys became a recording band once more, and in 2012, released *That's Why God Made the Radio* (Capitol). It sounds more like a new and relevant Beach Boys album than any released since 1985, and deservedly reached #3 on the U.S. album charts. That year was taken up with a fiftieth anniversary tour of the world, which was roundly cheered everywhere. Using Brian's live touring band as backing, he, Mike, Al, Bruce, and David appeared to be

enormously enjoying performing together.

The touring idyll had a limited lifespan, however, as Mike showed in June 2012, (midway through the fiftieth tour) when he booked dates for 2013, without Brian. Mike and Bruce returned to playing Beach Boys U.S. shows without the other members (David returned in 2015). Subsequent live shows by Brian saw Al and David on stage with him, all playing old Beach Boys songs.

The Beach Boys, being a family affair, will doubtless reconcile and fall out again for as long as they're able to perform and record. Who'd be surprised if there was a reunion sixtieth anniversary tour? Meanwhile, there will always be a Beach Boys gigging somewhere—and a new compilation album coming soon.

The Beach Boys at the Hollywood
Bowl, June 2, 2012.

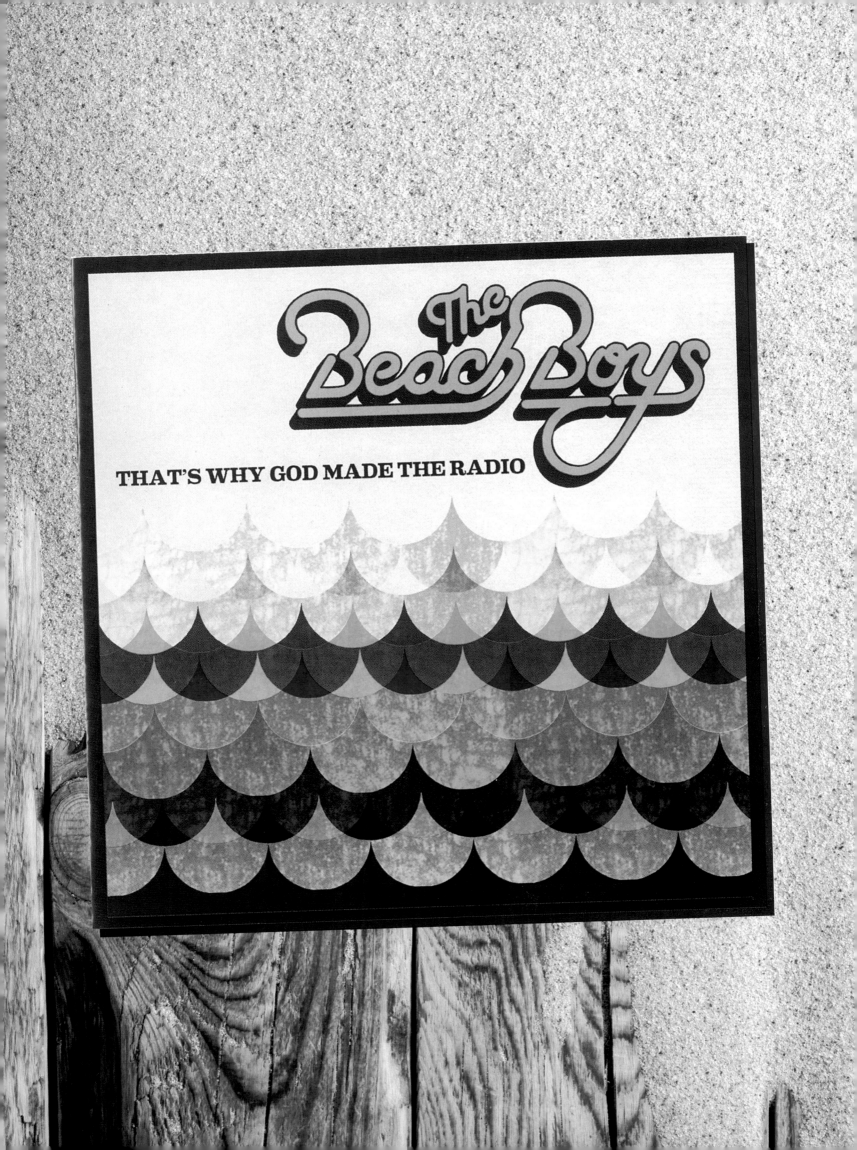

THAT'S WHY GOD MADE THE RADIO

CAPITOL, JUNE 2012

Producers	Mike Love (Executive), Brian Wilson
Engineers	Joe Thomas (listed as "recorded by"), Frank Pappalardo
Recorded	7/11, 3/12, Ocean Way Recording, Hollywood; Ben's Studio, Nashville; World Stage Studios, Burr Ridge, IL; Love Shack, Incline Village, NV; Chicago Recording Co., Chicago
U.S. Chart	#3 *Billboard*
Singles	"That's Why God Made the Radio," "Isn't It Time"

Side 1

1. THINK ABOUT THE DAYS
B. Wilson/J. Thomas

2. THAT'S WHY GOD MADE THE RADIO
B. Wilson/M. Love/J. Thomas/L. Millas/J. Peterik

3. ISN'T IT TIME
B. Wilson/M. Love/J. Thomas/L. Millas/J. Peterik

4. SPRING VACATION
B. Wilson/M. Love/J. Thomas

5. THE PRIVATE LIFE OF BILL AND SUE
B. Wilson/J. Thomas

6. SHELTER
B. Wilson/J. Thomas

Side 2

7. DAYBREAK OVER THE OCEAN
M. Love

8. BEACHES IN MIND
B. Wilson/M. Love/J. Thomas

9. STRANGE WORLD
B. Wilson/J. Thomas

10. FROM THERE TO BACK AGAIN
B. Wilson/J. Thomas

11. PACIFIC COAST HIGHWAY
B. Wilson/J. Thomas

12. SUMMER'S GONE
B. Wilson/J. Bon Jovi/J. Thomas

By the time the reconciled Beach Boys assembled to make this album, Brian Wilson was the healthiest and possibly happiest that he'd been since 1967. With a blissful marriage and young children at home, and having received mass adulation from fans and critics alike for a series of great live performances, he'd even had a couple of hit solo albums. Brian clearly enjoyed working with the longest-lasting collaborator he'd had since Mike and he first got together. Joe Thomas (whose River North label had released the last Beach Boys album) had moved in next door to Brian in 1997, in Chicago so that they could make *Imagination* (1998), and they'd continued to work together ever since. Every song on this, the first official album of new Beach Boys songs since 1992, apart from Mike's solo effort, was written by Brian and Thomas (sometimes with others), and had their roots in earlier solo Wilson albums. Thomas reminded Brian about songs they'd demo'd that were obviously Beach Boys numbers and hadn't been included on solo releases in the past. Thomas worked to broker a reconciliation between Love and Brian, and the result was this nostalgic album of self-referencing originals that includes musical contributions from David Marks and Bruce Johnston alongside Brian and Mike. The musical backing comes from Brian's touring band and a raft of other session players. There are enough musical reminders of past Beach Boys classics—a hook here, a guitar phrase there, harmonies swooping in wordless sound—to remind listeners that it's only when the Beach Boys get together that their true musical chemistry works. None of Brian's solo albums (nor those by Mike or Al) ever really get to be as reminiscent or redolent of past Beach Boys glories as this album does.

Discography

SINGLES: YEAR / A-SIDE B/W B-SIDE /(LABEL)

1961 Surfin' b/w Luau (Candix)

1962 Surfin' Safari b/w 409 (Capitol)

1962 Ten Little Indians b/w County Fair (Capitol)

1963 Surfin' USA b/w Shut Down (Capitol)

1963 Surfer Girl b/w Little Deuce Coupe (Capitol)

1963 Be True to Your School b/w In My Room (Capitol)

1963 Little Saint Nick b/w The Lord's Prayer (Capitol)

1964 Fun, Fun, Fun b/w Why Do Fools Fall in Love (Capitol)

1964 I Get Around b/w Don't Worry Baby (Capitol)

1964 When I Grow Up to Be a Man b/w She Knows Me Too Well (Capitol)

1964 Dance, Dance, Dance b/w The Warmth of the Sun (Capitol)

1964 The Man with All the Toys b/w Blue Christmas (Capitol)

1965 Do You Wanna Dance b/w Please Let Me Wonder (Capitol)

1965 Help Me, Rhonda b/w Kiss Me, Baby (Capitol)

1965 California Girls b/w Let Him Run Wild (Capitol)

1965 The Little Girl I Once Knew b/w There's No Other (Like My Baby) (Capitol)

1965 Barbara Ann b/w Girl Don't Tell Me (Capitol)

1966 Sloop John B. b/w You're So Good to Me (Capitol)

1966 Wouldn't It Be Nice b/w God Only Knows (Capitol)

1966 Good Vibrations b/w Let's Go Away for a While (Capitol)

1967 Then I Kissed Her b/w Mountain of Love (Capitol)

1967 Heroes and Villains b/w You're Welcome (Capitol)

1967 Wild Honey b/w Wind Chimes (Capitol)

1967 Darlin' b/w Here Today (Capitol)

1968 Friends b/w Little Bird (Capitol)

1968 Do It Again b/w Wake The World (Capitol)

1968 Bluebirds Over the Mountain b/w Never Learn Not to Love (Capitol)

1969 I Can Hear Music b/w All I Want to Do (Capitol)

1969 Break Away b/w Celebrate the News (Capitol)

1970 Add Some Music to Your Day b/w Susie Cincinnati (Brother/Reprise)

1970 Cottonfields b/w The Nearest Faraway Place (Brother/Reprise)

1970 Slip on Through b/w This Whole World (Brother/Reprise)

1970 Tears in the Morning b/w It's About Time (Brother/Reprise)

1971 Cool, Cool Water b/w Forever (Brother/Reprise)

1971 Wouldn't It Be Nice (Live) b/w The Times They Are a Changin' (Live) (Ode)

1971 Long Promised Road b/w Deirdre (Brother/Reprise)

1971 Surf's Up b/w Don't Go Near the Water (Brother/Reprise)

1972 You Need a Mess of Help to Stand Alone b/w Cuddle Up (Brother/Reprise)

1972 Marcella b/w Hold on Dear Brother (Brother/Reprise)

1973 Sail On, Sailor b/w Only with You (Brother/Reprise)

1973 California Saga: California b/w Funky Pretty (Brother/Reprise)

1974 Child of Winter (Christmas Song) b/w Susie Cincinnati (Brother/Reprise)

1975 Sail On, Sailor b/w Only with You (Brother/Reprise)

1976 Rock and Roll Music b/w T.M. Song (Brother/Reprise)

1976 It's O.K. b/w Had to Phone Ya (Brother/Reprise)

1976 Everyone's in Love with You b/w Susie Cincinnati (Brother/Reprise)

1977 Honkin' Down the Highway b/w Solar System (Brother/Reprise)

1978 Peggy Sue b/w Hey Little Tomboy (Brother/Reprise)

1979 Here Comes the Night b/w Baby Blue (Brother/Caribou/CBS)

1979 Good Timin' b/w Love Surrounds Me (Brother/Caribou/CBS)

1979 Lady Lynda b/w Full Sail (Brother/Caribou/CBS)

1979 It's a Beautiful Day b/w Sumahama (Caribou)

1980 Goin' On b/w Endless Harmony (Caribou)

1980 Livin' with a Heartache b/w Santa Ana Winds (Caribou)

1981 The Beach Boys Medley b/w God Only Knows (Capitol)

1981 Come Go With Me b/w Don't Go Near the Water (Caribou)

1985 Getcha Back b/w Male Ego (Brother)

1985 It's Gettin' Late b/w It's O.K. (Caribou)

1985 She Believes in Love Again b/w It's Just a Matter of Time (Caribou)

1986 Rock 'n' Roll to the Rescue b/w Good Vibrations (Live) (Capitol)

1986 California Dreamin' b/w Lady Liberty (Capitol)

1987 Wipe Out b/w N/A [with the Fat Boys] (Urban)

1988 Kokomo b/w Tutti Frutti (Elektra)

1988 Don't Worry Baby b/w N/A [with the Everly Brothers] (Capitol)

1989 Still Cruisin' b/w Kokomo (Capitol)

1990 Somewhere Near Japan b/w Kokomo (Capitol)

1990 Problem Child b/w N/A (RCA)

1992 Forever b/w Forever mixes [with John Stamos] (Brother)

1992 Hot Fun in the Summertime b/w Summer of Love (Brother)

1996 I Just Wasn't Made for These Times b/w Wouldn't It Be Nice (Sub Pop)

1996 I Can Hear Music b/w N/A [with Kathy Troccoli] (River North)

1996 Little Deuce Coupe b/w N/A [with James House] (River North)

2011 Cabin Essence b/w Wonderful (Capitol)

2012 That's Why God Made the Radio b/w Instrumental version (Capitol)

2012 Isn't It Time b/w California Girls, Do It Again, Sail On, Sailor (Live) (Capitol)

ALBUMS: YEAR / TITLE (LABEL)

1962 *Surfin' Safari* (Capitol)

1963 *Surfin' USA* (Capitol)

1963 *Surfer Girl* (Capitol)

1963 *Little Deuce Coupe* (Capitol)

1964 *Shut Down Volume 2* (Capitol)

1964 *All Summer Long* (Capitol)

1964 *Beach Boys Concert* (Capitol)

1964 *The Beach Boys' Christmas Album* (Capitol)

1965 *The Beach Boys Today!* (Capitol)

1965 *Summer Days (and Summer Nights!!)* (Capitol)

1965 *Beach Boys' Party!* (Capitol)

1966 *Pet Sounds* (Capitol)

1966 *Best of the Beach Boys* (Capitol)

1967 *Smiley Smile* (Capitol)

1967 *Best of the Beach Boys Volume 2* (Capitol)

1967 *Wild Honey* (Capitol)

1968 *Best of the Beach Boys Volume 3* (Capitol)

1968 *Stack O' Tracks* [instrumental compilation] (Capitol)

1968 *Friends* (Capitol)

1969 *20/20* (Capitol)

1970 *Sunflower* (Brother/Reprise)

1970 *Good Vibrations* [compilation] (Capitol)

1970 *Live in London* (Capitol)

1971 *Surf's Up* (Brother/Reprise)

1972 *Carl and the Passions—"So Tough"* (Brother/Reprise)

1973 *Holland* (Brother/Reprise)

1973 *The Beach Boys in Concert* (Brother/Reprise)

1974 *Endless Summer* [compilation] (Capitol)

1975 *Spirit of America* [compilation] (Capitol)

1975 *Good Vibrations – Best of the Beach Boys* (Brother/Reprise)

1976 *15 Big Ones* (Brother/Reprise)

1977 *Beach Boys Love You* (Brother/Reprise)

1978 *M.I.U. Album* (Brother/Reprise)

1979 *L.A. (Light Album)* (Brother/Caribou/CBS)

1980 *Keepin' the Summer Alive* (Brother/Caribou/CBS)

1981 *Ten Years of Harmony* [compilation] (Brother/Caribou/CBS)

1982 *Sunshine Dream* (Brother/Caribou/CBS) (Capitol)

1983 *Rarities* (Brother/Caribou/CBS) (Capitol)

1985 *The Beach Boys* (Brother/Caribou)

1986 *Made in the USA* [compilation] (Capitol)

1989 *Still Cruisin'* (Capitol)

1991 *Lost & Found (1961–62)* [compilation] (DCC Compact Classics)

1992 *Summer in Paradise* (Brother Entertainment)

1993 *Good Vibrations: Thirty Years of The Beach Boys* [box set] (Capitol)

1996 *Stars & Stripes Vol. 1* (River North)

1997 *The Pet Sounds Sessions* [box set] (Capitol)

1998 *Endless Harmony Soundtrack* (Capitol)

1998 *Ultimate Christmas* [compilation] (Capitol)

1999 *The Capitol Years* [box set] (Capitol)

1999 *The Greatest Hits–Volume 1: 20 More Good Vibrations* (Capitol)

1999 *The Greatest Hits–Volume 2: 20 Good Vibrations* (Capitol)

2000 *The Greatest Hits–Volume 3: Best of the Brother Years 1970–1986* (Capitol)

2001 *The Very Best of the Beach Boys* (EMI)

2001 *Hawthorne, CA* [compilation] (Capitol)

2002 *Classics Selected by Brian Wilson* [compilation]
    (Capitol)

2002 *Good Timin': Live at Knebworth, 1980* (Brother/Eagle)

2003 *Sounds of Summer: The Very Best of the Beach Boys*
    [compilation] (Capitol)

2005 *The Platinum Collection* (Sounds of Summer Edition)
    [compilation] (EMI)

2006 *Songs from Here & Back* (Hallmark)

2007 *The Warmth of the Sun* [compilation] (Capitol)

2008 *The Original U.S. Singles Collection the Capitol Years
    1962–1965* [box set] (Capitol)

2009 *Summer Love Songs* [compilation] (Capitol)

2011 *The Smile Sessions* [box set] (Capitol)

2012 *That's Why God Made the Radio* (Capitol)

2012 *Fifty Big Ones* [compilation] (Capitol)

2013 *Live–the 50th Anniversary Tour* (Capitol)

2013 *Made in California* [compilation] (Capitol)

2014 *Keep an Eye on Summer–the Beach Boys Sessions
    1964* [compilation] (Capitol)

2014 *Live in Sacramento 1964* (Capitol)

SOLO DISCOGRAPHY

Al Jardine Singles:

2002 PT Cruiser b/w PT Cruiser (a capella) (CQ)

2011 Don't Fight the Sea b/w Friends (a capella) (Capitol)

Al Jardine Albums:

2001 *Live in Las Vegas* (Jardine Tours)

2010 *A Postcard from California* (Jardine Tours)

Bruce Johnston Singles:

1962 Do the Surfer Stomp (Part One) b/w Do the Surfer
    Stomp (Part Two) (Donna)

1962 Soupy Shuffle Stomp b/w Moon Shot (Donna)

1963 The Original Surfer Stomp b/w Pajama Party (Del-Fi)

1977 Pipeline b/w Disney Girls (1957) (Columbia)

1977 Rendezvous b/w I Write the Songs (Columbia)

Bruce Johnston Albums:

1962 *Surfer's Pajama Party* (Del-Fi)

1963 *Surfin' Round the World* (Columbia)

1977 *Going Public* (Columbia)

Mike Love Singles:

1967 [+ Brian Wilson] Devoted to You b/w Gettin' Hungry
    (Capitol)

1974 I Can't Leave You Alone b/w Rain (Delta France)

1981 Runnin' Around the World b/w One Good Reason
    (Boardwalk Entertainment Co.)

1981 Looking Back with Love b/w One Good Reason
    (Boardwalk Entertainment Co.)

1982 [+ Dean Torrence, Endless Summer Beach Band]
    Da Doo Ron Ron b/w Baby Talk (Hitbound)

1983 Jingle Bell Rock b/w Let's Party (Creole)

2006 Santa's Going to Kokomo b/w N/A (M.E.L.E.CO)

Mike Love Albums:

1981 *Looking Back with Love* (Boardwalk Entertainment Co.)

1983 [+ Dean Torrence] *Rock 'n' Roll City* (Realistic)

1996 *Catch a Wave* (M.E.L.E.CO)

1998 [+ Bruce Johnston and David Marks of The Beach Boys]
    Salutes NASCAR (Union 76)

Brian Wilson Singles:

1966 Caroline No b/w Summer Means New Love (Capitol)

1967 Gettin' Hungry b/w Devoted to You (with Mike Love)
    (Capitol)

1987 Let's Go to Heaven in My Car b/w Too Much Sugar
(Sire)

1988 Love and Mercy b/w He Couldn't Get His Poor Old Body
    to Move (Sire)

1989 Melt Away b/w Being with the One You Love (Sire)

1995 Do It Again b/w Til I Die, This Song Wants to Sleep
    with You Tonight (MCA)

1998 Your Imagination b/w Happy Days (Giant)

2004 Wonderful b/w Wind Chimes (Nonesuch)

2004 Good Vibrations b/w In Blue Hawaii (Nonesuch)

2005 What I Really Want for Christmas b/w We Wish You a
    Merry Christmas, Brian's Christmas Message (Sony
    BMG)

2008 Midnight's Another Day b/w That Lucky Old Sun,
    Morning Beat (Capitol)

Brian Wilson Albums:

1988 *Brian Wilson* (Sire)

1995 *I Just Wasn't Made for These Times* (MCA)

1995 *Orange Crate Art* [+ Van Dyke Parks] (Warner Bros)

1998 *Imagination* (Giant)

2000 *Live at the Roxy Theater* (Brimel)

2002 *Pet Sounds Live* (Sanctuary)

2004 *Gettin' in Over My Head* (Warner Bros)

2004 *Brian Wilson Presents SMiLE* (Nonesuch)

2005 *What I Really Want for Christmas* (Arista)

2008 *That Lucky Old Sun* (Capitol)

2010 *Brian Wilson Reimagines Gershwin* (Disney)

2011 *In the Key of Disney* (Disney)

2015 *No Pier Pressure* (Capitol)

Carl Wilson Singles:

1981 Hold Me b/w Hurry Love (Caribou)

1981 Heaven b/w Hurry Love (Caribou)

1983 What You Do to Me b/w Time (Caribou)

1983 Givin' You Up b/w It's Too Early to Tell (Caribou)

Carl Wilson Albums:

1981 *Carl Wilson* (Caribou)

1983 *Youngblood* (Carbou)

2000 [Beckley-Lamm-Wilson] *Like a Brother* (Transparent Music)

Dennis Wilson Singles:

1970 Sound of Free b/w Lady (Stateside; UK only)

1977 River Song b/w Farewell My Friend (Caribou; Europe only)

1977 You and I b/w Friday Night (Caribou)

Dennis Wilson Albums:

1977 *Pacific Ocean Blue* (Caribou)

2008 *Pacific Ocean Blue 30th Anniversary Edition Inc. Bambu* (the Caribou Sessions) (Caribou/Sony Legacy)

Filmography

YEAR / TITLE / STUDIO

1965 *The Girls on the Beach* (Paramount)

1965 *The Monkey's Uncle* (Walt Disney Productions)

1985 *The Beach Boys: An American Band* (High Ridge Productions)

1996 *The Beach Boys: Nashville Sounds* (Delilah Films, Disney Channel, BMG)

1998 *The Beach Boys: Endless Harmony* (Capitol)

1998 *The Beach Boys' Lost Concert 1964* (Brother,SabuCat Productions)

2003 *Good Timin': Live at Knebworth 1980* (Eagle Rock Ent., Brother Records)

2003 *Surfing USA: Featuring the Hits of the Beach Boys* (Passport Video)

2004 *The Beach Boys' Good Vibrations Tour 1976* (Eagle Vision USA, Brother Records)

2006 *The Beach Boys in London 1966* (Rex Features)

2012 *The Beach Boys Live in Concert: 50th Anniversary Tour* (SMC Recordings)

Bibliography

AUTHOR / TITLE / (PUBLISHER, YEAR)

Kinglsey Abbott, *Back to the Beach* (Helter Skelter, 1997)

Keith Badman, *The Beach Boys: The Definitive Diary of America's Greatest Band on Stage and in the Studio* (Backbeat, 2004)

Peter Ames Carlin, *Catch a Wave: The Rise, Fall & Redemption of Beach Boys' Brian Wilson* (Rodale, 2006)

Mark Dillon, *Fifty Sides of The Beach Boys: The Songs That Tell Their Story* (ECW, 2012)

Steven Gaines, *Heroes & Villains: The True Story of The Beach Boys* (Da Capo Press, 1995)

Timothy White, *The Nearest Faraway Place: Brian Wilson, The Beach Boys, and the Southern California Experience* (Henry Holt, 1995)

Paul Williams, *Brian Wilson & The Beach Boys: How Deep is the Ocean?* (Omnibus, 1997)

Websites of Note

www.beachboys.com

www. beachboysarchives.com

www. esquarterly.com

www. forums.stevehoffman.tv

www. mountvernonandfairway.de

www. smileysmile.net

www.rollingstone.com/music/artists/the-beach-boys

OTHER ONLINE SOURCES

www.abilitymagazine.com/past/brianw/brianw.html

www.cinetropic.com/blacktop/people/

www.campaignstops.blogs.nytimes.com/2012/07/02/ be-true-to-your-school/?_r=0

www.rockcellaramagazine.com (interviews with Tony Asher and David Marks)

www.uncanny1.blogspot.co.uk/2005/04/peter-reum-collection.html

www.blog.wfmu.org/freeform/2005/10/im_a_genius_ too.html

www.uspto.gov/web/offices/com/sol/foia/ttab/ 2eissues/2002/75405215.pdf

Picture credits